SHERIDAN'S DRAMATIC WORKS

WITH

A SHORT ACCOUNT OF HIS LIFE

The Dramatic Works

of

𝕽𝖎𝖈𝖍𝖆𝖗𝖉 𝕭𝖗𝖎𝖓𝖘𝖑𝖊𝖞 𝕾𝖍𝖊𝖗𝖎𝖉𝖆𝖓

with

A Short Account of His Life

By G. G. S.

VOL. I.

London: Samuel Bagster & Sons Limited
New York: James Pott & Co.
MCMII

PREFACE

THE Memoir prefixed to the present edition of Sheridan's Dramatic Works contains the most striking circumstances that marked the eventful life of the author. These are necessarily condensed, and such only recorded as are based upon unimpeachable testimony; the numerous apocryphal anecdotes which have found their way into circulation having been intentionally rejected. The object of the editor has been to place before the public both the Memoir and the Plays in as authentic a form as existing materials permit. The difficulties attendant upon such a task may be gathered from the facts hereinafter narrated.

G. G. S.

CONTENTS

VOL. I

BIOGRAPHICAL MEMOIR

	PAGE
Sheridan, his birth	10
Sent to Harrow	13
First attempts in literature	13
Visits Bath	16
Elopes with Miss Linley	25
Duel with Captain Matthews	43
Domestic circumstances	51
Comedy of the " Rivals "	53
Its popularity	55
The " Duenna "	59
Correspondence between Linley and Garrick . . .	63
Rauzzini's career	65
Garrick resigns Drury Lane	67
Purchase of the theatre	68
The " Trip to Scarborough "	70
Comedy of the " School for Scandal "	70
Its striking features	71
Falsehoods respecting it	85
Jealousy of Cumberland	87
Remarks on the play	88
Retirement of Mr. King from the stage	98
Story of Sheridan and Palmer	100
Gentleman Smith	106
Dodd and Parsons	107
Mismanagement at Drury Lane	110
Further purchase of theatrical property	112

Contents

	PAGE
Monody on the death of Garrick	113
The "Critic"	113
Its impression on the public mind	116
Bannister, Waldron, Farren, and Miss Pope	117
Anecdote of Sheridan	118
Essay on absenteeism	122
State of the political world	124
Elected for Stafford	126
His first speeches in the House	127
Moves for a better regulation of the police	129
Bill for preventing desertion	131
Opposes Fox on the Marriage Act	131
Attacks Rigby, Paymaster of the Forces	132
Declares against the American War	133
Unpopularity of Lord North	136
Rockingham Administration	136
Appointed one of the Under-Secretaries of State	136
Coalition	137
Collision with Pitt	138
Becomes Secretary of the Treasury	139
Struggles on the East India Bill	139
Bitterly opposes Pitt's measures	140
Re-elected for Stafford	141
Distinguishes himself on the Westminster scrutiny	141
The "Rolliad"	142
Quarrel with Mr. Rolle	145
Vigorous speech on Irish Commercial Propositions	146
Charges against Warren Hastings	147
Sheridan's splendid speech on the occasion	154
Eulogium passed upon it by Burke, Pitt, and Fox	154
Impeachment of Warren Hastings	164
Account of the trial	165
Eagerness of the public to hear Sheridan	168
His eloquent address	173
Exultation of his family	177
Illness of the King	178
Account of the malady from Miss Burney's Memoirs	179
The Regency Question	184
Views of Sheridan on the subject	185

Contents

	PAGE
Debates in the House	187
His Majesty's restoration to health	194
Death of Sheridan's father	194
The French Revolution	196
Assiduity of Sheridan in his parliamentary duties	199
Secures his re-election at Stafford with difficulty	202
Virulence of Horne Tooke	203
Burke's opposition to the French Revolution	204
His breach with Sheridan	204
Separation of Fox and Burke	205
Rebuilding of Drury Lane	210
Death of Mrs. Sheridan	211
Serious aspect of public affairs	213
Debates in Parliament	214
Declaration of war with France	220
Schism amongst the Whigs	220
Sheridan's memorable speech	220
His reply to Lord Mornington	227
Drury Lane finished	229
"The first of June"	229
Debts of the Prince of Wales	230
Progress of Warren Hastings' trial	232
Irritated state of public feeling	234
Violent conduct towards the King in his progress to the House	235
Pamphlet of Mr. Reeves	237
Second marriage of Sheridan	238
Tom Sheridan	241
Mutiny in the Channel fleet	250
Ireland's Shakespeare forgeries	251
Speeches in Parliament	255
Anecdote of Pitt and Sheridan	257
Ministry of Addington	258
State of parties	258
Offer of a place to Tom Sheridan	259
Sheridan appointed Receiver-General of the Duchy of Cornwall	259
Becomes Treasurer of the Navy	260
Loses office on the death of Fox	260

Contents

	PAGE
Destruction of Drury Lane Theatre by fire	260
Mr. Whitbread	262
Plan for a third theatre	262
Mr. Canning	263
Sheridan's last speech in Parliament	263
Close of his political career	264
Summary of his character	265
His procrastination	269
Opening of the new theatre at Drury Lane	275
Lord Byron	276
Distresses of Sheridan	277
Illness	280
Death and funeral	283

DRAMATIC WORK

| The Rivals, a Comedy | 287 |

The Life of
Richard Brinsley Sheridan

(1751–1816)

SCARCELY anything remains at the present hour to attest the superiority of Richard Brinsley Sheridan over the great men of the times just passed away, but his contributions to the dramatic literature of the country, yet was he acknowledged to be at one period of his existence the most gifted genius of his age. Unfortunately for his memory, his last and least happy moments are those best remembered. He has been judged of when the decay of his intellect, the carelessness, nay, even the recklessness of his conduct, and the perplexities in which he was involved, had changed the character of the man. He has been regarded as the dissipated, thoughtless butterfly that passed through an ephemeral existence ; as one who was merely a brilliant ornament of society, or the boon companion of an idle hour. Far superior, however, was he to almost all those great personages who figured with him on the stage of existence in those qualities which are most highly prized in the busy section of the world.

His life is a romance. Even those who are wont to receive with incredulity the narrative of the biographer, believing him either a panegyrist labouring to exalt the hero who has excited his fancy, or the promulgator of some visionary doctrine, must acknowledge that the incidents which marked the career of Sheridan are too singular not to be recorded, and that they are of sufficient importance to be narrated by different individuals according to the respective views they entertain of the many events in which, from his position in the world, he was necessarily involved. If genius of the highest order in literature, if the eloquence that enchants, rivets the attention, and likewise touches the human heart, if the mingling in every question that agitates an empire, and produces an influence upon it, if splendid success followed by the sad vicissitudes of Fate are ever objects of our curiosity, they are in no one instance more singularly exemplified than in Sheridan.

He lived in an age of excitement, of which those who are now in the meridian of their days can, from the repose which they have enjoyed, form but a feeble idea. He was one of the most active, the most intelligent, the most fascinating of those who have stamped their names upon that singular page of history. There was no event in which he was not a leader, there was no great question, whether foreign or domestic, that he did not investigate and pronounce an opinion upon, which was listened to with respect and admiration by a large portion of the nation. His voice was the guide of a great and influential party; he was the attached friend of a band of patriots; and through good and evil repute supported, with manly ardour, a cause which did not bring with it the emoluments of the world, nor did he leave the camp when it was unguarded by some, and almost betrayed by others.

The Life of Sheridan

Professor Smyth thus speaks of him : " There were three others that flourished at the same time with him, the great minister and splendid debater, Mr. Pitt, the great philanthropist and orator, Mr. Fox, the great philosopher and enlightened statesman, Mr. Burke ; but he who to a certain degree might be said to unite the powers of all was Mr. Sheridan. He had not in such high superiority the distinguishing qualities of each—he had not the lofty tone and imposing declamation of Pitt; he had not the persuasive vehemence of Fox ; he had not the inexhaustible literature and ready philosophy of Burke ; but when he spoke on a great occasion, and prepared himself with all the necessary knowledge, nothing appeared wanting to the perfect orator. Grace of manner, charm of voice, fluency of language, and above all a brilliancy of sarcasm, a wit and a humour, and again a felicity of statement that made him the delight of every audience, and that excited the admiration of his opponents themselves."

The eulogium pronounced upon him by Lord Byron is now somewhat trite, but it is most true : " Whatever Sheridan has done or chosen to do, has been, *par excellence*, always the best of its kind. He has written the best comedy, ' The School for Scandal ' ; the best opera, ' The Duenna '—in my mind far before that St. Giles' lampoon, the ' Beggar's Opera ' ;—the best farce, ' The Critic '—it is only too good for an afterpiece ;— and the best address, ' The Monologue on Garrick ' ; and to crown all, delivered the very best oration, the famous Begum speech, ever conceived or heard in this country." These, however, are but a portion of the claims which he has to the highest consideration ; for scarcely had he attained the foremost rank amongst the comic writers of the age, when he astonished and

The Life of Sheridan

delighted the statesmen who surrounded him with the clearness of his political views, developed with all the power and splendour of eloquence. His friends had but just marvelled at the dexterity with which he gained an influence over the heir apparent to the throne, and were canvassing the merits of the advice which guided that prince through paths of considerable difficulty, when even his opponents were unanimously praising him in the loudest language for the exhibition of the purest patriotism, and admiring the conduct that he pursued during one of the most perilous moments that ever occurred in the annals of England—the Mutiny at the Nore.

The circumstances that are detailed in the following pages will, we think, plead an apology for many of the errors that have been strongly condemned; it will be found that a large portion of his pecuniary embarrassments did not originally spring from improvidence, but from the peculiar sources of his means, and from the unexpected position in which, at the very outset of his life, he found himself. He was placed, in an unaccountable manner, at the head of a great establishment, which seemed to yield unceasing means of expenditure, from whose treasury he was enabled to draw almost without acknowledgment; it appeared to offer endless wealth—the very purse of the Fortunatus of his childish days was in his hands. It was not only the inexhaustible vein of daily treasure, but it enabled him to multiply his means; to create new shares, to issue debentures, and to follow the thousand devices of the skilful financier was, for a length of time, as easy as to draw a cheque upon his banker. It afforded him a marriage settlement, or a new edifice; hence the mind became vitiated, false and factitious views of property took possession of it.

The Life of Sheridan

All was, however, paper money, based upon no solid means; it lured the credulous victim on, until he expected at every step more gold—he found at last that his wealth was visionary, and when compelled to acknowledge the melancholy truth, it was too late to recede. Harassed at every step, he had recourse to deception until it became systematic; he lost his caste in society, he sought relief in dissipation, and when his home was invaded by his angry creditors, he rushed to places where he gradually learnt habits that undermined his constitution and weakened his intellect. If, however, Sheridan was to be blamed, how much more so were his friends! how much more the public! It is a deep reflection upon the morals and upon the character of the country that such a man was allowed to suffer distress and misery; the selfishness of the great, the heartlessness of society, the mammon worship of the many, were never more conspicuous than in its treatment of its devoted servant.

In this country virtue and talents may be respected by the few—wealth by all; he who loses the one may in vain possess the other; his welcome in that world which hung upon his shadow is past, the good that he has done is forgotten. Such was the fate of Sheridan; those who had been the warmest admirers of his splendid talents were at first amused with the narratives of his cleverness in eluding the vigilance of his numerous creditors, but gradually they spoke of his imprudence, and then learnt to treat him with contempt. He had to stoop to the meanest subterfuges to escape from present embarrassment, or to degrade himself by the vilest cunning for a momentary supply of funds. How humiliating to his own mind must have been the comparison of the days when listen-

[5]

ing senates were hushed when he spoke !—how fearful
to him must have been the remembrance of those
brilliant hours of his youth, when he was the theme
of general observation ! Consider him, however, in
what light we may, still did he maintain some
superiority over all those by whom he was surrounded, and in almost every scene of his eventful life
he was an actor who obtained and excited the wonder,
if not the admiration, of his contemporaries.

Even the romantic incidents attending upon his
private life are such only as occur to men unlike the
ordinary class of fellow-beings. The celebrated object
of his choice, the clever manner in which he contrived
to outwit his rivals in love, becoming not only the
theme of conversation in a fashionable watering-place,
but of newspaper controversy, drew upon him at an
early age the general attention. From that period
every circumstance of his life became public property ;
indeed it was then evident that his lot could not be
cast in obscurity, but that he had that within him,
which, when duly exercised, would lead to his filling a
distinguished position in society. How, too, did the
bold daring with which he undertook the management
of a great theatrical establishment tell upon the public
mind, for all knew that he must be dependent on his
own abilities for his financial resources ! Surrounded
at an early age by men of the highest talent, he was
quickly remarked amongst them for the brilliancy of
his conversation, his flashes of wit, and the ease and
elegance of his manner. These qualifications, which
made him so delightful in society, are too apt to
render their possessor self-indulgent, vain, and careless,
nor was Sheridan on these points unlike the rest of
his fellow-beings. Gradually faults began to ripen into

The Life of Sheridan

vices; the feebleness with which he resisted the first
inroads upon his original sense of honour and of
virtue, led to a recklessness and sensuality which
eventually were remembered, when his brighter
qualities were somewhat dimmed. As the generation passed away in which his nobler characteristics
had been developed they were almost forgotten, and
those who were rising in the world saw only that
state which was, in comparison, one of degradation,
and hence they estimated him less than those who
had been dazzled by the early lustre of his career.

Valuable, doubtless, would be considered the moral
lessons deducible from a scrutiny into his errors and
defects; but sufficient for us is it in our sketch to
relate the prominent circumstances of his life, to
delineate him with that fair and honest colouring
which is required for truth ; more consonant would it
be with our feelings to throw a veil over his follies and
inconsistencies rather than to scan them too deeply ;
the brilliancy of his talents, and the severity of his misfortunes, command for the thoughtlessness of Richard
Brinsley Sheridan, oblivion—for his sorrows, respect.

He has found two biographers, both of whom have
entered with some degree of warmth into his political
career. The first, Dr. Watkins, was a Tory of the old
school ; the other, a Whig, of equally uncompromising
caste. They have seen through glasses which operate
on every subject of their examination with power of a
totally different kind ; the same topic is magnified or
diminished according to the respective instrument
that each holds. Much is to be said in praise of the
diligence with which Dr. Watkins has investigated the
numerous great questions which engaged the attention
of Sheridan, but his strong bias shines forth on all

[7]

The Life of Sheridan

occasions. He views everything as a good, consistent follower of Pitt would naturally do, he thinks only of the heaven-born minister, he insinuates that his opponents were actuated by malevolence, were besotted in ignorance, and were worthy condign punishment. His detestation of the French Revolution was only surpassed by his terror lest parliamentary reform should ever be brought about in England. From so decided a partisan there was little to be expected, and he has throughout evinced too much of the politician of the humblest grade to be the judge of one who had any pretension to rank amongst statesmen. Of his private life he has drawn but a feeble sketch ; whatever he knew and gave was derived from Mr. Samuel Whyte, who had for a short period been Sheridan's teacher.

Moore's Life has greater claims to our consideration. Although it has the internal evidence of its being a laboured panegyric upon the great Whig statesman Fox, it furnishes us with a consistent narrative of the most remarkable events in which Sheridan became a partaker ; still they are more or less tinted with the colouring which, as a decided Whig, Moore was likely to make use of. The private life is of a most poetic character. It is the work of a rich fancy, rendering everything it touches more beautiful than nature in her sweet simplicity usually attempts. He sought from the immediate family and friends materials for his publication, and of course received from them only such as were likely to embellish his narrative, and produce the most favourable effect. It is not to be supposed that truth has ever been wantonly sacrificed, but much has been suppressed, and much has been overcharged ; so that a picture somewhat gaudy, but

The Life of Sheridan

bearing the general character, has been produced. Mrs. Lefanu, the youngest sister of Sheridan, communicated the romantic details of the love affair in which Sheridan was so early in life involved, and they are necessarily tinctured with the feeling which an affectionate relation would naturally wish should be experienced by all those who would read the memoirs. The great advantage which Moore had was free access to all the manuscripts that Sheridan left behind him. Of these he has admirably availed himself : he has shown us the gradual development of the "School for Scandal" from the first germ ; he has exhibited to us that it was the slow and laborious effort of long consideration ; that it reached by a gradual process that perfection to which it ultimately attained. From the evident study bestowed upon this and his other plays, Moore has attempted to deduce, and his opinion has been followed by others, that Sheridan was not a man of quick ideas, of rapid and vigorous fancy, but that all he did was carefully and slowly prepared, patiently digested and long paused upon before it was made public. That this may have been the case in his early career, and that in his latter days he may have had recourse to his memory rather than to his imagination may be granted, but no man was possessed of greater readiness in his best days, and few have exhibited more quickly unpremeditated wit, bursts of genius, and glow of fancy.

A most interesting narrative has been drawn up by the distinguished Professor of History at Cambridge, who lived under the roof of Sheridan, as the tutor of his son Thomas, and has been read by a few. It is eloquent, as everything must be from that ornament of our literature, Professor Smyth.

[9]

The Life of Sheridan

We have also a slight sketch by the hand of Leigh Hunt. The modesty with which he has given it would forbid any attempt to find fault with it, but when we remember the position he holds, as a poet and a critic, that " nihil non tetigit quod non ornavit," we must be excused from expressing our regret that he has so cursorily glanced at the dramatic works of Sheridan, and so heedlessly admitted, as facts, the wanton assertions of those who have pretended to be acquainted with the circumstances of his life. The few observations on the education of Sheridan are erroneous, for although he gave little or no attention to classical knowledge, he was not so thoroughly incapable as he has described him to have been ; nor ought the epithets, applied to the gentleman who fought two duels with Sheridan, to have been given without some inquiry as to the propriety of their adoption. There is, however, such polish and so much fancy in the little brochure that it will be perused with infinite pleasure.

Sheridan was born in Dublin in the year 1751. His family boasted on both sides genius. His grandfather, Dr. Sheridan, was the friend—nay, it is said, the instructor—of Swift, and was not only distinguished for his classic attainments, but "for such a ready wit and flow of humour, that it was impossible for any, even the most splenetic man, not to be cheerful in his company." He was not a fortunate man, and by no means a careful one. He lost his appointment as one of the Court Chaplains by a somewhat ludicrous incident. He was called upon to preach before the Lord-Lieutenant, and as he had not prepared himself for such an event, he hastily snatched up a sermon, innocent enough of politics, but the text of which

The Life of Sheridan

was, "Sufficient unto the day is the evil thereof." Unfortunately for him, the day on which he delivered a discourse so headed, was the first of August, the anniversary of the accession to the throne of George the First, an occasion on which every species of flattery to the powers in authority would have been much more acceptable. He was, therefore, suspected of Jacobinism, and lost all chance of rising in his profession. Thomas, the third son of Dr. Sheridan, and the father of Richard Brinsley Sheridan, was distinguished as an actor, a teacher of elocution, and as the author of a pronouncing dictionary that has, from its first appearance, been generally received as a useful addition to our literature. Although an unsuccessful person on the great stage of life, he played his part with much energy, and his name has descended to posterity amongst those who have been useful in their generation.

It is one of the pet theories of the day, that men of genius have had on the female side a parent much above the ordinary class of women in intellectual power, and certainly Sheridan is one of the instances that may be adduced. The authoress of so many works of merit deserves a niche in the Temple of Fame. It is, however, not to be forgotten that one of her plays, "The Dupe," was condemned for some passages that were considered as offensive to the laws of decorum. "The Discovery" was more fortunate. It was hailed as a "moral, sentimental, yet entertaining performance," but the length and languor of its scenes became somewhat insupportable. Garrick it was who bore the whole onus of the play, and performed a pedantic character, considered to be quite unsuited to him, in such a way as to elicit infinite entertainment. He seemed entirely to have relinquished his natural ability, and to have assumed an air of unutterable dulness. The younger Colman says, "He made the twin stars which nature had stuck in his head look like two coddled gooseberries." Her "Memoirs of Sidney Biddulph" have been much admired, not only for their power of awakening our sympathy for the sorrows of man upon this transitory globe, but for the beautiful language in which they point out the blissful rewards of a hereafter to those who, by their conduct, may deserve them.

Amongst other productions of her pen "Nourjahad" is particularly distinguished, alike for the development of the story and the gracefulness of its diction, and even to the present hour it enjoys a high degree of popularity amongst youthful readers, who, if they are not able to detect the moral of a tale that shows that the gifts of perpetual youth and of endless riches, if not properly estimated, will produce sensuality and brutality, are at any rate delighted with the beautiful pictures of oriental manners that she has so admirably delineated.

In his seventh year Sheridan was placed, together with his brother, under the tuition of Mr. Samuel Whyte, of Dublin ; they were the first two pupils he had. Their mother, in giving them to his care, made use of an expression which has been oftentimes repeated as if it had been applied to Sheridan in the latter days of his boyhood. She pointed out to Mr. Whyte that in the profession he had undertaken patience was absolutely necessary. "These boys will be your tutors in that respect. I have hitherto been their only instructor, they have sufficiently exercised mine, for two such impenetrable dunces I never met

The Life of Sheridan

with." From such an expression, at such an age, it would be most unfair to form an opinion of the intellectual capabilities of a child.

On his parents settling in England which was in the year 1762, Harrow was selected as the best school for his education. Here he exhibited none of that superior intellect for which his future life was to be distinguished. Dr. Parr has given evidence as to his deficiency in those studies which were the pride of that seminary, but observes, " He was a favourite amongst his schoolfellows, mischievous, and his pranks were accompanied by a sort of vivacity and cheerfulness. He was a great reader of English poetry, but was careless about literary fame ; he appears to have been removed too early from school." He, however, in after life was, according to the same testimony, given to classic reading, and was well acquainted with the orations of Cicero and of Demosthenes, and impressed Dr. Parr with an idea that he was possessed of considerable classic attainments. Mr. Roderic, Dr. Sumner's assistant during the time that Sheridan was at Harrow, says "that he was a shrewd, artful, and supercilious boy, without any shining accomplishments or superior learning."

During his residence at Harrow he lost his excellent and amiable mother, who died at Blois, where the family had for some time resided, in the year 1766.

Whilst at Harrow he formed an intimacy with a fellow-pupil, Mr. Halhed, with whom he entered into literary partnership, which was not dissolved by their both quitting their school, the one for Oxford, the other for Bath. Together they laboured upon a farce in three acts, called " Jupiter," from which they anticipated to reap a sum of no less than £200 ; but they were doomed to disappointment, for it never was brought before the public, and whatever of merit it may have possessed we are unable to judge, for, with the exception of some extracts which Moore has given, we are not in possession of any remains of a burlesque which has been supposed to have remained long on the memory of Sheridan, and to have been the model on which the "Critic" was founded. A miscellany was projected by the friends, but it did not live beyond one number ; this was but poor, if we may be allowed to form a judgment from the short specimen that has been preserved. A collection of occasional poems, and a volume of crazy tales, were amongst the dreams that flitted across the imaginations of the enthusiasts, but beyond fancy's first sketch it would appear that they were not allowed to proceed.

One, however, of the united productions of these aspirants to literary fame was actually committed to the press, and has reached us ; it has been the means of exhibiting positive proof that they were indifferent judges of that which was likely to impress the public with a favourable opinion of their merits. They selected a Greek author but little known, Aristænetus, and rendered his Greek prose into English verse. The facetious Tom Brown had previously translated, or rather imitated, some select pieces from the epistles of this author, but the young poets thought that he had failed in giving the elegance and the wit of the original. They stated that "their object was not so much to bring to light the merits of an undistinguished author, as to endeavour to introduce into the language a species of poetry not frequently attempted, and but very seldom with success, that species which has been called the *simplex munditiis* in writing, where the

The Life of Sheridan

thoughts are spirited and fanciful without quaintness, and the style simple, yet not inelegant." There is a great variation of the metres employed, and each epistle has its own particular measure, and it would be difficult to point out upon what particular species of poetry they relied for their claim to success. The Epistles of Aristænetus are altogether unknown, and what could have tempted young and cultivated minds to bestow a thought upon a writer who had neither a name amongst classical authors, nor a single recommendation from a modern critic, we are utterly at a loss to imagine. We can only ascribe it to an enthusiastic taste for compositions which occasionally captivate youth, and to which we are doubtless indebted for Moore's translation of Anacreon, and for his juvenile poems, which are admired at the commencement of our career in life. They were compelled to soften many passages which were indelicate in the original, and to suppress others as indecent. The preface, to which the initials " H. S." are added, is concluded by a passage informing us that the original is divided into two parts, the present essay containing only the first ; by its success must the fate of the second be determined. Carefully did they watch the impression made on the public by their labours ; they saw that they were unsuccessful, and they wisely attempted no more. There is but one epistle, "The Garden of Phyllion," that possesses much merit, and this is spoilt by the introduction, not only of language somewhat too glowing, but of libertinism totally uncalled for in a descriptive pastoral. The Tenth Epistle has some striking passages ; but with every wish to view the first productions of youth with kindness and lenity, we

The Life of Sheridan

cannot but express our gratification that the second part never appeared, and that the first has been but little read. One of the reviews of the period has very justly said, "We have been idly employed in reading it, and our readers will in proportion lose their time in perusing this article."

In the year 1771 Sheridan's father took his young family to Bath, there to reside whilst he was fulfilling his theatrical engagements elsewhere. No place could have been more unfortunately selected for the *début* in life of a young man ; for whatever may have been the charm of society there, nothing could by possibility be more destructive to habits of industry and the exercise of the higher qualities of the mind and the heart than the unvarying monotony of indolence and selfishness in which the visitors of that once fashionable watering-place constantly indulged themselves. The lounge in the pump-room and in the streets of Bath may have furnished young Sheridan with sketches of those characters which have rendered his dramas the admiration of those who are initiated into society, but it was the very worst school for the education of a man whose destiny was forcibly urging him on to figure as one of the most prominent men in public life. From all quarters of the globe congregated not only the invalid to gain health from the thermal springs, but the idle, the dissipated, and also the lovers of the arts. Bilious East Indians, Irish fortune-hunters, gouty statesmen, ladies of rank, " chiefly remarkable for the delicacy of their reputation," went there to seek relief from ennui. To furnish relief for them, there was an admirable theatre, time out of mind the nursery for the London stage, and concerts, such as were not to be outrivalled in

The Life of Sheridan

Europe, and private parties of every description, where music, dancing, or poetry was the ruling passion. Every aspirant to fame wrote poetry, in some guise ; nor was Sheridan the last amongst those who sought for a laurel from the reigning Queen of Bath, Lady Miller. This lady, so admirably described to us by Horace Walpole and by Madame D'Arblay, held at her house at Bath Easton, every Thursday, a "fair of Parnassus." We are told by the latter lady "that, notwithstanding Bath Easton is so much laughed at in London, nothing is here more tonish than to visit Lady Miller, who is extremely curious in her company, admitting few people who are not of rank or fame, and excluding of those all who are not people of character very unblemished." Horace Walpole says, "All the flux of quality contended for prizes gained for rhymes and themes ; a Roman vase, dressed with pink ribbons and myrtle, received the poetry which was drawn out at every festival. Six judges of these Olympic Games retired and selected the brightest composition, which was rewarded by permission for the author to kneel and kiss the hands of Lady Miller, who crowned the victor with myrtle." This Lady Miller, whose reputation had spread far and wide as the ruling star of Bath, was a round, coarse, plump-looking dame, whose aim it was to appear a woman of fashion, and succeeded only in having the appearance of an ordinary woman in very common life with fine clothes on. Her manners were bustling, her air mock important, and appearance very inelegant. She was, however, extremely good-humoured and remarkably civil.

Many are the pieces of poetry which Sheridan,

The Life of Sheridan

scarcely then in his twentieth year, produced. Amongst them the exquisite stanzas :—

> " Dry be that tear, my gentlest love,
>   Be hushed that struggling sigh,
> Nor seasons, day, nor fate shall prove
>   More fixed, more true than I.
> Hush'd be that sigh, be dry that tear,
> Cease boding doubt, cease anxious fear,
>   Dry be that tear.
>
> Ask'st thou how long my love will stay
>   When all that's new is past?
> How long—ah, Delia, can I say
>   How long my life will last?
> Dry be that tear, be hush'd that sigh
> At least I'll love thee till I die,
>   Hushed be that sigh.
>
> And does that thought affect thee too,
>   The thought of Sylvio's death,
> That he who only breath'd for you,
>   Must yield that faithful breath?
> Hushed be that sigh, be dry that tear
> Nor let us lose our Heaven here,
>   Dry be that tear."

In a poem addressed to Lady Margaret Fordyce are those lines which have been so universally admired:—

> " . . . Marked you her cheek of rosy hue,
> Marked you her eye of sparkling blue?
> That eye, in liquid circles moving,
> That cheek abashed at Man's approving ;
> The one, Love's arrows darting round,
> The other, blushing at the wound :
> Did she not speak, did she not move,
> Now Pallas—now the Queen of Love !"

The rest of the poem is very indifferent, and it appears strange that lines of such singular beauty should have been introduced. Amongst the light trifles published, one is to be noticed as exhibiting his varied talent. It was written on the occasion of the

The Life of Sheridan

opening of that splendid pile of buildings, the Upper Assembly Rooms, September 30, 1771. It is entitled "An Epistle from Timothy Screw to his Brother Henry, Waiter at Almack's," of which the following is an extract :—

"Two rooms were first opened—the long and the round one
(These Hogstyegon names only serve to confound one),
Both splendidly lit with the new chandeliers,
With drops hanging down like the bobs at Peg's ears :
While jewels of paste reflected the rays,
And Bristol-stone diamonds gave strength to the blaze :
So that it was doubtful, to view the bright clusters,
Which sent the most light out, the ear-rings or lustres.

  · · · · · · · ·

Nor less among you was the medley, ye fair !
I believe there were some beside quality there.
Miss Spiggot, Miss Brussels, Miss Tape, and Miss Socket,
Miss Trinket, and aunt, with her leathern pocket,
With good Mrs. Soaker, who made her old chin go,
Four hours, hobnobbing with Mrs. Syringo :
Had Tib staid at home, I b'lieve none would have miss'd her,
Or pretty Peg Runt, with her tight little sister," &c. &c.

The allusions are to the splendid ball-room and to the octagon-room, two of the most perfect specimens of domestic architecture which we possess. The chandeliers, which still remain, were once considered perfect models, and as *chef-d'œuvres* of the art of glass-making. They have been so thoroughly surpassed by modern productions, as to excite our wonder that they should still be retained.

Besides the motley group that lounged in the Crescent, the Circus, or the Parades, there were many individuals of great talent with whom Sheridan had the opportunity of mixing. He, however, to judge from his letters, had no wish to be intimate with any of them, and speaks of Mr. Wyndham and Mr. Luttrel, a brother of the colonel, as the only acquaintance he had made. Amongst those who were there was the pious and clever Hannah More; the lively Mrs. Thrale; Fanny and Harriott Bowdler, both blue-stockings of the deepest dye; Anstey, the author of the "Bath Guide," "with an air, look, and manner, mighty heavy and unfavourable"; Mrs. Dobson, the translator of Petrarch; Mr. Melmoth, the Pliny Melmoth, "thinking nobody half so great as himself, therefore, playing first violin without further ceremony"; Cumberland, "so querulous, so dissatisfied, so determined to like nobody and nothing, but himself"; Dr. Harrington, "dry, comic, and very agreeable," and a whole host of people who have been celebrated in their day, but whose memory, alas! has faded away.

But the great and ruling passion at Bath was music. The public concerts were delightful recreations, they were the first in England; the private concerts were as detestable, although first-rate talent was engaged, and there were amateurs of high consideration. There was Jerningham, the poet, "a mighty gentleman, who looks to be painted, and is all daintification in manner, speech, and dress, singing to his own accompaniment on the harp, whilst he looks the gentlest of all dying Corydons." Miss Latouche singing "not in your Italian style—no, that she hates, and holds very cheap—but all about Daphne and Chloe, Damon and Phyllis"; but the parties in which they sung, were usually all "confusion worse confounded." "There were quartettos and overtures by gentlemen performers whose names and faces I never knew; such was the never-ceasing battling and noise of the card-room, that a general humming of musical sounds, and now and then a twang, was all I heard," says

The Life of Sheridan

Madame D'Arblay. The concerts, however, in the great Assembly-Room were of the highest character. Here the works of such composers as Rauzzini, Jackson, the Linleys, and Dr. Harrington were for the first time produced, in a style that had never yet been equalled; here talent of this kind found its devoted admirers. Miss Guest, afterwards the celebrated Mrs. Miles, and her father, were heard with rapture, and many of those artists whose talents have commanded the admiration of Europe.

Amongst those who sang, not only at the oratorios at Bath, but who had gained a high reputation in all musical circles, was Miss Linley, the daughter of the eminent composer, upon whom Nature seems to have lavished her richest treasures, and Art to have nobly seconded her.

This young lady was destined to have a lasting influence upon the conduct, the talents, and the happiness of young Sheridan. Various are the versions of the love tale, and difficult, most difficult, is it to arrive at the real truth of the affair. At lovers' perjuries they say Jove laughs; and there were, and there are, many who look upon the whole of this singular event as a tissue of absurd longings after notoriety on the part of more than one of the individuals engaged in it. Miss Linley was, beyond a doubt, one of the most accomplished, as well as beautiful, young women ever seen.

At the early age of sixteen she was surrounded by a host of admirers, and there is but little doubt that she was one of the most decided coquettes that ever existed, but beyond this pretty piece of female folly we sincerely believe that there was no indiscretion; though a letter written by herself, addressed to Miss

The Life of Sheridan

Saunders, would almost lead us to imagine even something beyond it, if that letter be genuine. She was admitted to be a model of personal beauty, and the charms of the Fair Maid of Bath were universally acknowledged. As a public singer, she was naturally exposed to allurements and temptations, and was very probably obliged to listen to offers which, in her heart, she might disdain. The catalogue of her lovers is somewhat long. Halhed, the poetic partner of Sheridan, was not only one, but even Sheridan's own brother Charles entertained a passion for her. Norris, who was supposed to have sung himself into her affections; Mr. Watts, a gentleman commoner of Oxford; Mr. Long, a man of large fortune; Sir Thomas Clarges, and several others less known to fame, swelled up a long list. But every student at Oxford, where she sang at the oratorios, was enchanted with this beautiful girl, to whom the title of the divine St. Cecilia was unanimously given. Nothing seemed to fright the University from its propriety so much as a rumour that was industriously circulated, that one youth, happier than the rest, had found the soft hour when she had listened, and had consented to accompany him to Scotland, and that a splendid fortune was the result of this matrimonial adventure.

Whatever may have been the merits of these candidates for her love, neither poetry in the shape of Halhed, music in that of Norris, nor wealth in others, had power to move her. Whatever may have been the earlier fancies of her heart—and there seems, from her own confession, to have been some—Richard Brinsley Sheridan had silently, and unsuspiciously, succeeded in winning her affections, and in wooing

[22]

her for his bride. He contrived, for all is fair in love, to mystify Halhed, to blind his brother Charles, to make the man she fancied that she loved actually odious in her eyes, and by dint of some persuasive power, which lovers only understand, wove a web around her from which there was no possibility of escaping, and eventually carried her off, in spite of parents and of lovers, of threats and of swords.

Amongst the characteristics of the ancient city of King Bladud is a lively curiosity, and an innate love of becoming intimately acquainted with the particularities of everybody and everything, which furnishes forth rich food for constant prattle. Anything connected with an individual so gifted as Miss Linley, naturally excited the peculiarly inquisitive thirst after subjects for conversation, and soon there arose this matter of a singularly gratifying description for them, of which they failed not to avail themselves ; and their appetites were richly tickled by a series of occurrences that involved Miss Linley, Sheridan, and Mr. Matthews, a gentleman of fortune, as principals ; and as accessories, the master of ceremonies, Captain Wade, Captain Paumier, and several men moving in the highest circles ; and they were commented on in the *Bath Herald*, conducted by Meyler, a man of considerable ability, and in the *Bath Chronicle*, under the direction of Richard Crutwell.

Captain Matthews was the possessor of a large property in Wales, and usually passed the season at Bath in the enjoyment of those gratifications which the fashionable city afforded. He was not altogether, what Leigh Hunt has designated him, a married blackguard, but a man of elegant exterior, and, whatever may have been his folly with regard to Miss Linley,

The Life of Sheridan

of kindly disposition, of lively manners, and of agreeable conversation, nor was he deficient in intellectual power; and had he bestowed as much time on the cultivation of any of the arts or sciences as he did upon whist, he might have become a useful member of society; but to this game his life was devoted, and the treatise, for a long period the whist-player's grammar, which he wrote upon it, evinces that he did not consider it as a means of passing an idle hour, but as a study requiring observation, memory, and the powers of calculation. When the events about to be narrated were almost forgotten, and the obloquy which had been heaped upon him in certain circles was somewhat washed away by the healing hand of time, Captain Matthews became the centre of a circle, every member of which entertained a strong regard for him, and listened with respect and confidence to his own relation of all the facts, which were much at variance with those detailed by Moore, in his Life of Sheridan, and by those who were, from their connection with Sheridan, inclined to believe the statement which from the beginning he had made. Led away by the opinion that prevailed at that period that every female who came prominently before the public was open to the attentions of any man of sufficient fortune to make a handsome settlement, Captain Matthews became a professed admirer of Miss Linley. Admitted into the bosom of the family, he, according to the assertion of Sheridan and of Miss Linley, forgot his own position as a married man, and with more than the usual licence of the times persevered in offers, which, at any rate, were received at first with love and affection, but afterwards with indignation and with expressions of abhorrence. In

The Life of Sheridan

public he was her constant shadow, and appeared determined to prevent any other man from approaching her too nearly, and this, it was said, arose from a wish on his part to make it appear that he had succeeded in the lawless object of his incessant desire, and that having failed to make any impression upon her by entreaties, by presents, by threats of the committal of suicide, he sought to accomplish his wishes by the ruin of her character, and the dissemination of the vilest calumnies, which would for ever blast her reputation. To her father she dared not breathe a syllable against this individual, for he was courted and respected by her family; but at length she was determined to disclose to Sheridan, who had already gained her heart, the painful position in which she was placed. After a consultation with his sister, the singular step of a flight to the Continent was resolved upon, an elopement took place, and a marriage at a village in the neighbourhood of Calais was the consequence; but as it was deemed right to keep the ceremony a secret, she afterwards went to a convent at Lisle, there to remain till such time as Sheridan might publicly claim her as his wife.

Miss Linley's extraordinary letter, which has fortunately been preserved, will best explain her share in these events.

"Bath, *May* 2, 1772.

"After so long a silence, and after the many unfavourable reports which must, I dare say, have prejudiced my dear friend against me, how shall I endeavour to vindicate a conduct which has but too much deserved her censure? But if my dear friend will suspend her judgment till I have made her acquainted with my real motives, I flatter myself she will rather be induced to pity than condemn me.

[25]

The Life of Sheridan

"At the time I wrote last, my mind was in a state of distraction not to be conceived; but I little thought then I should ever be forced to the cruel necessity of leaving my friends, and becoming an exile from everything I hold dear.

"In your answer to that letter, you hinted that you thought I loved Mr. R——, and that that was the cause of my uneasiness; but in that you, as well as many others, have been deceived. I confess myself greatly to blame in my behaviour to him; but I cannot explain myself on this subject, without acquainting you with the first cause of every uneasiness and indiscretion I have since been guilty of. Let me, then, my dear girl, beg your patience; for, though my story is long, and not very enlivening, yet such is the affection I have for you that I cannot bear to think it possible, by the various reports which are so industriously propagated, I may entirely lose your good opinion and esteem—a thing, of all others, I should most regret. Excuse my being tedious; and when you know the motive which induced me to take this last step, I flatter myself you will once more restore me to your friendship.

"At the age of twelve years, I was brought from the country, where I had been all my life, and introduced into public, with a heart capable of receiving the softest impressions, and too sincere ever to suspect deceit in another. I was led into scenes of dissipation, when reason and experience were not allowed to assist me in the many temptations which ever surrounded a young girl in such a situation. But, though my credulity often made me feel for the pretended distresses of others, yet my heart was entirely free from love, nor could I be seduced by flattery and compliments. I always considered them as words of course; and never looked upon those people as my friends who made too much use of them.

"In an evil hour my father was introduced to Mr. Matthews, as one who wished to serve him. My father, who is, like me, too apt to believe every one his friend who professes himself so, gladly embraced the opportunity of gaining the friendship of a man who had it in his power to be of service to him in his business : little did he think he was seeking the serpent who was designed to sting his heart. Mr. Matthews, from the first moment he saw me, resolved to make me his prey, and (child as I then was) left no means untried to make himself master of my affections, thinking but too justly that an impression fixed so early in life could not easily be removed. If it were possible to describe the many arts he made use of to effect this end, you would, I am sure, at once excuse me ; but as these are not to be conceived by any one but those who are capable of acting so basely, I must still rely on your goodness.

"For three years he never ceased his assiduities to me ; and though at times my conscience would upbraid me, yet by his respectful behaviour, his counterfeit distress, and by averring sentiments foreign to his heart, he made me, instead of flying from him, not only pity him, but promise him my friendship. This was my first fault. He saw too plainly that he was not indifferent to me, and made use of every artifice to increase my regard.

"About this time the people began to take notice of his particular behaviour to me, and my friends all spoke to my father to hinder my seeing him ; but my father, thinking that my youth was a sufficient safeguard for me, and unwilling to lose, as he thought, a good friend, took no notice of this first alarm. I then began to feel myself, for the first time, wretchedly involved in an unhappy passion for a man whom (though I thought him equally to be pitied) yet it was criminal in me even to think of. When he went into the country for the summer, I resolved, whatever it cost me, to tear him from my heart, and when he returned, to avoid him everywhere. With these resolutions I consoled myself till winter. When he returned, he had not been in town a week before we had repeated invitations to his house. Conscious that I could never forget him, if I was always to be exposed to his solicitations, I informed my mother of everything he had said to me, and, at the same time, told her how far he had gained my heart.

"Oh, my dear friend, had my mother but then acted properly, I had now been happy; but she, too much attached to interest, laughed at my uneasiness, and told me that novels had turned my head; and that I fancied, if any one was civil to me, he must certainly be in love. She desired I would put such thoughts out of my head; for no man could think seriously of such a child. Thus was I again led into temptation, and exposed to all the artifices of a man whom I already loved but too well, and who was but too sensible of it. I could not fly from the danger. After my first reproof, I was ashamed to mention it again to my mother, and I had everything to fear from my father's violent temper.

"For another year we went on in the same manner; till, at last, finding it impossible to conquer my inclinations, he soon brought me to a confession of my weakness, which has been the cause of all my distress.

The Life of Sheridan

That obstacle removed, many others fell of course, and the next season he prevailed on me to meet him at the house of a friend, as we were not permitted to talk together in public. During this time I had many offers of marriage very much to my advantage; but I refused them all. So far had he gained my love, that I resolved never to marry.

"About this time, Mr. Long addressed me. You know by what means I was induced to suffer his visits, though you do not know likewise that another great motive was the hope of forgetting Matthews, and retiring into solitude. After I had consented to receive Mr. Long's visits, I forbade Matthews ever to speak to me, to the consequences of which you yourself were witness. He immediately pretended to be dying, and by that artifice very nearly made me really so. You know how ill I was for a long time. At last he wrote me word, that he must see me once more; that he would then take a final leave of me, and quit the kingdom directly; but he could not resolve to go without seeing me. I was weak enough to comply with his request, as I thought it would be the last time.

"Some way or other, my mother was told of it, when she taxed me with it. I immediately confessed everything that had passed since I first acquainted her with his behaviour. She was at first greatly enraged; but on my telling her how unexceptionably he had behaved, she was pacified, and consented to conceal it from my father. And indeed, my dear, had any impartial person been present at our meeting, they would have thought Matthews the most unhappy but amiable man in the world. His behaviour was always consistent with the strictest honour; nor did he ever, in the smallest degree, give me any reason to think he had any intentions that were in the least alarming to my virtue. Deceived by such conduct, his merit shone more conspicuous; nor did I wish to get the better of my passion for one whom I thought every way so worthy of it. I considered myself as the cause of all his wretchedness, and thought it would be the height of cruelty if I did not endeavour to alleviate it. But to proceed; my mother resolved to see Matthews herself, and therefore insisted that I should write, and desire to see him again that evening. I did so, and my mother went in my place. You may imagine he was very much surprised at seeing her. She went with a full resolution to upbraid him; yet so far did his arts prevail, that he not only made her forgive but pity him, and promise that this should never make any alteration in our behaviour to him; and we would still continue our visits and intimacy with him. He promised, however, that he never would for the future attempt to see me.

"About this time my marriage with Mr. Long broke off, and my father went to London to commence a lawsuit. During the time he was absent I went on a visit to Mr. and Mrs. Norton, where you saw me. She had been informed by undoubted authority that my father would not only lose his suit, but that I should be exposed to the public court, as Mr. Long had been informed of my meeting Matthews, and intended to make use of that as a plea in court. This being told me suddenly, and at a time when my spirits were greatly distressed, flung me into a high fever. I lost my senses some time, and when I recovered was so weak, and had such strong symptoms of a rapid decline that, when my father returned, I was sent to the Wells to drink the waters. While I

The Life of Sheridan

was there I was told that Matthews, during my illness, had spoken disrespectfully of me in public, and had boasted it was owing to my love for him I was so ill. This behaviour from one for whom I had suffered so much shocked me greatly, and I resolved in my first heat of passion that he should not have it in his power to triumph over my weakness. The resentment I felt was of service to me, as it roused me from a state of stupid despondence, which perhaps would have occasioned my death. It was then that you received my first letter, which must have shown you in what a wretched state of mind I was.

"When I had so far recovered my spirits and health as to be able to walk and ride, I became acquainted with Mr. R——, who from the first time he saw me was particular in his behaviour to me. I did not at first observe it, and as I thought him an agreeable man, and one who I was told bore an unexceptionable character, I did not avoid him so much as I certainly ought. I wished, likewise, by turning my attention to him, to eradicate every impression of Matthews; but though Mr. R—— behaved with the greatest delicacy, I found it impossible for me to love him. I went on in this manner some time, and by Mr. R——'s attention to me incurred the ill-will of all the ladies, who did not spare to censure my conduct; but as I was conscious in my own heart of no ill, and wished to convince Matthews he had not so much reason to boast of his conquest, I paid very little attention to the envy of the women.

"Mr. R—— had not, as yet, made any professions; but one day he confessed to me that he loved me, but that it was not in his power to marry publicly, as he was entirely dependent on his father, except a pension

The Life of Sheridan

which he had ; but, at the same time, begged me to consent to marry him privately, and to go off with him to any part of the world, till his father died, when he said he would marry me again in the face of the world. This proposal, had I loved him, I should certainly have rejected ; but in the state of mind I then was, I was very angry, and refused seeing him for a great while.

" At this time Mr. and Mrs. Norton came over to be with me, as they had heard of R——. Through his means Mr. R—— entreated me to forgive him, and permit him to be on the footing of a friend, and assured me I never should have further cause to be offended with him. As Mr. Norton, under whose protection I then was, had no objection, and as I really had an esteem for Mr. R——, and thought him a good young man, I consented, and we continued to walk and ride together, but never without Mr. Norton. I was thus situated when Matthews came to the Wells in his road to Wales. He had been extremely ill at Bath, and when I saw him in the public walk at the Wells I could scarce keep myself from fainting. There was such an alteration in his person that I could not believe it possible. He spoke to me once in the walk, and asked me if I resolved to be his death, declared his illness proceeded from the accounts he had heard of me and R——, and that he was now going into the country to die. You may be sure I was greatly affected with his words ; but, as I had suffered so much in my reputation by being seen with him, I would not stay to explain myself or upbraid him with his behaviour to me ; I merely told him that the only way to convince me of his sincerity was to leave me and never see me more. I left him immediately and went home, where, soon after, a lady informed me he had fainted in the Long Room, and that his friends had taken him to Wales, given over by all. This news made me relapse, and had very nearly cost me my life, till I heard again that he was well and in good spirits, laughing at my distress and exulting in the success of his scheme. This once more raised my resentment, and I was resolved to encourage Mr. R—— ; and though I could not consent to go off with him, I told him (with my father's consent) that when it was in his power, if he still retained his love for me, and I was free from any other engagements, I would marry him. When I returned to Bath he followed me, but, as he was very much talked of, I would not suffer him to be so particular. When he was going to D——, he begged me to give him a letter to you, that he might, by you, sometimes hear from me, as I refused to correspond with him. As I wished to have my dear girl's opinion of him, I was not unwilling to trust him with a letter, in which I mentioned something relative to my misfortunes, but luckily mentioned no names, nor could he, if he had read it, understand whom or what it meant. He wrote to me that he was in D——, but never mentioned your name, which I was surprised at, and as I had not heard anything from you, was a good deal hurt, thinking you would not keep your word with me. In answer to his letter I desired to know if he had seen you, and begged to be informed of some other circumstances in his letter which made me uneasy. To this I received no answer, and the account you gave me afterwards convinced me that he was like all other men—deceitful. I then gave him entirely up, and contented myself with thinking how unworthy all men were of a woman's affection !

The Life of Sheridan

"I was in this state of mind when Matthews returned; when, in spite of all I could do or say, I was obliged to visit them, and scarcely a day passed without my having some conversation with him. In these conversations he cleared himself of the imputations alleged against him, and set my conduct in such a point of view, that he made me appear the criminal, and himself the injured person. This and being constantly with him, joined to his engaging behaviour, soon regained him that love which had never been quite extinguished. That gained, I was soon prevailed on to see him, but this did not hinder him from behaving so particular in public that at last everybody talked of it, and many people spoke to my father.

"I was one night going to bed, when I heard my father and mother talking very loud, and my name and Matthews's were repeated very often. This induced me to listen, and I heard my mother tell my father that I was miserable, and that Matthews was equally wretched; that we had loved one another for these some years, and that she was sure it would be my death. My father seemed sometimes to pity and sometimes to condemn me, but at last he resolved I should never see him again. In the morning, when I came to breakfast, my spirits were low, and I could not refrain from tears; this soon brought on an explanation with my father, to whom I confessed everything that had passed. His behaviour was tender to a degree, and by that method he gained more upon me than if he had treated me harshly. Anger I can withstand, but tenderness I never could. My father, after many arguments, wherein he convinced me of the folly, if not wickedness, of such a connection, made me promise never to see him more, and told me he would break

off all intercourse with the family immediately. In
the afternoon of this day Mrs. Sheridan called, by
Matthews's desire, to know the reason why they had
not seen me that day.

"Old Mr. Sheridan (who is now in Dublin) is my
father's particular friend. When they came to settle
in Bath, the strictest intimacy commenced between
our families. Miss Sheridan is the only person
(besides yourself) that I would place any confidence
in ; she is one of the worthiest girls breathing, and
we have been always united in the strictest friendship. The same connection subsists between our two
younger sisters. There are two brothers, who, on our
first acquaintance, both professed to love me ; but,
though I had the greatest esteem for them, I never
gave either of them the least hope that I should ever
look on them in any other light than as the brothers of
my friend ; I own I preferred the youngest, as he is
by far the most agreeable in person, understanding,
and accomplishments. He is a very amiable young
man, beloved by every one, and greatly respected by
all the better sort of people in Bath. He became
acquainted with Matthews, and was at first deceived
in him, but he soon discovered the depravity of his
heart, under the specious appearance of virtue which
he at times assumed ; but, perceiving the attachment
between us, he resolved to make use of a little art to
endeavour, if he could, to save me from such a villain.
For this purpose, he disguised his real sentiments,
and became the most intimate friend of Matthews,
who at last entrusted him with all his designs in regard to me, and boasted to him how cleverly he had
deceived me ; for that I believed him to be an angel.

"Excuse my being thus tedious, but it was necessary

to let you so far into my connection with the
Sheridans, before I could account for my behaviour
latterly.

"When Mr. Sheridan came to me in the evening, I
only told him something had happened to make me
uneasy; but bid him tell Matthews I would write to
him. I accordingly wrote, and told him every circumstance that had happened, showed him how impossible
it was for us to continue any such connection, and
begged (for still I thought him worthy) that he would
write to tell me he was convinced by my arguments,
and that we might part friends, though unhappy ones.
He wrote to me and comforted me greatly by assuring
me of his approbation of my conduct, and that he was
ready to acquiesce in anything to make me happy,
as he was unwilling to see my father. Mr. Sheridan
was appointed to settle everything; he accordingly
came to my father, and told him what Matthews had
said, and that he intended to write to my father and
bind himself in the most solemn manner never to see
me again. My father was satisfied with this, and
pitied Matthews greatly. He kept his word, and my
father was happy that he had settled everything so
amicably.

"Mr. Sheridan was with me every day, and did
everything in his power to make me happy. He said,
if Matthews ever broke his word to my father, he
never would be seen with him again; as he had engaged him in the affair, he was resolved to act the part
of a man of honour. I applauded his sentiments, but
said I thought it impossible that Matthews ever
should. The next day convinced me how cruelly I
had deceived myself. I received a letter from
Matthews, wherein he told me he was going to

The Life of Sheridan

London, but would return in less than two months, and if I did not consent to see him sometimes, he would shoot himself that instant. He said my answer would determine his fate. This letter flung me into fits, as I must either break my word to my father, or consent to the death of the man on whose life my own depended. At last I wrote and expostulated with him once more on the baseness of such a proceeding. This letter, instead of having the wished effect, produced another still more alarming; in this he flung off the tender behaviour for which I always loved him, and put on the language of a tyrant—told me he would see me, that no father on earth should hinder him, and if I would not consent, he would take me off by force. I answered this with some warmth, as I began to see I had been deceived in him. I then insisted he should never write to me again; but he contrived to make me read a letter directed in another hand, wherein he told me we had both been deceived through some mistake; said he had something to communicate of the utmost consequence to my future happiness; and if I would indulge him with ten minutes' conversation, he never after would desire to see me again; but if I refused this last request, I must expect the worst.

"Terrified as I was, with no friend to advise me, I at last consented, and appointed an hour, but the moment he saw me he locked the door, and drawing a pistol from his pocket, uttered the most horrid imprecations, and swore if I would not bind myself by the most solemn oaths to see him again on his return from London, he would shoot himself before my face. Think, my dear girl, on my cruel situation; what could I do? Half distracted, I told him I

The Life of Sheridan

would do anything rather than see him commit so rash an action. This was Saturday, and I promised him (if I was alive) to see him on Wednesday evening during the concert. On this condition he let me go.

"I was to spend the day with Miss Sheridan, who was ill with the toothache. All the time I was with her I was resolving in my own mind what way I was to act. To break my word with my father was impossible. If I did not see Matthews, I expected worse to ensue. What resource was there left? At length (I tremble while I write) I came to the horrid resolution of destroying my own wretched being, as the only means to prevent my becoming still more guilty, and saving my parents from still more distress. With these horrid thoughts I searched Miss Sheridan's room for some laudanum, which I knew she had for the toothache; I found a small bottle full, and put it in my pocket.

"The next day (Sunday), after church, I left my mother and sisters walking. I sat down, made my will, and wrote a letter to my father and one to Matthews. While I was about it, Mr. Sheridan came in; he had observed me taking the laudanum, and when he saw me writing he seemed very much alarmed. At last, after swearing him to secrecy, I told him what I intended to do, and begged him to take charge of the letters. He used every argument in the world to dissuade me from it; but finding them all useless, he entreated me at least not to take it till the afternoon, as he then would tell me something which he was sure would make me lay aside such thoughts entirely. Fearful of his betraying me, I consented; but the moment he was gone took half the quantity, and after dinner, finding it had no effect, I took the rest.

My fears were true. He had gone to Dr. Harrington and Dr. W., and begged of them for God's sake to go to our house that night, in case I should have taken it before he returned in the evening. When he came I was on the settee in a state of lethargy. He immediately ran for the doctors ; but before they could give me any assistance, I dropped down, as they thought, dead. I lay for some time in that dreadful state, till by force they opened my teeth and poured something down my throat, which made me bring up a great deal of the poison.

"To describe the distress of my family at this time is impossible ; but such a scene by all accounts cannot be conceived or imagined. It was happy for me that I was insensible of it, as it would certainly have had a severer effect upon me than all the poison.

"After I had taken everything that was proper, I was put to bed, where I passed the night in the most dreadful agonies of mind at the thoughts of what would be the consequence of this affair.

"Monday evening, Sheridan came to me. He expostulated with me with the greatest tenderness, and showed me the dreadful crime I had been about to commit, and for one who was every way unworthy of my least consideration. He then told me every circumstance relative to myself which Matthews had told him. He showed me letters he had received from him, and wherein his villainy was fully explained.

"Judge what must be my feelings on finding the man, for whom I had sacrificed life, fortune, reputation, everything that was dear, the most abandoned wretch that ever existed. In his last letter to Sheridan he had told him that I had given him so much trouble that he had the greatest inclination to give me up, but his vanity would not let him do that without having gained his point. He therefore said he was resolved the next time I met him to throw off the mask, and if I would not consent to make myself still more infamous, to force me, and then leave me to repent at leisure. He then told how he had acted on Saturday, and that I had promised to see him on Wednesday. He then said he would sufficiently revenge himself for all the trouble I had given him ; but if I changed my mind, and would not see him, he was resolved to carry me off by force. The moment I read this horrid letter I fainted, and it was some time before I could recover my senses sufficiently to thank Mr. Sheridan for his opening my eyes. He said he had made Matthews believe he was equally infamous, that he might the sooner know his designs ; but he said it was not in his power to appear on a friendly footing any longer with such a villain. Mr. Sheridan then asked me what I designed to do. I told him my mind was in such a state of distraction, between anger, remorse, and fear, that I did not know what I should do ; but as Matthews had declared he would ruin my reputation, I was resolved never to stay in Bath. He then first proposed my going to France and entering a convent, where he said I should be safe from all kind of danger, and in time I might recover my peace and tranquillity of mind ; his sister would give me letters of recommendation to St. Quintin, where she had been four years, and he would go with me to protect me ; and after he had seen me settled, he would return to England and place my conduct in such a light that the world would applaud and not condemn me.

" You may be assured I gladly embraced his offer,

as I had the highest opinion of him. He accordingly settled everything ; so that we resolved to go on that fatal Wednesday which was to determine my fate. Miss Sheridan came to me, approved the scheme, and helped me in putting up my clothes. I kept up my spirits very well till the day came, and then I thought I should go distracted. To add to my affliction, my mother miscarried the day before, owing to the fright of Sunday. The being obliged to leave her in such a situation, with the thoughts of the distress in which my whole family would be involved, made me almost give up my resolution ; but, on the other hand, so many circumstances concurred to make it absolutely necessary, that I was, in short, almost distracted.

" At last Sheridan came with two chairs, and having put me half fainting into one, and my trunks into the other, I was carried to a coach that waited in Walcot Street. Sheridan had engaged the wife of one of his servants to go with me as a maid without my knowledge. You may imagine how pleased I was with his delicate behaviour. Before he could follow the chairs he met Matthews, who was going to our house, as I had not undeceived him for fear of the consequence. Sheridan framed some excuse, and after telling him that my mother had miscarried, and that the house was in such confusion it was impossible for him to go in, begged he would go to his sister's, and wait there till he sent for him, as he had an affair of honour on his hands, and perhaps should want his assistance ; by this means he got rid of him.

" We arrived in London about nine o'clock the next morning. From London we went to Dunkirk by sea, where we were recommended to an English family, who treated me very politely. I changed my name to

Harley, as I thought my own rather too public. From thence we proceeded to Lisle, where by chance Sheridan met with an old schoolfellow, who immediately introduced us to an English family, with whom he boarded. They were very amiable people, and recommended us to a convent, which we resolved to accept without going farther.

"Adieu! my dear girl, and believe me yours,

"E. LINLEY."

Miss Linley was at that time but eighteen years of age, and was under articles of apprenticeship to her father until the age of twenty-one, but she was in possession of £3000, which she had obtained under singular circumstances. Mr. Long, a man of fortune, had wooed her for his wife, but she had avowed to him that, if obliged to marry him, she could never bestow her affections on him; he not only resigned himself to his disappointment, but actually took it upon himself to be the responsible cause of the breaking off the match, and paid the sum mentioned as an indemnity for the breach of covenant. Mr. Linley went to Lisle, and, after an explanation with Sheridan, it was resolved that his daughter should fulfil her engagement to him, and they returned together to England.

Scarcely had the elopement become known in Bath, than Matthews, breathing nothing but fury and rage, inserted an advertisement in the *Bath Chronicle*, in which he stated that Mr. Richard Sheridan had left behind him a letter "to account for his scandalous method of running away from the place by insinuations derogatory to his character, and that of a young lady innocent as far as relates to him or to his knowledge";

The Life of Sheridan

and then bestows on him the most scurrilous epithets,
and denounces "some malevolent incendiaries concerned in the propagation of this infamous lie," whom
he threatens to chastise in the most public manner.
Sheridan having read these accusations in France, and
received letters containing the most abusive threats
from Matthews, he determined to meet his opponent
face to face, and declared that he would not lie down
to sleep until he had obtained an ample apology. The
details of the first duel are of the most extraordinary
character, and reflect no honour either upon the principals or their seconds, and the long war of words
subsequent to it is scarcely intelligible.

Their first meeting in Hyde Park was a most ridiculous *rencontre* ending in nothing ; and, fearful of observations, they thence retired to a coffee-house ; and
the scene that ensued, of which we have a minute
description furnished in a published letter of Sheridan,
is one over which the biographer may as well draw a
veil, as so much of mystification exists that it would
be difficult to arrive at a fair conclusion. The most
favourable inference is that Sheridan, unacquainted
with the law of duelling—he could not be of fencing,
for he had been a pupil of Angelo's—rushed in upon
Matthews's guard somewhat unseasonably, and at the
point of the sword obtained an apology. Be the circumstances what they may, the partisans of each of
the duellists were busily occupied in relating the affair
according to their own views ; each insinuating that
much was withheld by the other. The apology, however, was ample. Matthews retracted what he had
said, and begged pardon for the advertisement in the
Chronicle. A second duel was determined on, according to Moore's version of the tale, in consequence of

the coolness with which Matthews found himself received in Wales, and the interference of a Mr. Barnett, whose duelling propensities were to be gratified, whilst the mortification of his principal was to be thus relieved; but those who read even Sheridan's own statement must acknowledge that the first duel was, to the duellists of that day, little more than a disgraceful scuffle, and that the fact of Sheridan's breaking his adversary's sword was quite enough to justify a second meeting. The following letter addressed to Captain Knight must be read:—

"SIR,—On the evening preceding my last meeting with Mr. Matthews, Mr. Barnett[1] produced a paper to me, written by Mr. Matthews, containing an account of our former meetings in London. As I had before frequently heard of Mr. Matthews's relation of that affair, without interesting myself much in contradicting it, I should certainly have treated this in the same manner, had it not been seemingly authenticated by Mr. Knight's name being subscribed to it. My asserting that the paper contains much misrepresentation, equivocation, and falsity, might make it appear strange that I should apply to you in this manner for information on the subject; but, as it likewise contradicts what I have been told were Mr. Knight's sentiments and assertions on that affair, I think I owe it to his credit, as well as my own justification, first, to be satisfied from himself whether he really subscribed and will support the truth of the account shown by Mr. Matthews. Give me leave previously to relate what I have affirmed to have been a real state of our meeting in London, and which I am now ready to

---

[1] The friend of Matthews in the second duel.

The Life of Sheridan

support on my honour, or my oath, as the best account
I can give of Mr. Matthews's relation is, that it is almost
directly opposite to mine.

"Mr. Ewart accompanied me to Hyde Park, about
six in the evening, where we met you and Mr.
Matthews, and we walked together to the ring. Mr.
Matthews refusing to make any other acknowledgment
than he had done, I observed that we were come to
the ground : Mr. Matthews objected to the spot, and
appealed to you. We proceeded to the back of a
building on the other side of the ring ; the ground was
there perfectly level. I called on him, and drew my
sword (he having previously declined pistols). Mr.
Ewart observed a sentinel on the other side of the
building ; we advanced to another part of the park.
I stopped again at a seemingly convenient place : Mr.
Matthews objected to the observation of some people
at a great distance, and proposed to retire to the
Hercules' Pillars till the park should be clear. We did
so. In a little time we returned. I again drew my
sword ; Mr. Matthews again objected to the observation of a person who seemed to watch us. Mr. Ewart
observed that the chance was equal, and engaged that
no one should stop him, should it be necessary for
him to retire to the gate, where we had a chaise and
four, which was equally at his service. Mr. Matthews
declared that he would not engage while any one was
within sight, and proposed to defer it till next morning.
I turned to you and said that 'this was trifling work,'
that I could not admit of any delay, and engaged to
remove the gentleman (who proved to be an officer,
and who, on my going up to him, and assuring him
that any interposition would be ill-timed, politely
retired). Mr. Matthews, in the meantime, had re-

turned towards the gate ; Mr. Ewart and I called to
you, and followed. We returned to the Hercules'
Pillars, and went from thence, by agreement, to the
Bedford Coffee House, where, the master being
alarmed, you came and conducted us to Mr. Matthews
at the Castle Tavern, Henrietta Street. Mr. Ewart
took lights up in his hand, and almost immediately on
our entering the room we engaged. I struck Mr.
Matthews's point so much out of the line, that I
stepped up and caught hold of his wrist, or the hilt of
his sword, while the point of mine was at his breast.
You ran in and caught hold of my arm, exclaiming,
' Don't kill him.' I struggled to disengage my arm,
and said his sword was in my power. Mr. Matthews
called out twice or thrice, ' I beg my life ! ' We were
parted. You immediately said, ' There, he has begged
his life, and now there is an end of it ' ; and on Mr.
Ewart's saying that when his sword was in my power,
as I attempted no more, you should not have interfered, you replied that you were wrong, but that you
had done it hastily and to prevent mischief—or words
to that effect. Mr. Matthews then hinted that I was
rather obliged to your interposition for the advantage ;
you declared that ' before you did so, both the swords
were in Mr. Sheridan's power.' Mr. Matthews still
seemed resolved to give it another turn, and observed
that he had never quitted his sword. Provoked at this,
I then swore (with too much heat, perhaps) that he
should either give up his sword and I would break it,
or go to his guard again. He refused ; but on my per-
sisting, either gave it into my hand, or flung it on
the table, or the ground (which, I will not absolutely affirm). I broke it, and flung the hilt to the
other end of the room. He exclaimed at this. I

took a mourning sword from Mr. Ewart, and pre-
senting him with mine, gave my honour that what had
passed should never be mentioned by me, and he might
now right himself again. He replied that he 'would
never draw a sword against the man who had given
him his life': but, on his still exclaiming against the
indignity of breaking his sword (which he had brought
upon himself), Mr. Ewart offered him the pistols, and
some altercation passed between them. Mr. Matthews
said that he could never show his face if it were
known how his sword was broke—that such a thing
had never been done—that it cancelled all obligations,
&c. &c. You seemed to think it was wrong, and we
both proposed, that if he never misrepresented the
affair, it should not be mentioned by us. This was
settled. I then asked Mr. Matthews whether (as he
had expressed himself sensible of, and shocked at, the
injustice and indignity he had done me in his advertisement) it did not occur to him that he owed me
another satisfaction; and that, as it was now in his
power to do it without discredit, I supposed he would
not hesitate. This he absolutely refused, unless
conditionally: I insisted on it, and said I would not
leave the room till it was settled. After much altercation, and with much ill-grace, he gave the apology,
which afterwards appeared. We parted, and I returned immediately to Bath. I there, to Colonel
Gould, Captain Wade, Mr. Creaser, and others, mentioned the affair to Mr. Matthews's credit—said that
chance had given me the advantage (Mr. Matthews
had consented to that apology), and mentioned nothing of the sword. Mr. Matthews came down, and
in two days I found the whole affair had been stated
in a different light, and insinuations given out to

the same purpose as in the paper, which has occasioned this trouble. I had undoubted authority that these accounts proceeded from Mr. Matthews, and likewise that Mr. Knight had never had any share in them. I then thought I no longer owed Mr. Matthews the compliment to conceal any circumstance, and I related the affair to several gentlemen exactly as above.

"Now, Sir, as I have put down nothing in this account but upon the most assured recollection, and as Mr. Matthews's paper either directly or equivocally contradicts almost every article of it, and as your name is subscribed to that paper, I flatter myself that I have a right to expect your answer to the following questions. First,

"Is there any falsity or misrepresentation in what I have advanced above ?

"With regard to Mr. Matthews's paper—did I, in the park, seem in the smallest article inclined to enter into conversation with Mr. Matthews ? He insinuates that I did.

"Did Mr. Matthews not beg his life ? He affirms he did not.

"Did I break his sword without warning ? He affirms I did it without warning, on his laying it on the table.

"Did I not offer him mine ? He omits it.

"Did Mr. Matthews give me the apology, as a point of generosity, on my desisting to demand it ? He affirms he did.

"I shall now give my reasons for doubting your having authenticated this paper.

"1. Because I think it full of falsehood and misrepresentation, and Mr. Knight has the character of a man of truth and honour.

" 2. When you were at Bath, I was informed that you had never expressed any such sentiments.

" 3. I have been told that, in Wales, Mr. Matthews never told his story in the presence of Mr. Knight, who had never there insinuated anything to my disadvantage.

" 4. The paper shown me by Mr. Barnett contains (if my memory does not deceive me) three separate sheets of writing-paper. Mr. Knight's evidence is annexed to the last, which contains chiefly a copy of our first proposed advertisements, which Mr. Matthews had, in Mr. Knight's presence, agreed should be destroyed as totally void ; and which (in a letter to Colonel Gould, by whom I had insisted on it) he declared upon his honour he knew nothing about, nor should ever make the least use of.

"These, Sir, are my reasons for applying to yourself, in preference to any appeal to Mr. Ewart, my second on that occasion, which is what I would wish to avoid. As for Mr. Matthews's assertions, I shall never be concerned at them. I have ever avoided any verbal altercation with that gentleman, and he has now secured himself from any other. I am your very humble servant,

" R. B. Sheridan."

The second duel took place near Bath : there is something exceedingly ludicrous in the descriptions which have appeared of this ferocious *rencontre*. Captain Matthews was anxious to have recourse to pistols, fearful that Sheridan, if the sword was employed, would again rush in upon him, and that an ungentlemanly scuffle would be the consequence ; he was, however, overruled, not by any arguments or by any decision, but by Sheridan drawing his sword and advancing upon Matthews in a vaunting manner. According to the *St. James's Chronicle* of July 4th, "Both their swords breaking upon the first lunge, they threw each other down, and with the broken pieces hacked at each other rolling upon the ground, the seconds standing by quiet spectators." The newspapers teemed with the marvellous deeds of valour of both parties, but the favourite was young Sheridan. The letter of Mr. Barnett, the second of Matthews, descriptive of the scene, was not so satisfactory, however, to this hero of the drama as might be expected; for he declared that Mr. Matthews discovered as much genuine cool and intrepid resolution as man could do, and that Sheridan's wounds, which were proclaimed to be of a most terrific character, were but skin deep, and that the fist or the hilt of the sword was as likely to have produced them as the weapons used.

Certain it is that the second duel was received as a most apocryphal proof of the gallantry of Sheridan; and it is an undeniable fact that Matthews's version of the story was essentially different. There are many now resident in Bath who remember to have heard him repeat his tale, in a consistent manner, and who imagine that Moore was made acquainted with it.

Matthews, who, even in his days of wrath, looked upon Sheridan as an exceedingly delightful companion, and as a lover of practical jokes, always spoke of the duel as a specimen of the exhibition of these qualifications. He stated that a friendly communication actually passed between them on the night previous to the duel, amounting to an invitation from Sheridan to sup with him and the seconds; that

The Life of Sheridan

Sheridan remained at table drinking claret until the time of appointment; that when he quitted it, he walked up Milsom Street, and observing Captain Matthews's chaise waiting at the door to take him to the spot, he reeled into it himself, and insisted upon his seconds following his example; he then desired the driver to proceed to the ground, which Matthews could not have reached in time had not the carriage of Captain Paumier taken him there. He found Sheridan in a high state of excitement from potations deep. The duel soon commenced, and, as described by Barnett, Sheridan rushed upon him and tried to wrest his sword out of his grasp; he succeeded in breaking it, and then fell down dragging Matthews upon him. A few slight wounds were made, but the blood, of which so much had been spoken, was, in fact, the claret discharged from the stomach of Sheridan. It would be impossible to arrive at any just conclusion from the statement of both parties. The reply of Sheridan to the injurious reports in several papers was so long delayed that it was at last forgotten. He had requested Woodfall to print, in the *Morning Advertiser*, the articles that reflected upon his own conduct, promising to send his refutation; unfortunately, his request was complied with, and the statements of his opponents were more largely promulgated, whilst his defence, from his indolence, was never to be read. Sheridan, however, became the theme of conversation and of curiosity: thus his first step in life led to notoriety, and in the minds of many to reputation, which he fortunately was capable of maintaining.

Immediately after the public announcement of their marriage, the young couple lived for a short time in

retirement at East Burnham, and it was soon generally promulgated that the fair siren had retired from
the musical world. The cause was by some said to be
her own dislike of appearing before large audiences;
by others, the delicacy of feeling on the part of
young Sheridan. The reputation which her talents
had acquired, the curiosity which her adventures
had excited, led every one to be anxious that Mrs.
Sheridan should continue a profession which she had
so much ornamented. She was, indeed, under an
engagement to sing at the Triennial Festival at
Worcester, and the remuneration to which she would
have been entitled was one thousand pounds for
twelve nights, and this not for one year only, but
for several seasons; besides which, it was averaged
that a large sum would be produced by a benefit;
but notwithstanding the assistance of Lord North,
at that time Chancellor of the University of Oxford,
who was called into the negotiation, that she might
sing at the meeting, the determination was inflexibly
adhered to, and Sheridan would not listen to any
proposal that would lead to her reappearance. The
stern moralist, Dr. Johnson, spoke of this resolution
to Boswell with expressions of approbation, when he
learnt that a young man without a shilling would not
permit his wife to become the public gaze.

From this time forward, it would appear that
Sheridan had made up his mind to depend upon his
own mental resources for his success in life, and to
strain every nerve to acquire wealth, although, alas!
for his own peace of mind and happiness, he knew
little of the art by which, when once gained, it is to be
kept. The first great result of this resolution was the
production of one of the best comedies ever penned,

The Life of Sheridan

and which, in spite of many deserving claimants to public approbation, has outlived the greater number of its successors.

The "Rivals" was first performed at Covent Garden the 17th of January 1775, and on that eventful night was proclaimed a failure. It was scarcely borne with, and all Sheridan's fond anticipations were nearly overthrown. The unfavourable reception was attributed to its being double the length of any acting comedy; to Sir Lucius O'Trigger, as being a national reflection, and likewise to the representative of Sir Lucius O'Trigger, Mr. Lee, for in this he so miserably acted as to call down shouts of disapprobation. Fortunately, on the following night, Mr. Clinch was his substitute; and so well did he satisfy Sheridan, that he prepared for Mr. Clinch's benefit the humorous farce of "St. Patrick's Day; or, The Scheming Lieutenant," which was brought out successfully in the following May. It, however, wanted any great claim to favour, and must be considered rather as a piece written for a particular occasion than as a dramatic effort. Not so with the "Rivals"; this was a masterpiece of art on which young Sheridan had bestowed time and labour.

The comedy was brought out with all the strength of the company; Shuter was the representative of the impetuous and boisterous Sir Anthony Absolute; Quick was the Acres; Lewis, Falkland; and Mrs. Green, Mrs. Malaprop; a prologue written by Sheridan was spoken by Woodward and Quick, under the characters of a Serjeant-at-Law and an Attorney; Woodward presents himself as counsel for the poet; but notwithstanding he stated that he never faced a milder jury, the storm of disapprobation commenced so early

The Life of Sheridan

as to justify the observation afterwards made by
Sheridan in his preface, that much of it must have
arisen from virulence of malice rather than severity of
criticism. On the tenth night Sheridan produced
another prologue, which was admirably delivered by
Mrs. Bulkley, whose Julia appears to have been a
marked favourite with the audience. Both of the
prologues are well written, and though they are not
peculiarly adapted for the particular play which they
ushered in, but might belong to any comedy for which
the favour of an audience is to be solicited, they show
that Sheridan had capacity which stood in lieu of
experience, and that he had the judgment which prevented the natural vanity of a young author from
becoming offensive. The epilogue was also spoken
by Mrs. Bulkley, and deserves to be preserved as one
of those lively and clever specimens of a style in which
Sheridan would have excelled had he bestowed some
portion of time on its cultivation. It is an epigrammatic, terse, and well-turned compliment to the gentler
sex. The moral of his comedy is, that on the world's
great stage woman rules :—

> " One moral's plain, without more fuss,
>   Man's social happiness all rests on us ;
>   Through all the drama, whether damned or not,
>   Love gilds the scene, and women guide the plot."

Mrs. Sheridan's family ascribed this epilogue to her,
so highly did they estimate her abilities ; however, no
doubt exists but that Sheridan himself composed it.
He had the gratification to find his play gradually grow
in public estimation, and it was received in the provinces with great enthusiasm. Of course, in Bath it
was speedily produced, and as the theatrical tribunal
in that city was looked up to as of the highest order,

its success there gave the greatest satisfaction. Mr. Dimond, afterwards the proprietor of the theatre, produced a great impression; Keaseberry, the Acres, was an admirable comic performer, and, as acting manager, bestowed great pains upon it. At Bristol, Mrs. Canning was much admired in Julia. During the popularity of the "Rivals," Sheridan's father, who had for some years been estranged from Brinsley, and who obstinately refused a reconciliation, went to the theatre, accompanied by his daughters, to judge for himself of its merits. His son placed himself at the side scene opposite his parent, and continued throughout the performance to gaze at him with tenderness and affection. On his return home he was overpowered with emotion, and, in reply to some inquiries from Mrs. Sheridan as to the cause of his apparent agitation, observed that he painfully felt that his father and sisters should sit before him and he be unable to join them.

It would be a task of no small difficulty at this time of day to criticise the "Rivals," to hold up to admiration the scenes which are most deserving praise, or to point out the delicate touches which distinguish each character. We cannot, however, refrain from making an observation in reply to those who have studied the beautiful imaginings of Sheridan, and have found several of those defects, which certainly may exist in the most carefully digested works. They have pointed out that every individual who appears on the scene is a wit of his kind, and that the humblest personage, be he a coachman, a usurer, a valet, or an humble friend, is a humorist in his way, and occasionally much too clever for his situation. To a certain extent this may be correct; but we shall never find a single smart

The Life of Sheridan

saying, a jest, or a sneer put into the mouth not
adapted for it. Not one single phrase is misplaced ;
if it came from any one person but the one for whom
it was written it would appear like a daub upon a
picture. Not one of his personages but is perfectly
distinct in his conversation from his neighbour ; a
clever thing becomes doubly so if appropriate to the
situation of him who speaks it, and this is precisely
the case with these dramas. Nobody else could utter
the things which the Coachman or Fag says in the
first scene ; neither Acres nor Sir Lucius O'Trigger
could be borne with if they had not each their own
sly hits and extravagant observations, adapted with
admirable judgment to their respective positions, and
the characteristics by which they are distinguished.
Mrs. Malaprop has been censured by critics as an
outrageous caricature ; but there are those in Bath to
whom it has been handed down that there was an
original from whom a tolerably well-drawn portrait
was taken, and that a lady who distinguished herself
as a minuet dancer was as remarkable for the singular
"choice of epitaphs" as the She Dragon whom
Sheridan has given to the world. We must confess
we find it much more difficult to discover the history
of his marriage, and the duel in which he was involved, in the drama. It is true that he has laid the
scene in Bath, with which he was familiar, and where
such persons as an Irish fortune-hunter, a booby
squire, a female matrimonial adventurer with a
marriageable niece, an irritable country gentleman,
and a love-sick youth were likely to rendezvous ; but
why on this account it should be found to correspond
with his own romantic adventures we cannot imagine.
The clever touches at the state of society in that

fashionable town, its lounges, its early hours, its circulating libraries, its abbey thickly peopled with the dead, are the natural results of the observation which even a superficial stranger might make, without it being attributed to him that a love of scandal and of satire was predominant in him. The least interesting of his delineations, Falkland and Julia, partake of the same talent ; and although they have been objected to as unnecessary to the general action of the comedy, yet they exhibit an intimate acquaintance with the springs that guide the lover's heart, and the peculiar form of jealousy which is held up to reprobation is one that required castigation. The language which the lovers express themselves in has been considered to exhibit false finery by one who has himself given to the world much more elaborate ornament and much more of false taste than any other author of our age.

The youth of Sheridan must be borne in mind when we pass any critical remarks upon the " Rivals," and we then shall be disposed to view it as the production of natural genius. At the age of twenty-three, a comedy remarkable for its wit, its ingenuity, and its knowledge of the world must be the result of innate powers. There had been no time for deep observation, reflection, and the study of human nature. There must have been a quick perception of character, a power of adaptation, and a rapid insight into the effects produced upon an audience by dramatic skill. We find individuals brought before us whom we recognise as the fair objects of legitimate comedy, their peculiarities, their foibles presented to us so as to excite our laughter, without any of that harshness or asperity which demands severe chastisement. In the midst of all their extravagances they have some re-

deeming good qualities, which make us pleased that
they sufficiently suffer by the exposure of their follies,
and the same holds good with his more matured
comedy, the "School for Scandal." If the "Rivals"
does not abound with the same sparkle, if there be less
polish in the dialogue, if the turn of satirical wit be
less epigrammatic, there is much more of the character
of common life about it, there is more ingenuity in the
several contrivances, the peculiarities of each individual lead to more decided ends, and are more skil-
fully combined to produce an effect. It is more like
the usual comedies of the stage, and there are more of
those conventional personages to whom time has reconciled us, and given to them its acknowledged sanction. We have had most of them placed before us
by other comic writers, but they have not been so
dexterously managed, nor have they appeared in so
vivid a light, or been so cleverly brought together.
The materials are of a very slight texture, yet the
whole is woven into a solid fabric well suited to the
ordinary taste. We are told that Sir Anthony Absolute and Mrs. Malaprop remind us of honest Matthew
Bramble and his sister Tabitha, and that Acres is a
distinct descendant of Sir Andrew Aguecheek. Granted
that it is so, the greater the praise due to Sheridan in
having placed in so ingenious a form before us our old
favourites ; and as much right have we to complain of
the want of variety in the lovely flowers that are
created by the hand of nature, because the petals of
some of them are distinguishable in shape only by
very slight apparent variations, and yet when we examine them we find they possess colouring totally distinct, and qualities quite at variance. The Irish fortune-
hunter, the romantic loving girl, the poltroon, and the

The Life of Sheridan

dictatorial father, are subjects with whom we daily
meet in novels and in plays; but it cannot detract
from the originality of Sheridan that he has ingeniously introduced them into a drama, made them act
and react upon each other, until they produce a most
agreeable impression upon the mind, and give us
rational amusement by the display of the singularities
which it is the peculiar province of the dramatist to
depict.

The "Duenna" was brought out on the 21st of
November 1775, and immediately became a favourite
with the public; it had, at the outset, a much longer
career than the "Beggar's Opera," which was looked
upon as the most successful drama of its class ever
placed upon the stage. For the progress of the composition, dramatic, poetic, and musical, a reference
must be made to Moore, who has given the letters
which passed between Sheridan and Linley previous
to its performance. We believe that the popularity of
this opera has never been exceeded, and even to this
hour the common quotations from its songs prove
how much they were in the thoughts of every one.
Many sayings which have become proverbial, and
whose origin is altogether forgotten, have their source
from this old favourite of our forefathers, to which
they listened with rapture, and from which it was at
one period considered fashionable to repeat lines. Indeed, independently of the conversation, which is of
no ordinary cast, there are so many beautiful expressions in the songs, that we cannot be surprised at their
reception, nor that many should be committed to
memory. We are astonished at the many comments
which have been made as to the direct violation of
probability in the plot of the "Duenna." It is con-

The Life of Sheridan

tended that no Spanish nobleman would allow his
daughter to marry a Jew recently baptized, and that it
is inconsistent that Seville, the very seat of the Inqui-
sition, should be laid down as the scene of the adventure described. So far from a recently converted
Jew being an object of either suspicion or dislike,
every favour was shown in Spain to those who abandoned the faith of their fathers from conviction, and
they became persons of weight and respectability.
Nor do we see the force of the objection that a man
hackneyed in the world should marry an old duenna
instead of a young and lovely girl, whose description indeed he had just heard ; but the person who
had drawn the picture was the parent, and naturally
enough might have been supposed to have viewed his
own offspring with a father's predilection, whilst the
sordid lover only thought of the wealth he was to
obtain, and to him the want of beauty was a secondary
consideration. Whatever may be the objections which
have been raised, the " Duenna " has maintained a
high reputation ; and should we ever again have to
boast upon the stage the talents and the powers of
Leoni or Braham, it will again be brought forward, its
dialogue be listened to with delight, its airs refresh the
memories of the old, and kindle enthusiasm in the
young.

Neither prologue nor epilogue seems to have been
thought necessary for an opera, but a playful poetic
finale sung by the various characters on the stage
brings it to a happy conclusion. It appears that it
was first printed in 1794, but upon what authority we
cannot trace, for Sheridan himself disavowed ever
having revised any edition. In 1807, we learn from
Kelly that he performed the part, in the " Duenna," of

The Life of Sheridan

Ferdinand. It was customary with him, when he played at night, to read his part over in the morning, in order to refresh his memory; one morning, after reading the part of Ferdinand, he left the printed play of the "Duenna," as then acted, on the table. On his return home he found Sheridan reading it, and with pen and ink before him correcting it. He said to him, "Do you act the part of Ferdinand from this printed copy?" To this Kelly replied in the affirmative, and added that he had done so for twenty years. Then said he, "You have been acting great nonsense." He examined every sentence, and corrected it all through before he left him. The corrections Kelly preserved in Sheridan's own handwriting; but, he observes, what could prove his negligence more than correcting an opera, which he had written in 1775, in the year 1807, and then abusing the manner in which it was printed. Kelly, however, had many more opportunities of becoming acquainted with Sheridan's sins of omission, which he does not fail to communicate to his readers in those reminiscences which he has written to the great satisfaction of the lovers of music and the drama. Whatever may have been the carelessness with which the dialogue of the "Duenna" may have been produced, such was not the case either with the poetry or the music; they both of them are exquisite of their kind, and the airs were borrowed from Linley, Rauzzini, and Dr. Harrington. The letters which are preserved of all the parties interested in the success of the opera show that no pains were spared; in those of Sheridan, which are given by Moore, we see that he was laborious, anxious, and painstaking. We are let almost too much behind the scenes, for we find that Sunday was fixed for a

The Life of Sheridan

musical rehearsal, and we learn how much was done for the individuals who happened at that time to take a prominent lead; thus the fondness of Leoni for a flourish, in which he was followed by Braham, was to be indulged in; Miss Brown was to show off her execution, and as Mr. "Simpson's hautboy is to cut a figure, Echo, who is always allowed to play her part, is lugged in." Linley, upon whom all the music rested, seems to have amply fulfilled the expectations of his son-in-law, and to have taken up his ideas with great quickness. The finale to the first act, so generally admired, in which Isaac and Donna Louisa sing a duet, and after Don Carlos has sung the beautiful air, "Gentle Maid," join with him in a glee, is the idea of Sheridan carried out by Linley. Don Jerome's song, "Oh, the days when I was young," once in the mouth of every boy in the street, is another of Sheridan's hints. That beautiful air, "By him we love offended, how soon our anger flies," was originally composed by that celebrated master, Rauzzini, "Fuggiamo de questo loco in piena liberta." When we compare the trash usually composed for English operas with the exquisite specimens of taste with which Sheridan has adorned the "Duenna," we cannot but express our surprise that there should be found audiences to tolerate the vile nonsense. "Had I a heart for falsehood famed;" "Oh, had my love ne'er smiled on me"; "How oft, Louisa, hast thou told"; "I ne'er could any lustre see," may vie with any compositions of a similar character; they are delicate, polished, and refined; they are full of tenderness of expression, and awaken the gentlest emotions. Nor are the livelier songs to be passed over, for they are animated and full of joyous feelings.

The Life of Sheridan

The "Duenna," like the "Rivals," was produced at Covent Garden. We find, however, that Mr. Linley was most anxious to direct the attention of Garrick to his son-in-law, and to prepare the way for his being amongst those who offered their incense at the shrine over which he presided; and he seems gradually to have paved the road for his success at Drury Lane Theatre. There is a letter, amongst the mass of those collected in the Garrick correspondence, from Linley to Dr. Hoadley, and another also from him to Mr. Garrick. In the former he says, "I have engaged to assist my son-in-law, Sheridan, in composing an opera which he is to bring out at Covent Garden this winter. I am a good deal distressed that from some misunderstanding between him and Mr. Garrick, that he is not connected with Drury Lane House, for though I believe they are now on very good terms, yet Sheridan thinks that he has been so honourably treated by Mr. Harris that he ought not to keep anything that he has written from him. However, I hope Mr. Garrick will not take anything amiss in my assisting him on this occasion, for it is a matter of absolute necessity that he should endeavour to get money by this means, as he will not be prevailed on to let his wife sing." To Garrick he says, "I have promised to assist Sheridan in compiling—I believe this is the properest term—an opera, which I understand from him he has engaged to produce at Covent Garden this season. I have already set some airs which he has given me, and he intends writing new words to some other tunes of mine. My son has likewise written some tunes for him, and I understand he is to have some others from Mr. Jackson of Exeter. This is a mode of proceeding in regard to his composition which I by no means approve of. I think he ought first to have finished his opera with the songs he intends to introduce in it, and have got it entirely new set. No musician can set a song properly unless he understands the character and knows the performer who is to exhibit it. For my part I shall be very unwilling for either my own name or my son's to appear in this business, and it is my present resolution to forbid it ; for I have great reason to be diffident of my own abilities and genius, and my son has not had experience in theatrical compositions, though I think well of his invention and musical skill. I would not have been concerned in this business at all, but that I know there is an absolute necessity for him to endeavour to get some money by this means, as he will not be prevailed upon to let his wife sing, and indeed at present she is incapable, and nature will not permit me to be indifferent to his success. You are deservedly at that point of fame which few of the great geniuses the world has produced have arrived at— above the reach of envy—and are the protector of dramatic merit, in what place or shape soever you find it, and I look up to you as the patron and director of both theatres, virtually, if not officially. I hope Sheridan has done nothing to forfeit the protection you have hitherto shown him." These appeals to the generous and liberal feelings of the great Roscius were not in vain. Not only did he, wherever his influence extended, assist Sheridan in his way into literary society, but, when the time was fully come, placed him on a pinnacle where he should have established himself, without being dazzled with the *ignes fatui* that played before his sight.

From these letters we may fairly conclude that

The Life of Sheridan

Linley did not then sufficiently appreciate the value
of his son-in-law, that he was hardly satisfied with his
determination to prevent his daughter again appearing before the public, and that he was an unwilling
labourer with him in the vineyard which was to produce such a valuable harvest. It must indeed have
been gratifying to him to find that the " Duenna" was
hailed with such rapturous delight, and that it maintained a position on the stage for so many years.
Much is undoubtedly owing to the judgment and
musical talent of Linley ; some of the airs he introduced will ever be heard with delight. The air,
with Sheridan's touching words, " By him we love
offended," the production of the well-known Rauzzini,
was a favourite in the musical world throughout
Europe. It was the production of that great master
to whom England is so deeply indebted for some of
the first vocalists we have had ; for, together with his
own instruction, he instilled into the minds of his
pupils, amongst whom Braham is the last, to visit
Italy, to study at Rome under Latilla, or at Naples
under Monopoli, Finerolli, or Porpori, at that time
the most distinguished of music-masters. Rauzzini
himself, however, was unequalled as a musician ; from
his rich stores much has been gleaned up to the present hour. His career was a singular one. He was
a native of Rome, and from the exquisite sweetness
of his voice had been selected, in compliance with
the miserable taste of that age, to be rendered fit
for singing in a style then much admired, but which
modern judgment has rejected. He performed the
parts of the principal female, as no woman was
allowed upon the stage in the Holy City. His singular beauty became the theme of general conversation ;

he was courted and flattered everywhere. On his visit to Munich, a distinguished personage evinced such admiration and heaped such caresses upon him that the ruling prince gave him a delicate hint, to which he was compelled to pay attention, that the time had arrived when his talent had ceased to be attractive. Rauzzini, with some indignation, resented the want of hospitality, and serious results were apprehended, when an invitation to England induced him to undertake an engagement at the Italian Opera ; for the *furore* had spread to London, and his acting, his singing, and his compositions were at once fashionable. Garrick pronounced his " Pyramus " "the finest piece of representation he had ever witnessed on the Italian stage "; but, alas ! a change came over the "spirit of the dream "; the climate affected his voice, and he never perfectly recovered from its effects. He settled in Bath, where for years he continued to teach, to compose, and preside at the pianoforte at all the great musical festivals. Beloved by every one, he was the centre of a most accomplished circle, comprising all the taste and talent of Bath. At Christmas Eve, Billington, Storace, Mora, Braham, and all the first-rate musicians of the day assembled ; a concert, consisting of the " Messiah," was given to the public, from which Rauzzini drew a portion of his income. This, alas ! never equalled his expenditure, the consequence of which was the embitterment of his latter days ; but to the last he maintained a splendid establishment, and was looked up to as one of those to whom Bath was indebted for its popularity. Whenever the venerable old man took his accustomed seat in the orchestra, tokens of regard and respect awaited him, and to the last he preserved beauty of countenance of a striking character.

The Life of Sheridan

In the year 1775 Garrick decided to quit the scene
of his many triumphs, and to retire from the theatre
which he had for so long a period managed with
singular felicity. He had just then attained the sixtieth
year of his age ; and although whenever he appeared
before the public he met with an enthusiastic reception, he resolved to resign his position, and to place in
other hands the power he had so long wielded. He had
very lately gone to considerable expense for various
improvements in Drury Lane Theatre, hence his
determination appeared somewhat sudden, and produced considerable surprise. When it was whispered
who the individual was into whose guidance he was
likely to commit the management, much conversation
was naturally excited. Although it was known that
Garrick had always most favourably expressed himself
of the talent and character of the youthful author, and
had specially introduced him to the first literary men
of the day, it was likewise borne in mind that Sheridan's
father had never been on good terms with Roscius,
and that on several occasions he had expressed himself with considerable animosity against him, and had
shown a degree of haughtiness in his demeanour towards him that was likely to alienate the kind feelings
which actuated Garrick, who when, according to
Davies, he spoke to a publisher of Mrs. Sheridan's
comedy, the "Discovery," eulogised it in language of
the most favourable character, and even went so far
as to say that the play was one of the best that he had
ever read, and that money would be well laid out in
its purchase. It is true that from the elder Sheridan
there was little of rivalry to be dreaded by Garrick,
although he was occasionally thrust forward as his
equal. As a speaker and declaimer few were to be

compared with him; but his monotonous tones, his pedantic manner, and his studied action, came but badly into competition with the impassioned tones and the naturally expressed feelings of Garrick. However much the theatrical world was surprised at the predilection which the veteran master of the stage exhibited for the youthful aspirant, no one doubted that the choice had fallen upon one fully equal to the task he had undertaken. He had already shown a thorough knowledge of the stage, and had brought forward the labour of his intellect, with considerable acquaintance of the points which tell with an audience. He had evinced much skill in placing before the public the "Duenna"; he had contrived to unite the dialogue and the music in a more pleasing way than usual, and his assiduity peculiarly touched the fancy of Garrick, who would not listen to numerous applicants, who no sooner heard of the probable change than they stood forward in hopes of becoming his successor. Colman would have willingly been the purchaser, but was desirous of being the sole proprietor, and as this could not be arranged, he abandoned a negotiation which he had commenced. Most probably Sheridan would not have been his successor had not Garrick anticipated, from the kind manner and the thoughtlessness of his young friend, that he himself would continue to direct the theatre and to maintain an influence which he felt loth at once to abandon. In the month of June a contract was entered into by which Sheridan came into possession of two-fourteenths, Mr. Linley the same, and Dr. Ford three-fourteenths, making, for the purchase of Garrick's share, the total sum of thirty-five thousand pounds: the letters which passed between Sheridan

The Life of Sheridan

and Linley on the subject were placed in the hands of Moore, and were published by him in his biography.

Every one who looked on this transaction was astonished at the speculative disposition of Sheridan; they marvelled at the whole of this singular transition from nothingness to the possession of an immense property. Unaccustomed as they were in those days to the bold operations of which the present age affords such numerous instances, of purchases made without one single sixpence of money being advanced, all looked with an eye of wonder and suspicion at the sudden acquisition. It was already whispered that the young author lived far beyond his means; that he was associating with the great and the wealthy; that he ventured to entertain upon a liberal scale, and that there were no visible funds from which his wealth was drawn. Various have been the explanations offered, and many channels have been pointed at as those from which he was enabled to meet the demands which were made upon him. There is, however, little doubt that he was advised by some able financier at his first outset, and that from Garrick he experienced the most generous consideration; but with whatever assistance he was furnished, it was not sufficient, as the embarrassments which gradually grew upon him fully proved. From this period may be traced the commencement of those difficulties which harassed him in after life, and that carelessness which ended in a recklessness that almost became proverbial. The embarrassments which he had to encounter, and which he fought off with adroitness, with wit, with practical jokes, and with every species of cunning, have been the theme of the humorist for many a day, and anecdotes, which sprang out of them, have been repeated from father to son till they became the standing jest of families. His first commencement as a manager was not of that brilliant kind to give any promise of great improvement in the conduct of the theatre. An alteration of Vanbrugh's play, the "Relapse," was the first production, under the name of "A Trip to Scarborough"; it was brought out February 24, 1777. This was an unfortunate commencement; neither the public nor the actors were satisfied. On the second night there was a decided opposition to its performance, but the actors were taught that, whatever opinion they might themselves form of the merits of a piece, it was their duty to perform their parts with propriety and with energy. The "Tempest" was also brought forward; parts of Dryden's version were given, which, together with some songs by Thomas Linley, served for a short time to fill up the night; but still there was a general feeling that the public had lost by the exchange of managers, when the town was astonished and delighted by the production of a comedy that has deservedly gained for its author an undying reputation, the "School for Scandal."

On the 8th of May 1777, that inimitable comedy, which has become a standard play wherever the English language is spoken, the "School for Scandal," was first brought forward. There was no doubt, from the earliest moment that it was listened to, that it was one of those brilliant and captivating productions of the human mind that are to be classed amongst the results of that inspiration of real genius with which some individuals, more fortunate than the rest of our race, are occasionally gifted. It was felt throughout its performance that there were those qualities in

The Life of Sheridan

it which excite our admiration, and leave behind the
happiest impression. It is neither from the artifice of
the plot, the delineation of character, nor the exhibition of those strong emotions of the heart, which
either astonish us or awaken sympathy, that we derive
so much pleasure ; it is from the correct adaptation
of such person to the scene, and from the happy
management of incidents, which, though few in
number, always occur at the right moment, whilst
the light, airy, sparkling dialogue suits the understanding of every auditor. It may safely be
pronounced the genuine effusion of an imagination alive to conversational power and beauty,
and to the effect of striking contrasts. Moore
was enabled, through his influence with the remaining relations of Sheridan, to lay before the public a
large portion of the manuscripts which were originally
drawn up by the author. He has shown us how
gradually, from two distinct plays, he was led to produce a perfect one, and to incorporate in that the
leading ideas, which he had intended to work up into
two separate pieces. It altogether forms a literary
curiosity, and exhibits to us by what repeated efforts,
by what lengthened process, an author gradually
weaves one beautiful piece of workmanship out of the
various raw materials placed in his hands ; and we
draw the inference that the powers of man are very
limited, and that time, labour, and unceasing exertion
are necessary for a work which, at first sight, appears
easy of construction and simple in its development.
We do not, perhaps, feel that it adds to the interest
we take in the author ; we are disappointed to find that
the bright sparks which we fancied were struck off by
a moment's collision are the effects of slow hammer-

ing ; that a sparkling expression, seemingly so instantaneous and happy, has been at first a dull, dry
remark, gradually elaborated into the shape in which
it appears. The slow transformation of Solomon
Teazle, a widower, having had five children, talking
over his wife's extravagance with his butler, into the
elegant, high-minded, disappointed Sir Peter Teazle ;
of Plausible into Joseph Surface ; of a silly country
girl, ill-bred and impertinent, into the lively, elegant,
fashionable, but thoughtless Lady Teazle, is interesting
amongst the curiosities of literature, but by no means
impresses us with that feeling of admiration for him
whom we find so much an artist. We feel that we
have been admitted behind the scenes, where lately
we have seen a spectacle of gorgeous splendour, and
the gaudy trappings, the false jewels, and the sparkling
tinsel from which the magnificence of the decorations
was produced, present us with a contrast somewhat too
forcible to be pleasing. Much, therefore, as we feel
indebted to the biographer who has ransacked every
escritoire which might contain a memorandum of his
hero, we almost wish that he had not shown us every
erasure, every superfluity, every blot that could be
seen. As no man, let his position be the highest,
can conceal from those immediately around him his
peculiarities and his defects, so none can bear the
inquisitive examination of those who trace literary
history for perfection ; Minerva springs armed from
the head of no one but Jupiter. The only advantage
in the general view of Sheridan's character to be
gained by this exhibition is, that he was neither careless
nor indolent, as was generally supposed, but that he
laboured with assiduity and constant diligence, and
that although he might be desirous to astonish with

The Life of Sheridan

the rapidity of his productions, he was indebted for their perfection as much to art and laborious consideration as he was to nature and his own genius.

It is evident that there were two different sketches drawn up by Sheridan, which he afterwards blended. One of them was more properly the "School for Scandal," the other a two-act comedy for the Teazles. The following were the *dramatis personæ* of the latter :—

Sir Rowland Harpur	Old Teazle
—— Plausible	
Captain H. Plausible	Mrs. Teazle
Freeman	Maria

and the following was the opening scene :—

"ACT I

"SCENE I.—OLD TEAZLE (*alone*).

"In the year '44, I married my first wife ; the wedding was at the end of the year—ay, 'twas in December ; yet, before Ann. Dom. '45, I repented. A month before, we swore we preferred each other to the whole world—perhaps we spoke truth ; but, when we came to promise to love each other till death, there I am sure we lied. Well, Fortune owed me a good turn ; in '48 she died. Ah, silly Solomon, in '52 I find thee married again ! Here, too, is a catalogue of ills— Thomas, born February 12 ; Jane, born January 6 ; so they go on to the number of five. However, by death I stand credited but by one. Well, Margery, rest her soul ! was a queer creature ; when she was gone I felt awkward at first, and being sensible that wishes availed nothing, I often wished for her return. For ten years

[73]

more I kept my senses and lived single. Oh, block-head, dolt Solomon! Within this twelvemonth thou art married again—married to a woman thirty years younger than thyself; a fashionable woman. Yet I took her with caution; she had been educated in the country, but now she has more extravagance than the daughter of an Earl, more levity than a Countess. What a defect it is in our laws, that a man who has once been branded in the forehead should be hanged for the second offence.

" *Enter* JARVIS.

" *Teaz.* Who's there? Well, Jarvis?

" *Jarv.* Sir, there are a number of my mistress's tradesmen without, clamorous for their money.

" *Teaz.* Are those their bills in your hand?

" *Jarv.* Something about a twentieth part, sir.

" *Teaz.* What! have you expended the hundred pounds I gave you for her use.

" *Jarv.* Long ago, sir, as you may judge by some of the items :—' Paid the coachmaker for lowering the front seat of the coach.'

" *Teaz.* What the deuce was the matter with the seat?

" *Jarv.* Oh Lord, the carriage was too low for her by a foot when she was dressed—so that it must have been so, or have had a tub at top like a hat-case on a travelling trunk. Well, sir (*reads*), ' Paid her two footmen half a year's wages, £50.'

" *Teaz.* 'Sdeath and fury! does she give her foot-men a hundred a year?

" *Jarv.* Yes, sir, and I think, indeed, she has rather made a good bargain, for they find their own bags and bouquets.

The Life of Sheridan

"*Teaz.* Bags and bouquets for footmen !—halters and bastinadoes !

"*Jarv.* 'Paid for my lady's own nosegays, £50.'

"*Teaz.* Fifty pounds for flowers ! enough to turn the Pantheon into a green-house, and give a Fête Champêtre at Christmas.

"*Lady Teaz.* Lord, Sir Peter, I wonder you should grudge me the most innocent articles in dress—and then, for the expense—flowers cannot be cheaper in winter—you should find fault with the climate, and not with me. I am sure I wish with all my heart that it was spring all the year round, and roses grew under one's feet.

"*Sir P.* Nay, but, madam, then you would not wear them ; but try snow-balls and icicles. But tell me, madam, how can you feel any satisfaction in wearing these, when you might reflect that one of the rose-buds would have furnished a poor family with a dinner ?

"*Lady T.* Upon my word, Sir Peter, begging your pardon, that is a very absurd way of arguing. By that rule, why do you indulge in the least superfluity ? I dare swear a beggar might dine tolerably on your greatcoat, or sup off your laced waistcoat—nay, I dare say, he wouldn't eat your gold-headed cane in a week. Indeed, if you would reserve nothing but necessaries, you should give the first poor man you meet your wig, and walk the streets in your nightcap, which, you know, becomes you very much.

"*Sir P.* Well, go on to the articles.

"*Jarv.* (*reading*). 'Fruit for my lady's monkey, £5 per week.'

"*Sir P.* Five pounds for the monkey !—why 'tis a dessert for an alderman !

[75]

"*Lady T.* Why, Sir Peter, would you starve the poor animal? I dare swear he lives as reasonably as other monkeys do.

"*Sir P.* Well, well, go on.

"*Jarv.* 'China for ditto——'

"*Sir P.* What, does he eat out of china?

"*Lady T.* Repairing china that he breaks — and I am sure no monkey breaks less.

"*Jarv.* 'Paid Mr. Warren for perfumes—milk of roses, £30.'

"*Lady T.* Very reasonable.

"*Sir P.* 'Sdeath, madam, if you had been born to these expenses, I should not have been so much amazed; but I took you, madam, an honest country squire's daughter——

"*Lady T.* Oh, filthy; don't name it. Well, Heaven forgive my mother, but I do believe my father must have been a man of quality.

"*Sir P.* Yes, madam, when first I saw you, you were drest in a pretty figured linen gown, with a bunch of keys by your side; your occupations, madam, to superintend the poultry; your accomplishments, a complete knowledge of the family receipt-book—then you sat in a room hung round with fruit in worsted of your own working; your amusements were to play country-dances on an old spinet to your father while he went asleep after a fox-chase—to read Tillotson's Sermons to your aunt Deborah. These, madam, were your recreations, and these the accomplishments that captivated me. Now, forsooth, you must have two footmen to your chair, and a pair of white dogs in a phaeton; you forget when you used to ride double behind the butler on a docked bay coach-horse. . . . Now you must have a French hairdresser; do you

think you did not look as well when you had your
hair combed smooth over a roller ? . . . Then you
could be content to sit with me, or walk by the side
of the Ha ! ha !

"*Lady T.* True, I did ; and, when you asked me if I
could love an old fellow, who would deny me nothing,
I simpered and said, ''Till death.'

"*Sir P.* Why did you say so ?

"*Lady T.* Shall I tell you the truth ?

"*Sir P.* If it is not too great a favour.

"*Lady T.* Why, then, the truth is, I was heartily
tired of all these agreeable recreations you have so
well remembered, and having a spirit to spend and
enjoy fortune, I was determined to marry the first
fool I should meet with . . . you made me a wife, for
which I am much obliged to you ; and if you have
a wish to make me more grateful still, make me a
widow.

.   .   .   .

"*Sir P.* Then, you never had a desire to please me,
or add to my happiness ?

"*Lady T.* Sincerely, I never thought about you ;
did you imagine that age was catching ?   I think you
have been overpaid for all you could bestow on me.
Here am I surrounded by half a hundred lovers, not
one of whom but would buy a single smile by a
thousand such baubles as you grudge me.

"*Sir P.* Then you wish me dead ?

"*Lady T.* You know I do not, for you have made
no settlement on me.

.   .   .   .

"*Sir P.* I am but middle-aged.

"*Lady T.* There's the misfortune ; put yourself on,

or back, twenty years, and either way I should like
you the better.

.   .   .   .

Yes, sir, and then your behaviour, too, was different.
You would dress, and smile, and bow; fly to fetch
me anything I wanted; praise everything I did or
said; fatigue your stiff face with an eternal grin; nay,
you even committed poetry, and muffled your harsh
tones into a lover's whisper to sing it yourself, so
that even my mother said you were the smartest
old bachelor she ever saw—a *billet - doux* engrossed
on buckram ! ! ! ! ! !

.   .   .   .

Let girls take my advice and never marry an old
bachelor. He must be so either because he could
find nothing to love in women, or because women
could find nothing to love in him."

The scene, now so admirably elaborated into the
screen scene, was thus in the author's imagination, to
judge from the first draught.

"*Scene*—YOUNG PLIANT'S *Room*.

" *Young P.* I wonder her ladyship is not here; she
promised me to call this morning. I have a hard
game to play here, to pursue my designs on Maria. I
have brought myself into a scrape with the mother-in-
law. However, I think we have taken care to ruin
my brother's character with my uncle, should he
come to-morrow. Frank has not an ill quality in his
nature; yet, a neglect of forms, and of the opinion
of the world, has hurt him in the estimation of all his
graver friends. I have profited by his errors, and

The Life of Sheridan

contrived to gain a character, which now serves me
as a mask to lie under.

"*Enter* LADY TEAZLE.

"*Lady T.* What, musing, or thinking of me ?

"*Young P.* I was thinking unkindly of you ; do you
know now that you must repay me for all this delay,
or I must be coaxed into good humour ?

"*Lady T.* Nay, in faith you should pity me—this
old curmudgeon of late is grown so jealous that I
dare scarce go out till I know he is secure for some
time.

"*Young P.* I am afraid the insinuations we have
had spread about Frank have operated too strongly
on him—we meant only to direct his suspicions to a
wrong object.

"*Lady T.* Oh, hang him ! I have told him plainly
that if he continues to be so suspicious, I'll leave
him entirely, and make him allow me a separate
maintenance.

"*Young P.* But, my charmer, if ever that should be
the case, you see before you the man who will ever be
attached to you. But you must not let matters come
to extremities ; you can never be revenged so well by
leaving him as by living with him, and let my sincere
affection make amends for his brutality.

"*Lady T.* But how shall I be sure now that you
are sincere ? I have sometimes suspected that you
loved my niece.

"*Young P.* Oh, hang her ! a puling idiot, without
sense or spirit.

"*Lady T.* But what proofs have I of your love to
me, for I have still so much of my country prejudices
left, that if I were to do a foolish thing (and I think I

[79]

The Life of Sheridan

can't promise) it shall be for a man who would risk everything for me alone. How shall I be sure you love me ?

" *Young P.* I have dreamed of you every night this week past.

" *Lady T.* That's a sign you have slept every night for this week past ; for my part, I would not give a pin for a lover who could not wake for a month in absence.

" *Young P.* I have written verses on you out of number.

" *Lady T.* I never saw any.

" *Young P.* No—they did not please me, and so I tore them.

" *Lady T.* Then it seems you wrote them only to divert yourself.

" *Young P.* Am I doomed for ever to suspense ?

" *Lady T.* I don't know—if I was convinced——

" *Young P.* Then let me on my knees——

" *Lady T.* Nay, nay, I will have no raptures either. This much I can tell you, that if I am to be seduced to do wrong, I am not to be taken by storm, but by deliberate capitulation, and that only where my reason or my heart is convinced.

" *Young P.* Then, to say it at once—the world gives itself liberties——

" *Lady T.* Nay, I am sure without cause ; for I am as yet unconscious of any ill, though I know not what I may be forced to.

" *Young P.* The fact is, my dear Lady Teazle, that your extreme innocence is the very cause of your danger ; it is the integrity of your heart that makes you run into a thousand imprudences which a full consciousness of error would make you guard against.

The Life of Sheridan

Now, in that case, you can't conceive how much
more circumspect you would be.

" *Lady T.* Do you think so ?

" *Young P.* Most certainly. Your character is like
a person in a plethora, absolutely dying of too much
health.

" *Lady T.* So then you would have me sin in my
own defence, and part with my virtue to preserve my
reputation.

" *Young P.* Exactly so, upon my credit, ma'am."

.   .   .   .

We may see, in the following extract, the first germ
of one of the most striking passages of the play as it
now exists :—

" *Spat.* O Lud, ma'am, I'll undertake to ruin the
character of the primmest prude in London with half
as much. Ha ! ha ! Did your ladyship never hear
how poor Miss Shepherd lost her lover and her
character last summer at Scarborough ?—this was the
whole of it. One evening at Lady ——'s the conversation happened to turn on the difficulty of breeding
Nova Scotia sheep in England. 'I have known instances,' says Miss ——, 'for last spring a friend of
mine, Miss Shepherd of Ramsgate, had a Nova Scotia
sheep that produced her twins.' 'What !' cries the
old deaf dowager Lady Bowlwell, 'has Miss Shepherd
of Ramsgate been brought to-bed of twins ?' This
mistake, as you may suppose, set the company
a-laughing. However, the next day, Miss Verjuice
Amarilla Lonely, who had been of the party, talking
of Lady Bowlwell's deafness, began to tell what had
happened ; but, unluckily, forgetting to say a word

of the sheep, it was understood by the company, and in every circle many believed, that Miss Shepherd of Ramsgate had actually been brought to-bed of a fine boy and girl; and in less than a fortnight, there were people who could name the father and the farmhouse where the babes were put out to nurse."

The production of the "School for Scandal" was accompanied by one of the most exquisite poetic eulogiums ever penned. Sheridan presented the beautiful Mrs. Crewe with a revised copy of his drama, together with a poem, to which he attached the title of a portrait. There does not exist in the English language a more perfect model of elegant flattery clothed in suitable language, neither fulsome nor over-strained; he has most carefully avoided those hyper-bolic expressions which are found in the dedications of the dramatic writers who preceded him, and has cleverly shunned the errors into which they were usually betrayed. The dread of ridicule taught him to eschew those bolder flights in which they indulged, and he has contrived to surround the object of his admiration with those attributes which, even if they be painted in somewhat an exaggerated form, cannot fail to be looked upon with a partial eye. There is a sincerity of expression, and a chivalrous boldness in the ebullition of so much approbation, that we should be carried away by the high colouring used, even had we been inclined to censure it as somewhat too gaudy. Garrick wrote a prologue, not certainly in his best style, but well suited to the taste of the day; he alludes to Sheridan as a bard "too young to think that he

Can stop the full spring tide of calumny;"

The Life of Sheridan

and

> " Proud of your smiles, once lavishly bestowed,
>   Again our young Don Quixote takes the road ;
>   To show his gratitude he draws his pen,
>   And seeks this hydra Scandal in his den.
>   For your applause all perils he would through,
>   He'll fight—that's write—a cavalliero true
>   Till every drop of blood—that's ink—is spilt for you."

The epilogue was written by Colman, and was committed to the care of Mrs. Abingdon as Lady Teazle ;
it has remained a favourite, and, though only spoken
occasionally on the provincial stage, has much merit.
The parody on the beautiful lines in "Othello"—
"Farewell, the tranquil mind"—has been much admired, and the author has cleverly enough adapted
the glorious circumstances of war to those of fashionable life, and we hear that Lady Teazle's occupation
is o'er, if not with the same deep sympathy that we do
the pathetic adieu from the lips of "Othello," it is with
the feeling that both personages have, in their respective
ways, added to the common stock of enjoyment. We
unfortunately possess no printed copy of this play
authenticated by its author ; some incorrect editions
have been printed. The one which appeared in
Ireland in the year 1788 has been usually followed,
and although pronounced incorrect, it has greater
pretension to be "authority" than any we possess,
for it is taken from the manuscript which Sheridan
forwarded to his sister for the use of the manager
of the Dublin Theatre, who gave her one hundred
guineas and free admission for her family for the
privilege of performing it. Sheridan had made an
arrangement with Ridgway of Piccadilly for the purchase of the copyright, but when he was urged to
furnish the manuscript, his answer was "that he had

[83]

been nineteen years endeavouring to satisfy himself with the style of the 'School for Scandal,' but had not succeeded." It is a well-known fact that the last act of "Pizarro" was in an unfinished state on the very night of its first representation, and upon good authority it is affirmed, that notwithstanding the incessant labour which Sheridan had bestowed for a considerable length of time, the "School for Scandal" was announced for representation before the actors had received copies of their respective parts. Moore, on a reference to the original manuscript, found that the last five scenes bore evident marks of the haste in which they were finished, there being but one rough draught of them scribbled upon detached pieces of paper, whilst of all the preceding acts there were numerous manuscripts. On the last leaf appears in his own handwriting, "*Finished at last, thank God,*" to which the prompter has added "Amen, W. Hopkins." Great attention was bestowed on the production of the comedy; each was desirous of supporting the new manager. Garrick, as we learn from Murphy, was never known on any former occasion to be more anxious for a favourite piece; he was proud of the new manager, and in a triumphant manner boasted of the genius to whom he had consigned the conduct of the theatre. Amongst the praise which he bestowed upon Sheridan, a ready reply to a gentleman who wished to exalt the Roscius at the expense of the new candidate for fame has been recorded. "This is but a single play," observed the critic, "and in the long run will be but a slender help to support the theatre. To you, Mr. Garrick, I must say the Atlas that propped the stage has left his station." "Has he?" said Garrick; "if that be the case he has found another

Hercules to succeed him." Isaac Reed has, in the *Biographia Dramatica*, very slightly alluded to an assertion that has been made that the plan was taken from a manuscript which had been previously delivered at Drury Lane by a young lady, who afterwards died of a pectoral disease ; he observes that this is probably mere scandal, founded on envy of the great success of the piece. Dr. Watkins has somewhat laboriously expatiated on this report, and drawn upon himself the severe censure of Moore, who was enabled to detect the falsehood, and to show how utterly unfounded was the stupid rumour ; not content with borrowing this idea from Isaac Reed, and setting it off with as much ingenuity as he could muster, Dr. Watkins throws out a surmise that Mrs. Sheridan was the person to whom the rank of the first dramatic writer of the day ought to have been assigned. He indulges, too, in some hypercritical remarks, which are only worthy of notice as exhibiting the anxiety of the biographer to scrape up from every source some material for his labour, regardless both of the useless information he was bestowing and the nothingness of the detraction to which he was giving circulation. In spite of all that has been written, from the first night of its performance up to the present hour, the " School for Scandal " has maintained its position, and even when indifferently brought forward, proves an unceasing attraction. Its uninterrupted run, its certainty of producing money to the treasury, its collecting together all the playgoers, are the best proofs of the estimation in which it is held — its intrinsic merit carries everything before it. Cumberland, the irritable opponent of all merit but his own, has praised the judicious introduction of the screen ; but there is an anecdote on record that he was with his young family at an early performance of the "School for Scandal." They were seated in the stage-box; the little children screamed with delight, but the less easily pleased, fretful author pinched them, exclaiming, "What are you laughing at, my dear little folks? You should not laugh, my angels, there is nothing to laugh at!" and then in an undertone, "Keep still, you little dunces." When Sheridan was told of this, he said, "It was ungrateful of Cumberland to have been displeased with his children for laughing at my comedy, for when I went to see his tragedy I laughed from beginning to end."

There is another version of the story extant; for the friends of Sheridan were most anxious to find a reason for the hostile feelings which he was supposed to bear towards Cumberland, and which induced him to use such an unmerciful rod of flagellation in the "Critic." It is that Sheridan, being most anxious to collect the opinions of the acknowledged judges of dramatic merit, earnestly asked what Mr. Cumberland had said on the first night of the performance. "Not a syllable," was the answer. "But did he seem amused?" "Why, faith, he might have been hung up beside Uncle Oliver's picture. He had the damned disinheriting countenance, like the ladies and gentlemen on the walls; he never moved a muscle." "Devilish ungrateful that," said Sheridan, "for I sat out his tragedy last week, and laughed from beginning to end." Cumberland, however, most strenuously denied that he was present when the "School for Scandal" was first performed. The tragedy alluded to is said to be the "Carmelites," which was the theme of ridicule of Sheridan's friends. In the

The Life of Sheridan

"Rolliad" they heap upon it the most extravagant and ludicrous praise, calling Cumberland "the most exalted genius of the present age," and in describing this tragedy, say, "the beauties of which, we will venture confidently to assert, will be admired and felt when those of Shakespeare, Dryden, Otway, Southerne, and Rowe, shall no longer be held in estimation." Again, "Our readers, we trust, will pardon our having been diverted from the task we have undertaken by the satisfaction of dwelling upon a few of the many beauties of this justly popular and universally admired tragedy, which, in our humble opinion, infinitely surpasses every other theatrical composition, being, in truth, an assemblage of every possible dramatic excellence; nor do we believe that any production, whether of ancient or modern date, can exhibit a more uncommon and peculiar selection of language, a greater variety of surprising incidents, a more rapid succession of extraordinary discoveries, a more curious collection of descriptions, similes, metaphors, images, storms, shipwrecks, challenges, and visions; or a more miscellaneous and striking picture of the contending passions of love, hatred, pity, madness, rage, jealousy, remorse, and anger, than this unparalleled performance presents to the admiration of the enraptured spectator. Mr. Cumberland has been represented, perhaps unjustly, as particularly jealous of the fame of his contemporaries, but we are persuaded he will not be offended when, in the rank of modern writers, we place him second only to the inimitable author of the 'Rolliad.'" Such at any rate was the feeling which took possession of Sheridan's mind, that he gladly sought the opportunity of holding him up to public ridicule; whenever

The Life of Sheridan

the occasion offered, his name was dragged forth. It was also alleged that every piece presented at Drury Lane by Cumberland met with a decided refusal ; and the newspapers seemed willing to support the disappointed author. Criticisms, ill-natured, were hurled against the "School for Scandal," and comparisons were drawn between the moral tendency of the plays that issued from the prolific pen of Cumberland and those which Sheridan had furnished to the world. This only continued to aggravate the quarrel, and led to further jealousies, which soon exhibited themselves in the production of Cumberland upon the stage as Sir Fretful Plagiary.

It would be hypercriticism to descant upon the beauties and defects of a play that has undergone, from its very first appearance up to the present moment, investigation the most severe ; that has been the theme of every dramatic censor who has examined into its construction, or pointed to it as a fair subject of comparison with the works of those who have either preceded or succeeded its author. The too constant sparkle of the dialogue, the want of connection of the scandalous college with the plot of the play, the imitation of Fielding's Blifil and Tom Jones, the investment of such a libertine as Charles with qualities that make us forget his vices, and a vast number of incongruities have been very wisely and very learnedly pointed out, and have been descanted upon with very commendable severity ; but, after all, we are so charmed with the ingenuity, with the endless richness of the dialogue, that we are never tired with reading it, or with seeing it on the stage. We admire Sir Peter Teazle in spite of his uxoriousness, his old-bachelor ideas ; in the hand of any other dramatist he would have been ridiculous, but he is invested with a certain dignity, a tenderness of feeling, and a sense of honour, that although we must laugh at him when his unenviable position is discovered, we are glad to find that he is likely to become a happy husband, after all his mortifications. We are just on the point of thinking that Lady Teazle must become the victim of her taste for extravagance and shining in scandalous society, whilst we feel she deserves a better fate, when we gladly find that she is rescued from her false position. Even Joseph Surface is delightful to us; the duplicity of his conduct, the sentimental hypocrisy of his heart are so thoroughly laid open to us, that we are convinced that he cannot be ultimately successful; we are not so anxious for even-handed justice being done to him, as we are to the dramatic villain of a novel, and we are perfectly satisfied with the punishment he meets in the exposure of his schemes. Charles's irregularities do not shock or disgust us; they are punished by the reproaches which he has to encounter from every one. We are happy in the conclusion that everything that annoyed the different parties is amicably arranged; it is this that reconciles us to the fifth act, for at the end of the fourth act the denouement has taken place, the fall of the screen in a common play would have been the be-all and end-all, and, as occurs in the " Merchant of Venice," the act after the condemnation of the principal character, however beautiful is the poetry, the interest would altogether have ceased. Yet after this exciting scene we are pleased that there is another act to wind up the story, and to tell us how everybody has got out of the scrape. Of the original acting we have heard much. That Garrick was delighted with it, we may conclude

The Life of Sheridan

not only from Murphy's observations in his Life of the great actor, but from a letter from him which has been preserved, in which he makes some remarks upon the length of time the characters on the stage stood after the falling of the screen ; he observes "that they should be astonished, a little petrified, yet it may be carried to too great a length." The conventional points which have been handed down to us are not many in number, but such as they are they show that the manner of acting was carefully studied, and therefore are strictly preserved. The acting of the late Matthews in Sir Peter Teazle is said to have been in strict conformity with the early stage directions ; the pointing to the screen with the thumb, the leer and the movements of the elbows were precisely the same as practised by King, and as they usually convulsed the audience with laughter, we have a right to suppose that man, in different generations, expresses his feelings much in the same way. It has, however, been said that Sheridan was himself never satisfied ; he requested permission to read the part over to Matthews, with whose delineation he expressed himself by no means pleased.

The personation of Lady Teazle has been supposed to be one of extreme delicacy, and although we seldom find an actress of a certain grade who does not think herself fully equal to the task, yet the fastidious lover of good acting is very apt to require a lady of personal attractions, of good judgment, and of elegant manners, and he repudiates the flippant attempts which have occasionally been made to introduce her as a being made up of levity, imprudence, and assumption. There is to be found in *Blackwood's Magazine* for the year 1826, a remarkably well-written essay, "On

Cant in Criticism," elicited by some letters which
appeared from Miss Kelly to the stage manager of
Drury Lane Theatre, in consequence of an ill-natured
censure in which one of the newspapers indulged
upon the occasion of Miss Kelly's performance of
Lady Teazle. Of the high intellectual powers of Miss
Kelly no doubt can exist, of her capability of sustain-
ing some of the most difficult characters in a particular
department of the drama no one who has ever seen
her inimitable personations could express any hesitation, but that she does not possess the necessary
qualifications for Lady Teazle the letters we have
mentioned are an indisputable proof, and bear out
the remark that we are compelled to make, that the
many remarkable traits which are to be clearly painted
to the audience are beyond the power of many an
otherwise gifted actress. That Miss Kelly's reading
of the character should lead her to give an air of
rusticity to Lady Teazle, to assert that there is not a
single line in the whole play which describes her
either as a beautiful or an elegant woman, but, on the
contrary, as having been six months before a girl of
limited education and of the most homely habits, are
singularly opposed to the author's ideas, and to those
which have been entertained by all who have been
considered judges of pure and genuine comedy. The
invariable reading of the part has assigned to Lady
Teazle the graces and the manners of a woman of
fashion, of one who, with the quick perception of the
female character, has been enabled rapidly to assume
all the refinement and all the manners of the *haut ton*.
The first complaint urged against her by Sir Peter
Teazle is that, though wholly bred in the country,
"she plays her part in all the extravagant foppery of

the fashion and the town with as ready a grace as if she had never seen a bush or a grass plot out of Grosvenor Square"; "then the charming air with which she contradicts him"; the great satisfaction he has in quarrelling with her, as " she never appears to such advantage as when she is doing everything in her power to plague him"; his sarcasms on having made her "a woman of fashion, her elegant expenses, her luxuries"; and after the exposure in Joseph Surface's library, the spontaneous burst of admiration with which he rushes to a reconciliation on seeing her in another room. "She looks this way—what a re-markably elegant turn of the head she has—Rowley, I'll go to her," are all evidences that she possessed those charms which belong only to a superior woman, who had, if they were not natural to her, rapidly acquired the graces which fascinate mankind. There is, too, throughout an unmistakable lady-like bearing, there is a choice of language, a quick appreciation of the defects of others, much less bordering on ill-nature than is perceptible in any of the scandalous school, and a purer sense of honour, after the almost fatal error into which she had fallen, expressed in the determined tone of contrition, with a knowledge of the worldly views of man, which must impress us with the conviction of her being endowed with the per-ception of what was most appreciated in society, and with a tact of the highest order.

Probably there never was a dramatist who more thoroughly understood the exact province of comedy than did Sheridan, no one could excite in us more cheerfulness and mirth at the follies and inconsist-encies of human nature, no one could portray them better, and certainly no one has ever interested us

The Life of Sheridan

more, even in the imperfections and immoralities of
his personages. Whatever faults and vices they may
exhibit, they are portrayed so as to instruct our understanding, but not to shock our feelings. His object
has been to amuse, even where he censures, and the
punishment which he inflicts is that ridicule and exposure which are more mortifying than any indignation or anger. It is not only a picture of the manners
of the day in which he lived, but the general features
are those which will be perceptible in all ages and all
times, as long as there shall be a privileged class in
society distinguished from the others by social and
domestic differences. There will always be uxorious
husbands, confiding women, irascible fathers, careless
spendthrifts, romantic girls, hypocrites, and slanderers ;
such characters, modified by circumstances, and by
national habits, will exist in every age and in every
clime. He has not slightly sketched these characters,
but has displayed them in all their full vigour. He has
made them, by the skill of his dialogue, their own
painters : each betrays his own obliquities, there is no
forced effort to deceive the audience ; until the development of the plot is brought about, incidents
follow one upon another which explain the position
of each actor in the drama, and we are gradually led
on to take a warm interest in the success of each,
even when we find that we are bordering on dislike of
the selfishness and immoral tendency which are beginning to show themselves. It is not only the in-
ventive and creative faculty that we admire in the
fable, but the light play of wit with which the conversation abounds. We feel that we are in good company, that every man is striving to be clever and
entertaining to his neighbour, and there is nothing so

The Life of Sheridan

flattering to our vanity as to find that the amusing persons amongst whom we chance to be mingling are exerting themselves to please us, that they are unloading the stores of their intellect for the purpose of making us satisfied with ourselves. There is a disposition to heighten the effect by the sallies of a sportive wit, but there is no caricature, no exaggeration. There is nothing improbable, nothing but what may have occurred, everything is perspicuous and easily developed. We have neither our hopes nor our fears painfully excited, but everything that passes before us inspires us with the confidence that we have nothing to do but to laugh at the exposure of the follies of the world, the mistaken views of men, the rogueries of some, the foibles of others, and that these are often blended together in such a manner as to excite our mirth and our good feeling, and to dispel the gloom which the realities of life are too often calculated to collect.

In the same volume of the *Edinburgh Review* which contains an examination into the merits of Moore as the biographer of Sheridan, there is an essay on the works of Machiavelli, by Macaulay, which has been much admired for its depth of thought and its terseness of expression; a few sentences have been often quoted from it on the subject of Sheridan's plays, and Leigh Hunt, in his brief but brilliant sketch of Sheridan, has placed them in juxtaposition with an extract from one of Hazlitt's lectures on the comic writers. We have thus the bane and antidote before us. To the comedies of Machiavelli, the reviewer apportions the correct and vigorous delineation of human nature, and considers that this is the highest kind of excellence. He believes that comedy is corrupted by wit.

The Life of Sheridan

To Congreve and to Sheridan he imputes their having deeply injured the comedy of England. He admits that they were men of splendid wit and of polished taste, but that their indiscriminate prodigality of sparkling language produces a dazzling glare, and that they unhappily made all their characters in their own likeness. We must confess that we cannot assent to the axiom laid down that the real object of the drama is the exhibition of the human character. We would rather look to the comedy as not only a representation of what is amusing in character, and in the contrast of situations and combinations, but as a picture of the manners, the feelings, and the language of the class of persons who are painted. Most of Shakespeare's comedies are romantic love tales, there is no attempt at a skilful plot, they are made up of slight materials, the incidents are few, the conclusions are brought about in a very arbitrary way, probabilities overlooked, plots scarcely wound up, characters broadly delineated, and they are altogether compositions of an extraordinary kind, produced before the rules of art had yet "cabined, cribbed, confined" the human imagination. In the age in which Shakespeare lived, the lively, elegant and sparkling dialogue would have been less understood than quaint expressions, play upon words, and logical disquisitions. In the earlier stages of society nature had her freshness yet unaltered, and those who painted her met with those who could appreciate her beauties. As man changed by cultivation, by refinement, he began to admire art, and although he can still love the first early impression that was made upon his youthful heart, he looks to those artificial ornaments by which he has been surrounded as the chief source of his delight. Congreve, Wycher-

The Life of Sheridan

ley, Farquhar, had prepared the audiences before whom Sheridan's plays were produced to enjoy his brilliancy of wit and repartee. These did not corrupt the taste, they were adapted to it, they were precisely the food on which the public were anxious to live, they were the delicacies best suited to their already pampered appetites. They have continued to delight the rising generation for whom in vain has been prepared other luxurious viands. After the exciting melodramas of the German school, their exaggerated sentimentality, their mawkish sensibility; after the light intrigue of the French comedy, its good-natured gaiety and its enticing sensuality, we still can turn with redoubled pleasure to the epigrammatic points, the sparkling dialogues, the pungent satire of Sheridan. All may be too highly wrought, too elaborate, too ornamental, still are we delighted; we feel, whilst we pry into the follies and foibles of our brethren, that they are exhibited in their richest point of view; and even the hypocrisy of a Joseph, or the cowardice of an Acres, whilst we abhor them, are laughed at, because they are genuine, and whilst they seem to belong to human nature are the best of their kind.

No one is more likely to become *laudator temporis acti* than the theatrical amateur; the first impressions of life, the earliest illusions strike so forcibly upon the imagination that they are recollected at subsequent periods with all their freshness, and with a large proportion of the pleasure they first excited. Judgment has had but little to do with the verdict our senses have early pronounced, and when in later days we make comparisons, we naturally forget that we have, from the course of events, grown fastidious; that objects which surprised and delighted us have

The Life of Sheridan

become familiar, and have therefore lost that which was their principal charm—their originality. We are apt to fancy that the actors of the present day are far inferior to those who formerly delighted us ; we are alive to their defects, and are not struck with their peculiar merits. There can, however, be but little doubt that when the "School for Scandal" was originally produced, there was upon the boards of Drury Lane Theatre as complete a company as ever was collected together ; and that though some of the characters may have been filled at different periods by individuals of equal merit to them, yet that the play was performed in a most masterly manner and worthy the school of the never-dying Garrick. The Sir Peter Teazle was entrusted to King, who has been traditionally spoken of as one of the most perfect performers in his depart- ment, which was, however, somewhat limited. He had distinguished himself as Lord Ogleby, a character that Garrick had originally intended for himself, and which, with the assistance of Colman, had been rendered admirably adapted for the great master of his art ; but he excused himself on the plea that he was unwilling to study a new part. In fact, in his own farce, "Lethe," the character of Lord Chalkstone was sufficiently like to prevent his having any great desire to undertake the new one. No one could deliver such dialogue as is found in Lord Ogleby and in Sir Peter Teazle with greater point than Mr. King. He excelled in a quiet, sententious mode of expressing feeling and sentiment. There was an epigrammatic style in everything he uttered ; for although he could, when occasion required, give rapid utterance to his thoughts, he seemed generally to dwell upon his words, and then make all the happy points tersely and

The Life of Sheridan

Amidst shouts of applause the venerable old man made his bow, and retired to the green-room, where an affectionate compliment awaited him from his dramatic brethren, in the shape of a handsome silver cup, with an engraved motto from " Henry the Fifth," happily adapted to the occasion :—

> " If he be not fellow with the best king,
> Thou shalt find him the best king of good fellows."

From this cup his health was drunk, and he returned the compliment, almost overpowered with the intensity of his feelings, for as yet these marks of admiration and of approbation had not become common, they were the spontaneous tributes of high and honourable affection ; as such they were offered, as such accepted. The lavish manner in which stage compliments are now distributed, the hackneyed offerings, behind and before the curtain, which managers, actors, and audiences bestow in so many shapes, have rendered all such expressions so ludicrous that they are rather to be avoided than courted. With him it was naturally said that Sir Peter had quitted the stage. We have, however, seen many representatives who have delighted us. It is true that, at the present moment, Farren is the only actor who will leave behind him the impression of greatness ; he deserves to be recorded as one worthy to be ranked with any of his predecessors.

Palmer's Joseph Surface seems to have been perfectly unapproachable by any competitor. So admirable a hypocrite has never yet been seen ; his manners, his deportment, his address, combined to render him the very man he desired to paint. His performance on the stage bore a very strong similarity

The Life of Sheridan

to what he was famous for in private life; he was plausible, of pleasing address, of much politeness, and even of great grace. He was fond of pleasure, which he pursued with so much avidity as to be generally very careless of his theatrical duties, but when he had committed some gross absurdity, or had been, through complete neglect of his duties, on the verge of hearing a loud shout of disapprobation, "he threw up his eyes with an expression of astonishment, or cast them down as if in penitent humility, drew out his eternal white handkerchief to smother his errors, and bowed himself out of his scrapes." His plausibility and insidious arts shone forth in Joseph. Palmer opened the Royalty Theatre in 1787, in Wellclose Square, Goodman's Fields, in opposition to his former friends at Drury Lane Theatre, and, attempting to perform plays, he was served with a threatening notice from the proprietors of Drury Lane, Covent Garden, and the Haymarket, which obliged him to abandon his undertaking. He therefore changed his plan, but being ultimately unsuccessful he was compelled to return to Drury Lane. He was received before the curtain with the sincerest demonstrations of welcome; he felt that he was surrounded by his friends, and received the applause with all his usual mute expressions of gratitude, but the difficulty was to reconcile the manager. The meeting between the two men of address—Sheridan and Palmer—was, as Boaden narrates it, expected to produce something remarkable. Palmer, making a profound bow, approached the author of the "School for Scandal" with an air of penitent humility; his head declined, the whites of his eyes turned upwards, his hands clasped together, and his whole air exactly that of Joseph Surface before Sir Peter

The Life of Sheridan

Teazle. He began thus: "My dear Mr. Sheridan, if you could but know what I feel at this moment HERE" (*laying one hand upon his heart*). Sheridan with inimitable readiness stopped him: "Why, Jack, you forgot *I wrote it.*" Palmer, in telling the story himself, added that "the manager's wit cost him something, for I made him add three pounds per week to the salary I had before my desertion." There is one story related by Boaden which shows that Palmer was even superior to the manager. A friend complimenting him one day upon his address, he disclaimed any remarkable possession of the quality. "No," said he, "I really don't give myself the credit of being so irresistible as you have fancied me; there is, however, one thing in the way of address that I think I am able to do. Whenever I am arrested I think I can always persuade the sheriffs' officers to bail me." This feat, however, has been surpassed by a more modern actor of considerable talent, who not only persuaded the keeper of a spunging-house to be his bail, but to lend him two guineas to pay the attention of the servants of the establishment, whom, he declared, he knew not how sufficiently to recompense, they were so full of civility and sympathy. He actually paid them out of the loan with three shillings, pocketing the surplus for a future occasion, and not forgetting to drink the health of the lender, as a man who ought to be encouraged as a good master and an honest friend, having no confined notions.

On an occasion when a new play was to be produced at Drury Lane, and the greatest anxiety prevailed that it should be well brought out, it was pretty evident at the rehearsal that Palmer knew not one line of his part; but it was expected, as he was aware that great anticipation had been formed of its success, that he would study it, more particularly as it was one that would do him much credit, and with which he had appeared more than usually pleased. The house was sure to be crowded, for the boxes were fully taken, and the night for the performance had been for some time fixed. At three o'clock on the eventful day arrived, however, at the stage - door, a letter; it was presented by Powell, the prompter, in the presence of Michael Kelly, to Sheridan in due form. He perused it; it was from John Palmer, announcing, as a deplorable fact, that he was taken dangerously ill, and that his appearance that night might be fatal to him. Sheridan, knowing his man tolerably well, said, " I'll lay my life this is a trick of Plausible Jack, and that there is nothing the matter with him, except, indeed, not knowing a line of the part he has to act to-night. Let you and I call upon him," turning to Kelly, " and I am sure we shall find him as well as ever." They went to Lisle Street, where Palmer lived, but Kelly managed to slip away and act the good-natured part of preparing Palmer for the visit. He found him in the enjoyment of good health, a good dinner, and his social circle. He gave him the hint to clear away the table, and to do all he could to mystify Sheridan, who never would forgive him for postponing the play. Palmer seized the moment, swore endless gratitude for the kindness received from Kelly, rushed into his bedroom, was quickly enveloped in a dressing-gown, with a large woollen nightcap on, and a face of the most becoming length. At first he could not make up his mind as to the nature of the dangerous illness with which he was to be afflicted. A dreadful and most excruciating

The Life of Sheridan

toothache at last presented itself to his mind. His face was immediately swollen, a handkerchief tied to his jaw, and lamentable groans issued from the agonised sufferer. Sheridan arrived. He gazed with pity and with sympathy upon the admirable actor, who, with his hand upon the usual place, and with a white handkerchief at his eyes, assured the anxious manager that his suffering corporeal was not equal to his mental, in consequence of his conviction that it was injuring the establishment. Sheridan was completely taken in, kindly suggested the extraction of the tooth, and then to study the part and get perfect in the new play, and never had the slightest idea of the trick played upon him. One of the happy excuses which Palmer played forth on every occasion was the accouchement of his wife. He would postpone an engagement by sighing forth, with his white hand-kerchief to his eyes, " My best of friends, this is the most awful period of my life; I cannot be with you ; my beloved wife, the partner of my sorrows and my joys, is just confined." He was engaged to act at Reading for the benefit of a poor actor, and at the very moment of expectation a letter was despatched by Palmer instead of himself, announcing such an occurrence just to have taken place. It was read to the audience, who, of course, felt the deepest sympathy with him on such an interesting domestic occurrence, and all opposition was silenced. He merely smiled, with his usual bland benignity, when congratulated by Kelly upon the happiness of having a wife who, at least once in two months, rendered him a contented father.

During the period that Palmer attempted to perform at Goodman's Fields, the magistrates summoned him to appear before them, and calling upon him to show the licence by which he acted, threatened instantaneous committal unless it was produced. He bowed with excessive humility, and lamenting very much that he did not know that it was their wish that it should be laid before them, entreated their indulgence whilst he went home, which was but a short distance, for the important document. After some discussion this was assented to. Palmer's gratitude for this indulgence knew no bounds; he called upon Heaven to bless them for their kindness, laying his hand as usual upon that part of the chest where he supposed he had a heart, respectfully bowed, and departed upon his errand. The magistrates waited for a considerable length of time in the room at the tavern, discussing the weather and the political topics of the day, until at length their patience was exhausted; they rang the bell to order the waiter to go to Mr. Palmer's lodgings, and desire him to say they could wait no longer. The waiter, on trying to open the door to learn the pleasure of the quorum assembled, found that it was locked, and requested the party within to open it, and they then learnt that they were fairly locked in; for Mr. Palmer, fully aware that there was no such document in existence, and fearing that the magistrates would, as they had the power, actually commit him, had, on shutting the door, quietly turned the key in the lock, pocketed it, and had gone his way to follow his business, as "every man hath business," and was careful to attend to nothing but that, and to be seen by nobody until the storm had blown over. A more specious representative of Joseph Surface was not to be found, nor has any one ever won such laurels. He played the part naturally; indeed, study was always out of the question with him. It is a fact that on the occasion of the production of Hayley's tragedy of "Lord Russell" he was completely incapable of giving effect to the character of Lord Russell, as he had as usual neglected to study it; but as he knew the tragedy of the "Earl of Essex," and that there was some similarity in the fate of the two heroes, he very dexterously recited passages from that play, contriving to fit them in so that the audience never discovered his incapacity. With all his faults—and they were many—he was one of the greatest favourites of the public; he was always hailed with loud approbation; he appeared to have been made for the profession, and trod the stage as no other man could do. There was something in his departure from the great scene of life that created considerable sensation. He was performing at Liverpool the character of the Stranger, and had just pronounced the words, "there is another and a better world," when he was seized with a paroxysm from which he never recovered. It does not appear that, as has generally been received, he died instantaneously; but from the moment of his fall upon the stage there were but feeble indications of existence.

Charles Surface fell to the lot of William Smith, who has been characterised by Churchill, in the "Rosciad," as "Smith the genteel, the airy, and the smart." All agree that he was one of the most elegant men of the day; his acquirements were of no ordinary kind. He had received a first-rate education, and had completed his studies with much credit to himself at Cambridge. He was admitted into the highest circles of society, and was particularly remarkable for the elegance of his manners. He had many of those qualifications which enabled him to perform respectably in tragedy, but he never attained anything like excellence in that walk. In comedy, however, as the fine gentleman, his powers were universally acknowledged. The graces of his person, the elegance of his manners, and the dignity of his deportment, admirably qualified him for that character. The style of the man moving in good society, it must be remembered, was essentially different from what it now is. The dress, the distinctions, the acquirements necessary, were so unlike anything which we now see, that we can form but an indifferent idea of the qualifications demanded for the accomplished actor in this walk. There was more stage effect then even in private life; the powdered hair, the folding hat, the sword, the short breeches with buckles, the embroidered coat, the ruffles, and all the accessories of dress, served to distinguish the class; dancing a minuet, fencing, and fashionable raillery were amongst the indispensable accomplishments. To portray upon the stage a man of the true school of gentility required pretensions of no ordinary kind, and Smith possessed these in a singular degree, and he gave to Charles Surface all that finish for which he was remarkable. He had acquired the sobriquet of Gentleman Smith, from his unvarying exhibition of an air of distinction without any false assumption. He had made it an indispensable article of his agreement with managers that his face was never to be blackened, and that he was never to be lowered through a stage-door. He retired from the stage in 1787. The house was enormously crowded; and such had been the desire to be present amongst the fashionable admirers of Smith, that the

The Life of Sheridan

pit was for the occasion converted into boxes, but there was not room for the accommodation of all. He took his farewell, he said, after having served thirty-five campaigns under the ablest generals, Garrick and Barry, and now resigned the youthful gaiety of Charles Surface to younger blood. The modern style of fine gentleman is so distinct from that of the day in which the "School for Scandal" was produced that we cannot attempt to picture what then fascinated the audience, but the opinion of the playgoers of the day was that "the Charles of the 'School for Scandal' died with Smith"; but that for this "we are to blame the alteration of our dress, and the consequent familiarity of our manners." In a subsequent year he once again appeared, when his old friend King bade farewell to the stage. He was then living in retirement surrounded by all the comforts of life; still, anxious to assist a brother veteran upon whom fortune had not so kindly bestowed her blessings, he played Charles with great spirit, and gave an admirable picture of the gentleman of the old school, and although associations, ideas, and habits were much altered from what they had been when he was in his zenith, his audience caught the spirit of his acting, and their applause urged him on to exhibit a high flow of spirits. He concluded with some lines written for the occasion :—

> "At friendship's call, ne'er to be heard in vain,
> My spirits rise—Richard's himself again."

The two scandal-mongers, uncle and nephew, each having his characteristic line of tattle, of censoriousness, and slander, fell into the hands of two excellent comedians, Dodd and Parsons. They eagerly contributed to the amusement of the public; Dodd was the most

The Life of Sheridan

perfect fopling ever placed upon the stage, he was the most exquisite coxcomb, the most ridiculous chatterer ever seen, he took his snuff, or applied the quintessence of roses to his nose, with an air of complacent superiority, such as won the hearts of all conversant with that style of affectation. His walk upon the boards bespoke the sweet effeminacy of the person; the pink heels, the muslin of his cravat and frills are dwelt upon by the amateurs of the day as specimens of his understanding the range of his art. He is spoken of as "the prince of pink heels, and the soul of empty eminence." Parsons was the Crabtree, and was a perfect old detractor and crabbed calumniator; he was an actor of great merit too, but he never appeared to greater advantage than he did in the "Critic." He was the original Sir Fretful Plagiary, and from his delineation most of our modern actors have borrowed their idea; it was his last performance on the 29th of January 1795, and on the 5th of February he died. A compliment paid to his memory, on the opening of the Haymarket Theatre in the summer, was caught at by the audience with loud expressions of their concurrence in the sentiment. A prelude was written by Colman, entitled "New Hay at the Old Market"; the audience was supposed to be made acquainted with the wants of the concern, and a dialogue between Prompter and Carpenter occurs, during which the following expressions were used :—

"*Carpenter*. We want a new scaffold for the 'Surrender of Calais.'

"*Prompter*. Ah! where shall we get such another hangman? Poor fellow, poor Parsons! the old cause of our mirth is now the cause of our melancholy; he

[108]

who so often made us forget our cares may well claim a sigh to his memory.

"*Carpenter.* He was one of the comicalest fellows I ever see.

"*Prompter.* Ay, and one of the honestest, Master Carpenter. When an individual has combined private worth with public talent he quits the bustling scene of life with twofold applause, and we doubly deplore his exit."

The allusion here was to the play of the "Surrender of Calais," in which Parsons performed the chief workman at the gallows erected for the patriots who were to be hung by the decree of King Edward. The scene was an imitation of the grave-diggers in "Hamlet." On an occasion when the king, George the Third, had commanded the play, Parsons, instead of saying the words set down for him, "So the king is coming : an the king like not my scaffold, I am no true man," gave a new reading, which, as it was expressed with peculiar humour, and a saucy assumption of independence, excited great laughter, more especially from the monarch. Parsons exclaimed, "An the king were here, and did not admire my scaffold, I would say da—n't he has no taste." Such a liberty in the present day would most probably cause anything but a shout of approbation ; the actors in those times were a privileged class, for whom the public at large entertained a kind of affection, which they now and then gladly evinced. These two clever performers supported each other in the scandalous school with wonderful effect ; the dry sarcasm of Parsons had additional sting given to it by the thoughtless and impertinent volubility of Dodd ; youth and age each had their privileged sneer and jest ; the total insensibility to the wounds they were inflicting seemed in the one instance to arise from reckless folly, in the other, from cold, calculating ill-nature. As they are generally given at the present day, there is a want of unity in the two performers, each seems totally independent of the other, and they express their villainous fancies without that force and vigour which would arise from a mutual good understanding. The two characters are by no means so easily delineated as may be imagined, and considerable study is required to satisfy those who are neither pleased with buffoonery nor burlesque.

Baddeley is not to be forgotten as Moses. He had taken infinite pains to study the characteristics by which the Jews are distinguished from other nations, and was particularly happy in expressing them. He was to have appeared at Drury Lane on the 20th of November in this character, but whilst dressing for it was seized with a fit, and expired on the following day. He was originally a cook, and was employed by Foote, with whom he quarrelled, and challenging him to fight, the great comedian declined, saying "Here is a pretty fellow! I allowed him to take my spit from the rack, and stick it by his side, and now he wants to stick me with it." His bequest of a cake and wine for the green-room, on Twelfth-night, has tended to keep his memory alive. Lamash was an actor, too, of considerable experience and of much merit, and was, as the coxcombical valet and underbred fine gentleman, a great favourite.

Nothing could exceed the mismanagement which at this time marked everything that was attempted at Drury Lane Theatre; numerous were the letters addressed to Garrick. Mrs. Clive, the original Nell in the "Devil to Pay," once so great a favourite with the public, then residing in quiet tranquillity at Twickenham, yet anxiously turning her eyes to her favourite haunts of old, wrote to her old friend : " Everybody is raving against Sheridan for his supineness ; there never was in nature such a contrast as Garrick and Sheridan. What have you given him that he keeps so ?" But a letter from Hopkins, the prompter, will show what a change had taken place in a short time after the retirement of the great actor and manager. "We played last night 'Much Ado about Nothing,' and had to make an apology for three principal parts. About twelve o'clock Mr. Henderson sent word that he was not able to play. We got Mr. Lewis from Covent Garden, who supplied the part of Benedick. Soon after, Mr. Parsons sent word he could not play. Mr. Moody supplied the part of Dogberry ; and about four in the afternoon Mr. Vernon sent word he could not play. Mr. Mattocks supplied his part of Balthazar. I thought myself very happy in getting these wide gaps so well stopped. In the middle of the first act a message was brought me that Mr. Lamash, who was to play the part of Borachio, was not come to the house. I had nobody there that would go on for it, so I was obliged to cut his scenes in the first and second act entirely out, and get Mr. Wrighton to go on for the remainder of the part. At length we got the play over without the audience finding it out. We had a very bad house. Mr. Parsons is not able to play in the " School for Scandal" to-morrow night ; do not know how we shall be able to settle that. I hope the pantomime may prove successful, and relieve us from this dreadful situation." All these communications could not fail to be distressing to Garrick, who, independent of the large pecuniary interest he had at stake, felt very great anxiety for the welfare of Sheridan and his colleagues ; he ends a correspondence between himself and Mr. T. King, "Poor Old Drury, I feel that it will very soon be in the hands of the Philistines." The complaints against Sheridan were strongly urged. He neglected to open his letters ; they were collected into an indiscriminate heap, and oftentimes, when their accumulation rather alarmed the manager, they were consigned to the flames, and frequently communications of considerable importance were thus sacrificed. Authors not only complained of the loss or neglect of their manuscripts, but boldly asserted that their plots, their incidents, and their conversations were pilfered and brought out in such shapes that the parent only recognised his offspring by some unmistakable feature. Sheridan had occasionally to pay for this heedlessness, and under the name of gratuity, or the expression of admiration of a play not quite suited for the stage, was compelled to silence some urgent claimant with money. Occasionally this obtained for him the name of liberality ; but he soon found that more were ready to take advantage of his good nature than had any real claims upon it.

The year 1788 was remarkable in the life of Mr. Sheridan from the circumstance of his becoming still further committed to the speculation at Drury Lane Theatre, for he purchased Mr. Willoughby Lacy's interests, and for the introduction on the stage of a musical entertainment entitled the "Camp." It now appears that it was the work of his brother-in-law, Tickell, and what could have induced Sheridan to lend the lustre of his reputation to so worthless a piece of nonsense it is difficult to imagine. Tate Wilkinson has rescued him from the discredit of the authorship, and, therefore, it is unnecessary to say a word more than that this, together with the carelessness with which the theatre was managed under the father of Sheridan, excited some degree of displeasure amongst the *habitués* of Drury Lane; nor did the monody which he wrote on the death of Garrick, and which, with a musical accompaniment, was given the next year, please the public. There seemed to be a tendency to reaction in the theatrical world, and the playgoers were apparently preparing themselves for an outbreak against their newly established friend, when he succeeded in amusing the town with that which seldom fails to please — a caricature of an author whose irritability was the source of much ridicule, and a satire which travestied the dramatic compositions of the day with great humour and fidelity.

The farce called the "Critic" was brought out on the 30th of October, and was the last dramatic effort of this great genius; for "Pizarro" is only an adaptation to the English stage of a play of Kotzebue, and the larger proportion a complete translation. The period, however, at which it was placed upon the stage—whilst a species of enthusiastic loyalty to the king, a detestation of the ruler of France, and a host of concomitant events—together with the acting of Kemble, of Mrs. Siddons, of Mrs. Jordan, gave a popularity to it which probably has never been equalled.

The "Critic" has remained a favourite, even after the causes that gave rise to its being thoroughly appreciated have ceased. During the lifetime of

Cumberland, a satire such as this was certain to please; nor do we agree with one of his admirers, who sometime since prophesied "that the works of Cumberland will delight and edify remote generations when the attempt to render him contemptible, on account of some little infirmity in his temper, shall have lost its point and be forgotten." So far from being realised is this, that the author of the "West Indian" and of the "Jew" is almost unknown to fame. His plays are rarely acted, and then rather for the exhibition of some favourite actor; whilst the "Critic," although the parties at whom the sarcasms were levelled are not even thought of, and although the passages which are ridiculed are scarcely known to exist, proves attractive, and mirth and merriment are called forth by every scene of a burlesque which had neither plot, nor character, nor moral to develop. The audience troubles itself not for a single instant to comprehend the hidden meaning with which each scene is pregnant; it enters into a joke which one would imagine would only be intelligible to those who study dramatic lore; for the "Critic" is as much a satire upon the plays of the present day as it was upon those of the generation just passed away.

That Cumberland was the Sir Fretful Plagiary there cannot be the slightest doubt, and that Sheridan hit his peculiarities off in the happiest manner is equally true. There is a letter from Cumberland in the Garrick correspondence tendering a piece, probably the "Battle of Hastings," which had been rejected at Covent Garden, so much like what Sir Fretful would have written, that it is enough to stamp the similitude of the two; there is another from him to Garrick

The Life of Sheridan

complaining of Sheridan exactly like the man. "I read the tragedy in the ears of the performers on Friday morning. I was highly flattered by the audience, but your successor in management is not a representative of your polite attention to authors on such occasions, for he came in yawning at the fifth act, with no other apology than having sat up two nights running. It gave me not the slightest offence, as I put it all to the habit of dissipation and indolence, but I fear his office will suffer from want of due attention, and the present drop upon the theatre justifies my apprehension." His letters exhibit his character ; there is flattery of Garrick, self-conceit, insinuations against every one. Garrick indorsed upon the back of those he sent to him upon the subject of his tragedy, the " Battle of Hastings," " A true picture of the man." Of his inflicting upon his friends the horrors of listening to the reading of his plays, there are many stories on record. None, however, are better told than by Michael Kelly, who relates what occurred to himself and Bannister, who were invited to partake Cumberland's hospitality at Tunbridge Wells, but were condemned to hear him go through a manuscript play entitled " Tiberius." His sensitiveness upon the subject of his writings may have been excusable, but his envy of the success of any other dramatist, and his inveterate dislike to Sheridan, are sufficient grounds for his being held up to ridicule.

Vaughan was the person portrayed under the name of Dangle. He was always busied in the progress of the dramatic world, and exceedingly anxious to be considered as possessing great power with the press and with managers. He had occupied himself about

The Life of Sheridan

the Richmond Theatre, and had written some letters in the *Morning Post*. He was fairly characterised as a theatrical Quidnunc and a mock Mecænas. Colman had launched some shafts of ridicule against him in a periodical paper which he brought out under the title of *Genius*, where Vaughan figured as Dapper. The stupid nonsense so often quoted from Dr. Watkins, that the exposure of these foolish individuals to public ridicule is an offence to humanity, is scarcely worth refutation. These persons had made themselves public property. Their talents were never called in question ; but those offensive foibles, which led them to depreciate all but themselves, were held up as fair objects for merriment. The castigation they received was in proportion to their offences, and has served as an example to those who would thrust themselves impertinently forward without duly regarding the claims of others.

Some have supposed that there are sundry sly hits at Woodfall, who was the theatrical critic in the *Morning Chronicle*, to which allusion is made, but the well-known independence of character of that excellent man shields him from any attack. He was fully capable of asserting the rights of the press, and of maintaining that high position which, as a critic, he had taken up. His admirable letters to Garrick in the year 1776 show that, however willing to acknowledge the claims of genius, he would inflexibly maintain a straightforward integrity in the conduct of his journal, and that he would steadily adhere to truth.

Such was the impression left upon the public mind by the "Critic," so strongly were its points felt, that no tragedy could be offered to the managers for a long time after its production. Every author saw the ridicule which must attend a repetition of those turgid, incongruous, unnatural attempts which had so long usurped the place of tragedy. " Zorayda " was brought out, but was borne with for eight nights only. Its author was a man of considerable genius, had distinguished himself at Cambridge, having gained the Seatonian prize, but his heroine was found to be forestalled in Tilburina, and vain was the effort to restore to the stage any of those rhapsodies which Sheridan had thus banished. It would not be difficult for any one in the habit of reading the plays of the period to show the different passages that are burlesqued. Holcroft had at one time an idea of publishing a key to the "Critic"; such has been done for the " Rehearsal."

Parsons, as Sir Fretful Plagiary, quickly won the kindest interpretation of his peculiar view of the character, though he did not altogether please Sheridan. Miss Pope, as Tilburina, was hailed with great rapture ; every one in a moment recognised the heroine they had been accustomed to see whining, raving, and killing herself and her lover, in the last act of every tragedy that had been produced for a quarter of a century. Her entrance in white satin, stark mad, according to custom, was the signal for a loud and long burst of applause ; " nobody could ever desire to see anybody madder." She mangled her metre in the most approved fashion of the day. Bannister supported her with great tact as Don Ferolo Whiskerandos. His whimsical situation, his combat with the captain, " Am I a beef-eater now ? " furnished him with admirable opportunities for burlesque acting, of which he availed himself. Short as is the

The Life of Sheridan

part, it has always been a favourite with the public. The refusal to " stay dying all night," which was an impromptu expression of weariness the first night of dress rehearsal, was seized upon by Sheridan and immediately introduced. Indeed, several of the points were instantaneously struck off on that occasion. Mr. Waldron, as Sir Christopher Hatton, was more popular in that short and insignificant character than in any that he performed. It was said by Sheridan that he made more points by his toes than by his brains. The " Critic" loses nothing of its value by frequent repetition. Farren has in modern times been received as a skilful delineator of Sir Fretful Plagiary, and has deservedly been admired.

It is a well-authenticated fact that two days before the " Critic" was announced to be played Sheridan had not finished the last scene. Everybody was anxious and nervous ; Mr. Linley and Dr. Ford were in no enviable state—they were joint-managers, and responsible. The performers looked at each other with dread and dismay. King, who had the part of Puff to sustain, was the stage manager. It was his especial duty to find out Sheridan, and to weary him with remonstrances on the backward state of things, but matters went on much as usual. Sheridan came to the theatre, made the customary promise that he was just going home to finish it ; that, in fact, it was completed, and only wanted an additional line or two. His father-in-law, Linley, knew the only spur to his industry and his genius ; he therefore ordered a night rehearsal, invited Sheridan to dine with him, gave him a capital dinner, and proposed a lounge to Drury Lane whilst the supper was preparing. Sheridan assented, and they sauntered together up and down the stage previous to the rehearsal, when King stepped up to Sheridan, requested a moment's audience, and went with him into the small green-room, where there was a comfortable fire, a good arm-chair, a table furnished with pens, ink, and paper, two bottles of claret, a tempting dish of anchovy sandwiches, and the prompter's unfinished copy of the "Critic." King, immediately Sheridan entered the room, popped out, locked the door, when Ford and Linley made their pleasure known to him, that he was to finish the wine and the farce, but not to be allowed to stir out of the room until they were both at an end. Sheridan laughed heartily at the joke, set to in good earnest, and finished the work, to the great delight of all parties.

This last act contains an inimitable scene, almost unknown to the theatrical world, as it is rarely, if ever, performed. It boasts some of the most genuine hits at the winding-up of dramas and novels that have ever appeared. The family recognition of the Justice, and the wife of the highwayman, is admirable. It is a supposed hit at the tumid language of Home, the author of "Douglas," in the "Fatal Discovery," a tragedy of bombast and nonsense, which, singularly enough, was warmly patronised by Garrick, who had repudiated the popular play of "Douglas" as unfitted for the stage. We have had occasion to observe that there exists no copy of the "School for Scandal," excepting the Dublin edition, nor of the "Duenna," authorised by Sheridan himself; but fortunately we possess something like circumstantial evidence that the "Critic" was given in such a shape to the world as he could approve of; for, in the library of Mr. Henry Bohn, there exists a presentation copy to one

The Life of Sheridan

of the Duke of Marlborough's family with the undoubted autograph of the author. From this treasure
we are enabled to produce an authentic version. It is
a thin octavo volume, with a frontispiece beautifully
engraved, having the masks of tragedy and comedy
admirably executed, printed for T. Beckett, Adelphi,
Strand, 1781. There are no very striking differences
in the text from that which has been usually received
as genuine ; indeed, it is only in the stage directions
and in the printing of the dialogue that there is much
perceptible variation. Such, however, as is the original version, we have taken care that it should be
preserved in the present volume. One or two of the
passages, as they appear there, are rendered somewhat
striking by the introduction of italics and capitals ;
thus, the accusation that Sheridan plagiarised from his
fellow-labourers, who sent their plays for acceptance
at Drury Lane Theatre, is unhesitatingly met and
sneered at in the following dialogue, which is thus
printed :—

"*Dangle*. Sir Fretful, have you sent your play to
the managers yet ? or can I be of any service to
you ?

"*Sir Fretful*. No, no, I thank you ; I believe the
piece had sufficient recommendation with it. I thank
you, though I sent it to the manager of COVENT
GARDEN THEATRE this morning.

"*Sneer*. I should have thought now that it might
have been cast (as the actors call it) better at DRURY
LANE.

"*Sir Fretful*. O lud, no !—never send a play there
while I live, harkee ! [*Whispers Sneerwell.*]

"*Sneer. Writes himself !* I know he does !

"*Sir Fretful*. I say nothing—I take away from no

man's merit—am hurt at no man's good fortune—I
say nothing, but this I say—through all my knowledge of life I have observed that there is not a passion
so strongly rooted in the human heart as envy.

" *Sneer.* I believe you have reason for what you
say, indeed.

" *Sir Fretful.* Besides—I can tell you it is not always
so safe to leave a play in the hands of those who write
themselves.

" *Sneer.* What! they may steal from them, my dear
Plagiary.

" *Sir Fretful.* Steal! to be sure they may, and egad!
serve your best thoughts as gipsies do stolen children,
disfigure them to make them pass for their own.

" *Sneer.* But your present work is a sacrifice to Mel-
pomene, and HE, you know, never——

" *Sir Fretful.* That's no security — a dexterous
plagiarist may do anything. Why, Sir, for aught I
know, he might take out some of the best things in
my tragedy and put them into his own comedy."

From the same stores that were opened for the use
of Moore, and from which he has collected a vast
quantity of amusing information as to the early career
of Sheridan in the dramatic and literary world, have
been collected proofs that many things were commenced by him which were never thoroughly carried
out; several unfinished pieces attest his labours and
his talents. He had meditated over many designs, of
which slight sketches were drawn, the outlines of characters delineated, and heads of conversation prepared,
all of which never arrived at that degree of perfection
which would warrant their being given to the public
in any other character than as literary curiosities.
These, from the eminence of the author, are well

worth preserving. The memorandums of a comedy
entitled "Affectation," three acts of a drama, frag-
ments of epilogues, of poems, lead us to regret that
so early in life he abandoned for political strife the
Muses, who were so willing to hover around him and
lend him their influence.

About the year 1780 a change came over the spirit
of his dream. "That year a dissolution of Parliament
took place ; he felt 'aspiring passions' ; he bade adieu
to the triumphs which a theatrical auditory had
afforded him, and sought a new scene for the exhibition of talents which doubtless he felt that he
possessed, and wanted only an opportunity for their
display." Amongst his manuscripts are to be found
indications that, even whilst he was busy in the
theatrical world, he had bestowed some portion of
his time and attention to politics. A paper on absentee-
ism, embracing some views of the cruelty practised
by England upon the sister isle by restraining her
commercial freedom, and other proofs exist that he
did not entirely yield himself up to the fascinations of
the theatre.

The neglect, however, which necessarily followed
upon his new career was soon felt at Drury Lane
Theatre ; and it is to be inferred that, about this time,
those embarrassments commenced which haunted
and embittered his future life. Murmurs began to be
heard as to the payment of certain salaries—whispers
which gradually grew into loud complaints — that
there was no regular system followed in the management, and no regard paid to economy. The father of
Sheridan directed the affairs of Drury Lane with great
difficulty ; and at last so many obstacles were thrown
in his way by one set of persons, and so little apparent

The Life of Sheridan

wish to support him by those who had most interest in his management, that he was compelled to relinquish the undertaking. Sheridan himself seemed altogether careless ; invited into society by those who were delighted with his gaiety and his talent, he plunged into expenses for entertaining others, which very rapidly absorbed large sums of money, whilst the facility of drawing from the treasury led him to forget that it was only by persevering economy fortunes are to be realised, and those we love rendered independent of the pressure of want. Light-hearted, amiable, open to flattery, caressed for his talents by all who had any claim to public fame, he launched into the bustle of life. At the age of twenty-nine he had achieved a brilliant reputation, had gained an immense property, and was apparently master of large resources ; but he rushed upon an ambitious career which dazzled him; he abandoned that of which he was certain for that which was yet unknown. He neglected the business of that concern by which he could have gained, as Garrick had done before him, a splendid fortune, left it almost without management, content to be called the kind-hearted proprietor, and to draw money from it. An epilogue to Miss Hannah Moore's play of "Fatal Falsehood" from his pen, and a pantomime, "Robinson Crusoe ; or, Harlequin Friday," attributed to him, seem for a time to have been all that he considered necessary for him to do for the theatre.

The biographer who is endowed with Spurzheim's organ of comparison would feel some difficulty in assigning to Sheridan his proper rank as a statesman, if he sought to elucidate the circumstances of his political career by drawing a parallel between his

The Life of Sheridan

position and that of any of the distinguished men who at the present moment sway the public mind. Indeed, events are of so different a character that another race of individuals has sprung up, who would most probably have been little thought of had they attempted to bring themselves into notice at an earlier period. The eloquence which was required in the stormier moments of a nation's existence would now be of little avail. The passions are no longer to be aroused ; the reason is to be addressed. Men have time leisurely to reflect upon the nightly debates ; these are occupied with subjects which require facts, statistic details, and knowledge of business. Assiduity and practical information are more looked to than brilliancy of language or beautiful imagery. The representative of a manufacturing district, or a railway proprietor who can stutter forth his own conviction, commands more attention than the chaste speaker or the acute logician. Such, however, was not the case when Sheridan won the admiration of his country.

Politics were then more universally discussed ; all ranks of society engaged in public affairs ; the spirit of party ran high ; matters of the deepest happiness to the human race were boldly investigated. The attempt by one set of men to stifle the expression of the general voice had engendered a rankling hatred in the bosom of others and kindled the passions that were sought to be extinguished ; these, however, have now died away. In England, since the secession from active exertion for the party of the people of their last great leader, Sir Francis Burdett, there has been little of that enthusiasm which once animated the whole kingdom and led society to rank itself under two great sections, which, whatever might have been their subdivisions, represented, on one hand, the love of power, on the other, that of liberty. From the commencement of the great American War until the overthrow of Napoleon, there was a constant excitement in the public mind; the mightiest changes were going forward, and opportunities offered themselves to men to distinguish themselves more by their power of influencing others by personal ability and their more apparent qualifications than by their research, their inventions, or their discoveries. Above all, eloquence, which addresses itself at once to the senses and leads them onwards, was worshipped, and brought to its possessor not only admiration, but beyond that the actual affection of its auditors. No one more successfully obtained this than did Sheridan.

He was listened to, even by such a man as Professor Smyth, "as a being that belonged to another sphere, as one to whom no ordinary mortal was for a moment to be brought into likeness or comparison." Such was the wondrous power of Sheridan, that his vehement and affecting torrents of eloquence left an impression upon the mind that no subsequent series of events could ever efface; if, indeed, all that his eulogists have said of him be true, those who once listened to him have had a greater enjoyment than has fallen to the lot of the most enthusiastic admirer of public speaking. Yet, when Sheridan entered upon his career, he by no means gave promise of becoming so splendid an orator. There were, twenty years ago, at Bath, many who remembered him there as a young man walking about in a cocked hat and scarlet waistcoat, with his pockets most deplorably empty, trying various means of filling them and amusing himself. Amongst other thoughts that crossed his mind was a private play, but in rehearsal he was found incapable of filling any prominent position.

When, in 1780, Sheridan made his first address upon the subject of his return to Parliament for Stafford, in answer to a petition against his election, he was listened to with great attention, the House being uncommonly still while he was speaking, for his reputation had prepared for him a willing audience. He made, however, but little impression. It appeared to those who were anxious to judge of his real capabilities that nature never intended him for an orator; his enunciation was evidently very imperfect; he spoke as if his tongue was too thick for the due action of the muscles which close the teeth upon it; there was an indistinctness of which, indeed, he never got rid, so that his mental powers appeared to be very far superior to his physical qualifications. He was himself agitated during the delivery of· his speech, and upon its conclusion he went into the gallery where Woodfall was reporting, and with much evident anxiety tried to obtain from him his opinion of the probability of his ultimate success. With his usual frankness, Woodfall told him that he candidly advised him to stick to his former pursuits, for he had now got out of his depth. Sheridan, however, felt that within him which urged him on to future fame, and, resting his head upon his hand, exclaimed, "I know that it is in me, and out it shall come!" Woodfall was nearly right. Sheridan became, with as much labour as Demosthenes had employed, a great orator, and mind overcame the deficiencies of the earthly frame, but even to the latest moments he had occasionally a defect which, for a short time, impeded the power of producing an impression; but when carried away by his subject all minor thoughts were dissipated by the excitement of his language, the fervour of his manner, and the wondrous lustre and expression of his eye, so that when he ceased all seemed to wait with the hope of something more.

This first attempt made by Sheridan to address the House naturally excited great interest. He was heard with particular attention and unusual silence; he replied to a complaint against his election for Stafford by means of bribery and corruption; he defended his constituents from an accusation made by the lowest and most unprincipled voters. He thought it a great hardship, and wished that some adequate penalties should be inflicted on those who traduced and stigmatised a respectable body of men. Mr. Rigby did not allow these observations to pass unnoticed, but ridiculed the idea of any member being concerned for the character of his constituents. Mr. Fox threw his shield over the young member, and made some sarcastic remarks on the ministerial members, who chiefly robbed and plundered their constituents, and afterwards affected to despise them. Sheridan himself took the opportunity, on the next occasion of his addressing the House, which was a few evenings after, when he spoke on the vote of thanks to Earl Cornwallis and General Sir Henry Clinton for their conduct in America, to show that he was not likely tamely to submit to the taunts of Mr. Rigby. He apologised to him for not answering some things that had fallen from him in the same ludicrous strain in which he chose to view everything, excepting what related to his own immediate interest. He acknowledged the gentleman had a kind of drollery and humour, but he liked his ingenuity,

The Life of Sheridan

his humour, and his counsels better than his political arguments.

Sheridan's next speech, which occurred on the second reading of the bill for " The Better Regulation of His Majesty's Civil List," was the first indication that he gave of his readiness of reply, and of the happy tact with which he could seize on the observations of an adversary, and turn the weapons of ridicule upon the practised debater. Mr. Courtenay, instead of discussing a serious and grave question, which involved the characters of the ministry for retaining several useless, expensive, and inconvenient places, and diverting the money of the public from its proper channels into the purse of individuals, attacked the opposition members, and observed that " O liberty ! O virtue ! O my country !" had been the incessant, pathetic, but fallacious cry of former oppositions. The present, he was sure, acted on purer motives. They wept over their bleeding country ; yet the patriot " eye, in a fine frenzy rolling," deigned to cast a wishful squint on riches and honour enjoyed by the minister and his venal supporters. He compared their conduct to the sentimental alderman in Hogarth's print, who, when his daughter is dying, wears a face of parental grief and solicitude ; but it is to secure a diamond ring which he is drawing off her finger. He proceeded, in a ludicrous strain, to point out the anxious wish of the opposition to breathe a fresh air, but implored them not to put the drag-chain upon a rising state. Mr. Sheridan, after reproving Mr. Courtenay for the unsuitable manner in which he had introduced his opinion, observed that, if they could not act with dignity, they ought to debate with decency ; that he would not attempt seriously to reply to that which had an infusion of ridicule in every part; but two of his similes he must take notice of. The one was that the opposition was envious of those who basked in court sunshine, and were desirous only of getting into their places. To this insinuation he would reply, that though the sun afforded a genial warmth, it also occasioned an intemperate heat that tainted and infected everything that it reflected on; that this excessive heat tended to corrupt, as well as to cherish; to putrefy, as well as to animate; to dry and soak up the wholesome juices of the body politic, and to turn the whole into one mass of corruption. If those, therefore, who sat near him did not enjoy so genial a warmth as the honourable gentleman and those who, like him, kept near the nobleman in the blue riband (Lord North), he was certain that they breathed a purer air, an air less infected and less corrupt. The drag-chain of the gentleman's allusion was never applied but when a machine was going down hill, and then it was applied wisely. He concluded a felicitous speech by assuring the honourable gentleman that the most serious part of his argument appeared the most ludicrous.

It was on the 5th of March that the first parliamentary effort demanding talent and judgment was made by Sheridan, and the universal opinion expressed in favour both of the matter and manner of his speech gave him a decided position in the political world. Mr. Sheridan had previously given notice of his intention to bring forward a motion for the better regulation of the police of Westminster, and he took the opportunity of coming before the House with a well-digested view of the circumstances which had presented themselves during the month of June in the past year, when the metropolis was left for several days at the mercy of an ignorant and fanatic mob. His motions were :—

" 1. That the military force entrusted to his Majesty by Parliament cannot justifiably be applied to the dispersing illegal and tumultuous assemblies of the people, without waiting for directions from the civil magistrates, but where the outrages have broke forth with such violence that all civil authority is overborne, and the immediate subversion of all legal government directly threatened."

" 2. That the necessity of issuing that unprecedented order to the military, on the 7th of June last, to act without waiting for directions from the civil magistrates, affords a strong presumption of the defective state of the magistracy of Westminster, where the riots began."

" 3. That a committee be appointed to inquire into the conduct of the magistracy and civil power of the city of Westminster, with respect to the riots in June last ; and to examine and report to the House the present state of the magistracy and government of the said city."

The language he employed was not peculiarly striking, but it was to the point.

On the 13th of May, and on the 17th, the readiness of Sheridan excited much amusement in the House. On the first occasion he made some observations on lotteries, and concluded with observing, that " as the learned gentleman (the Solicitor-General) who brought in the bill had already on one occasion stood forward, not only as the *censor morum*, but as the *arbiter elegantiarum*, at once the Cato and the Petronius of the age, he hoped he would be active in his new

The Life of Sheridan

character, and join in putting a stop to lottery gaming, by bringing in a bill to abolish all the present lottery offices, and preventing the opening of any new ones in future."

On the other, on the bill for preventing desertion, Sheridan pithily observed "that the honourable gentleman (Mr. Penton) had omitted to take notice of one objection adduced by Mr. Dunning, which was, that when sailors, suspected to be deserters, were brought before a justice of the peace by virtue of this Act, though the suspicion turned out to be groundless, they might nevertheless, by authority of former statutes, be impressed. He ironically complimented the Board of Admiralty for the high sense they seemed here to entertain of the honour of British sailors ; it might be illustrated by a very trite anecdote of Julius Cæsar, for, like his wife, the character of our seamen must be as clear of suspicion as of impeachment ; they not only must not be deserters, but not suspected to be so."

A few words upon the bill to amend and explain the Marriage Act, brought in by Mr. Fox, gave that great leader of the opposition an opportunity of complimenting, somewhat insidiously, his friend Mr. Sheridan, who opposed Mr. Fox's favourite views. "He said his honourable friend (Mr. Fox), who brought in the bill, appeared not to be aware that, if he carried the clause enabling girls to marry at sixteen, he would do an injury to that liberty of which he had always shown himself the friend, and promote domestic tyranny, which he could consider only as little less intolerable than public tyranny. If girls were allowed to marry at sixteen, they would, he conceived, be abridged of that happy freedom of intercourse which modern custom had introduced between the youth of both sexes ; and which was, in his opinion, the best nursery of happy marriages. Guardians would in that case look on their wards with a jealous eye, from a fear that footmen and those about them might take advantage of their tender years and immature judgment, and persuade them into marriage as soon as they attained the age of sixteen. In like manner, young men, when mere boys, in a moment of passion, however ill-directed, or perhaps in a moment of intoxication, might be prevailed upon to make an imprudent match, and probably be united to a common prostitute."

Fox's reply to this was "that his honourable friend, Mr. Sheridan, had so much ingenuity of mind, that he could contrive to give an argument what turn he pleased ; he considered not, therefore, when what he said was really in support of domestic tyranny, he should ground it on a wish to preserve liberty." This terminated all that fell from Sheridan during his first session.

The second session was marked by no striking proof of his senatorial ability. He seemed to wait his opportunity, and to examine carefully the opinions and strength of parties. He once took occasion to reproach his former antagonist, Mr. Rigby, for the contemptuous manner in which he spoke of his constituents, when that gentleman, attempting to reply to a forcible speech of Mr. Fox on the prosecution of the American War, animadverted on the doctrine of taking counsel from their constituents, which he proclaimed unconstitutional, if not illegal. On one occasion Sheridan commented with much energy on some expressions which fell from Lord North, "that many of our best officers were unemployed and disgusted"; for it by no means appeared they had not just cause for their disgust; but the only speech worthy of being recorded is one upon a motion, made by Lord John Cavendish, of censure on Lord North. Here he had another opportunity of attacking Mr. Rigby, the paymaster of the forces. "Mr. Sheridan meant to speak to the purpose; but he wished not to be judged by the test laid down by the right honourable gentleman (Mr. Rigby), for he meant to give no offence in what he should say, though, it was true, the rule had been proposed from high authority; for undoubtedly, if the degree of offence which speeches gave was to be considered as the criterion of eloquence, the right honourable gentleman must be looked up to as the Demosthenes of that assembly. He had acted, how-ever, in that day's debate perfectly consistent; he had assured the House that he thought the noble lord ought to resign his offices; and yet he would give his vote for his remaining in it. The honourable gentle-man had long declared that he thought the American War ought to be abandoned; but he had uniformly given his vote for its continuance. He did not mean, however, to insinuate any motives for such conduct— he believed the right honourable gentleman to have been sincere; he believed that, as a member of Parliament, as a privy councillor, as a private gentle-man, he had always detested the American War as much as any man, but that he had never been able to persuade the paymaster that it was a bad war: and, unfortunately, in whatever character he spoke, it was the paymaster who always voted in that House. His attacks on the noble lord, he said, appeared only an ingenious method of supporting him ; it was figurative ; but *ay* and *no* were speeches that did not admit of a trope." Mr. Sheridan then attacked the language used by that honourable gentleman on all occasions when the constituents of that House were mentioned. "His manner of treating the late petitions on the American War was highly indecent, and at that time extremely impolitic. The people began to be sufficiently irritated ; gentlemen should be careful to drop no expressions of contempt towards them in that House. They had borne a great deal, and it might be imprudent to treat their patience with insult. The way to prevent the interference of the people, the way to destroy those associations and petitions, which seemed so offensive to the right honourable gentleman, was to endeavour to make Parliament respectable. Let that House show itself independent, let it show itself consistent, and the people will never think of interfering ; but if Parliament became contemptible in the eyes of the nation, the people would interfere, and neither threats nor influence would prevent them."

Sheridan was now fairly launched upon the troubled sea of politics. He had displayed that kind of talent which naturally made him an acquisition to either of the parties which sought to direct the affairs of this great empire. His eloquence, his tact, his elegance of manner, his brilliant conversation, all led to his being recognised as one who had a claim to rank amongst the leading men of the age ; but it was evident that he was much better adapted to become an independent chieftain than a partisan. Although he followed the footsteps of the Whigs, he occasionally deviated from their line of march ; and it was soon evident that he would act, think, and speak for himself, and that, though

The Life of Sheridan

he was bound in strict ties of regard and of friendship
to the great and good leader of the party, he would
even combat him, and, when the occasion required it,
would assert his own views in opposition to the man
who, from his position, was entitled to express the
opinions of a numerous body. The period was one of
great excitement. Men's minds were directed with
unusual energy towards the solution of a great difficulty.
A struggle carried on between the mother-country and
her excited offspring had tended to awaken, in England
and in the United States, the spirit of liberty, and a
hatred of despotic sway. Lord North, as the osten-
sible minister of the crown, had accumulated upon
himself the uncompromising hatred of a large portion
of the people. They had been urged on by the violent
declamations of Charles Fox, of Lord John Cavendish,
of Edmund Burke, and of the great leaders of the
Whig party. Sheridan took but little interest in this
inexhaustible theme for parliamentary eloquence;
and, notwithstanding the inducements he met with to
exert himself, he appears to have remained almost an
indifferent spectator of the struggle. There is, however, a rumour, "coming," as Moore says, "from an
authority worthy in every respect of the most implicit
belief, that the Government of the United States made
him an offer of £20,000 as a mark of the high estimation in which his talents were held, but that Sheridan
would not accept it." "With respect to the credibility
of the transaction," continues Moore, "it is far less
easy to believe that the Americans had so much money
to give, than that Mr. Sheridan should have been
sufficiently high-minded to have refused it."

He seemed at this period to be intent on learning
the tone and temper of the House. When he spoke,

The Life of Sheridan

it was with conciseness, and without any ambitious desire to win approbation; he felt the difficulties of his new position, and was determined to surmount them. His judgment and good taste drew upon him the notice and admiration of Charles Fox, who, already charmed with his talents, had bestowed upon him his warmest friendship.

Lord North's administration now drew to a close; the general murmuring against the war at last acted upon the supporters of the premier. On an address being moved by General Conway for a discontinuance of hostilities with America, Lord North's majority had dwindled down to a bare unit; on a similar resolution being again brought forward, he was left in a minority of nine. Mr. Sheridan made a speech on this occasion, in ridicule of Sir William Dolben, who intimated his intention of voting against the motion, although he had voted in its favour a few evenings before. This speech, which has not been recorded, is said to have been an admirable piece of satire. A few nights afterwards, Lord North announced that his administration had ceased to exist. Sheridan seems to have contented himself with general censure of the administration, but did not so virulently declaim against it as did others of the party into whose hands the reins of government now fell.

Such was, however, the respect in which Sheridan was held by his party, that when Lord North's ministry was overthrown, and the Marquis of Rockingham formed a new one from which the country anticipated great results, he was appointed one of the under-secretaries of state, a post which he had then reason to believe would be a permanent one; but in this he was doomed to disappointment. There were seeds of dissolution in that administration, which very rapidly sprung up and quickly choked the promising growth of the tree of Whiggism; but one short speech has been recorded to have been delivered by him in his new official position, and that upon a point which failed to interest the public. But he spoke briefly on another occasion, memorable in the annals of reform, when a young man, destined to rule the destinies of a mighty empire, and afterwards to oppose with all his strength the doctrines which he at first supported with zeal and enthusiasm—William Pitt—moved for a committee to inquire into the state of the representation.

The death of the Marquis of Rockingham led to such disunion that, after a short existence of four months, this administration was dissolved, and made way for that coalition which was execrated by the politicians of the day, and at this hour is looked upon as having so far shaken all confidence in the integrity of public men as to have laid the foundation for the formation of a party of the people, the principle of whose political creed was the distrust of both Whig and Tory.

Lord North and his opponent, Charles Fox, antagonists in every public measure that had ever been agitated, listening to the tone of the charmers who sang of the sweets of office, of the mutability of the people, and of the smiles from the throne, threw aside every idea of the moral strength of public opinion, and fraternised. It is universally allowed that on this occasion Sheridan upheld the dignity of the statesman's character, that he boldly proclaimed his dissent from this sacrifice of character, and that he held an interview with Fox, during which he vainly attempted to change his decision; it was terminated

The Life of Sheridan

by the remarkable expression of the great Whig leader, " It is as fixed as the Hanover succession."

Once only did Sheridan make any allusion to this coalition. The debate in which it occurred, on the preliminary articles of peace, is more remarkable from its bringing him into collision with Mr. Pitt, and his triumphant reply to some sarcasms which the future prime minister indulged in. The following portions of their speeches are amongst the reports of the House of Commons. " No man," observed Mr. Pitt, " admired more than he did the abilities of that right honourable gentleman, the elegant sallies of his thought, the gay effusions of his fancy, his dramatic turns, and his epigrammatic points ; and, if they were reserved for a proper stage, they would, no doubt, receive what the honourable gentleman's abilities always did receive, the plaudits of the audience ; and it would be his fortune ' *sui plausu gaudere theatri.*' But this was not the proper scene for the exhibition of these elegancies." To this Sheridan's instantaneous reply was : "On that particular sort of personality which the right honourable gentleman had thought proper to introduce, I need make no comment—the propriety, the taste, the gentlemanly point of it, must have been obvious to the House. But let me assure the right honourable gentleman that I do now, and will at any time when he chooses, meet it with the most sincere good humour. Nay, I will say more, flattered and encouraged by the right honourable gentleman's panegyric on my talents, if I ever again engage in the compositions he alludes to, I may be tempted to an act of presumption, to attempt an improvement on one of Ben Jonson's best characters— the character of the Angry Boy in the ' Alchymist.' "

The Life of Sheridan

During this unnatural coalition, Mr. Sheridan became secretary of the treasury; his coadjutor, Richard Burke, was the brother of Edmund. Of the businesslike manner in which he discharged the duties which devolved upon him, his warmest friends are necessarily silent; but his opponents speak of a laughable *affiche* which was found upon the doors of the treasury: "No applications can be received here on Sundays, nor any business done here during the remainder of the week." This was the first proof of his inaptitude to the discharge of public duty. Mr. Sheridan attempted, as did his colleagues, to justify their conduct in associating with that ministry, whose chief they had not only loudly denounced as dangerous, but actually declared their intention of impeaching for unconstitutional conduct. His speech was clever and ingenious, but failed to convince; he, in common with the rest of his party, lost caste by this inconsistent union. The only debate which he enlivened with his wit was the threatened taxation of tombstones, actually proposed by Mr. Coke of Norfolk as one which could meet with no objections. To which Sheridan replied, "that the only reason why the proposed tax could not be objected to was because those out of whose property it was to be paid would know nothing of the matter, as they must be dead before the demand could be made; but then, after all, who knows but that it may not be rendered unpopular in being represented as a tax upon persons who, having paid the debt of nature, must prove that they have done so by having the receipt engraved upon their tombs?"

The great struggle between parties took place on the celebrated India Bill, which has been universally acknowledged to have been a measure, introduced for the government of India, that would have given to the existing ministry such patronage and such power as to have rendered it independent both of the sovereign and the people. The advocates of Whiggism pronounce it a master-stroke of policy, for they hold that, as their doctrines are the only true principles upon which government should be carried on, they admire the minister who could have devised means which would have given their promulgators means of perpetuating themselves in office. These views were not satisfactory to the British people, who enthusiastically received the intelligence that the monarch had so influenced the House of Lords that the measures were rejected. The ministry that had been received with indignation was dismissed amidst expressions of triumph. Although Sheridan took no conspicuous part in the debates, he shared the odium of his party; he momentarily ceased to be a favourite with the people, who could not admire the fidelity with which he adhered to his friends and who learnt with regret that he lent his aid in the concoction of the obnoxious measure. Once again he was to be seen in the ranks of the opposition, leading a determined attack upon the young minister, Mr. Pitt, who, by a fortuitous occurrence of events, was hailed as the leader of a party at once supported by the king and the people. Sheridan was amongst the bitterest of his opponents; he lost no opportunity of assailing him with taunts and invectives. "How shuffling," exclaimed he, "is this conduct of a young minister, unhackneyed in the ways of man! This is an instance of duplicity scarcely to be paralleled by the most hoary hypocrite that ever guided the principles of a great nation. If, in the very onset, this young minister thus tramples on the constitution, what may you not expect from the audacity of his riper years ? " Nor was such a style of language disliked by the House of Commons, to whom Sheridan had rendered his eloquence not only tolerable, but almost necessary.

The determined energy of the king's conduct inspired Mr. Pitt with resolution. In spite of the hostility of the House of Commons, he continued to pursue his policy until a dissolution of Parliament would allow him to take the sense of the country ; for he felt assured that, whenever this occurred, he should be enabled to command a majority, for the clamour was loud, and the conduct of the coalition had shown too much of the old leaven of corruption, instead of the promised reform so long proclaimed. Sheridan, more fortunate than many of his co-mates, found himself in Parliament after a dissolution. Stafford, faithful to him, had returned him once again, and had shown a greater sympathy with their representative than many a borough that had vaunted its love of liberty and its disinterestedness. The next two sessions were not marked by any vigorous display of Sheridan's abilities. He made no bold attacks upon the minister, and in this conduct he was borne out by Fox, who almost absented himself from the field, and rarely made his appearance at all. Sheridan acted as a guerilla chief, occasionally hanging on the flanks of his enemy, making a bold excursion, showing his capability of injuring, but rarely committing himself to anything in the shape of a regular attack. The Westminster scrutiny, now a subject forgotten by all, was the one in which Sheridan most distinguished himself. Upon the general election, Lord Hood was declared duly elected ;

but there was a doubt raised by Sir Cecil Wray, who, together with Mr. Fox, were the other candidates. A scrutiny was demanded as to the legality of the majority of 235 which the latter claimed, to which the high bailiff assented. The opposition in the House of Commons sought to censure the high bailiff's conduct, and a long battle of words, renewed during the two subsequent sessions of Parliament, gave rise to two very clever speeches from Sheridan. He was also eloquent upon various reform questions, upon taxation, and upon questions connected with India. Throughout the whole of the period he gained upon the nation by his temperate zeal and, singular to say, by his apparent acquaintance with financial measures, and rose into consideration amongst the calculating politicians of the day for the soundness of his views and the carefulness with which he promulgated them. On one or two occasions he spoke with great deference of the prime minister, congratulating the country in rather an insidious way upon the consistency of his conduct as a parliamentary reformer. On one occasion he came into collision with Mr. Rolle, the member for Devonshire, afterwards known as Lord Rolle, and exhibited his usual tact in answering his charges, and denying his co-operation with those who had attacked him in the " Rolliad."

No ephemeral production ever produced a greater sensation than the "Rolliad." It was hailed with rapturous shouts of laughter ; impression after impression issued from the press. Not even the "Antijacobin" nor the "Rejected Addresses" was read by the whole nation with greater avidity. Though now slumbering in peaceful quiet and completely forgotten, it will amply repay the lovers of genuine mirth

The Life of Sheridan

by its happy vein of ridicule, its playfulness, its allusions to classic literature, and its sparkling satire. The name of Rolle is scarcely known to the present generation ; the only occasion on which it has come of late before the public was when, on the coronation of her Majesty, the venerable peer, the hero of the "Rolliad," stumbled on approaching to do homage to the queen. It was forgotten that he had ever been apostrophised thus :—

> " Illustrious Rolle, O may thy honoured name
> Roll down distinguished on the rolls of fame ;
> Still first be found on Devon's county polls,
> Still future senates boast their future Rolles,
> Since of all rolls, which in this world we see,
> The world has ne'er produced a roll like thee."

The work purports to be criticisms on a poem supposed to have been written upon the actions of Rollo, Duke of Normandy, from whom Mr. Rolle had imprudently boasted his descent. The quotations, the subject of the pretended exertion of the critic's art, alluded to the general supporters of the minister, who were handled with caustic severity and ludicrous animadversions ; to this was added a series of political eclogues, in which Mr. Rose, Mr. Banks, Lord Liverpool, Jekyll, and other prominent characters, were chastised with no measured hand for their political principles. The same volume contains some inimitable burlesque compositions, pretended to be written by candidates for the laureateship, vacant by the death of William Whitehead. They are supposed to be such odes as are written by the laureate on such an occasion as a birthday by a number of candidates for the post. The persons selected for this medium of holding them up to ridicule were the most remarkable men of the day, all of whom were treated with

The Life of Sheridan

much humour, and with that species of lashing which has always been considered fair in political warfare. Sheridan's brother-in-law, Tickell, General Fitzpatrick, George Ellis, Dr. French Laurence, and Joseph Richardson, took a very active portion of these publications upon themselves, and were the authors. They formed themselves into a club, and continued to exercise their ingenuity in tormenting their public opponents. The relationship in which Sheridan stood with one of those who were most actively employed, and his well-known mental resources, led to the suspicion that he was a member of the coterie, and that he gave to their united efforts his own acknowledged powers; and those who will bestow some little time on the perusal of the criticisms may fancy that they can detect "the fine old Roman hand."

Sheridan went considerably out of his way to clear himself from the suspicion of being one of the tormentors of Mr. Rolle, and took a very early opportunity of denying in the House his connection with the critics. He had spent some part of the previous summer in Lancashire, and had paid so much attention to the state of the Manchester manufacturers as to have excited some foolish jealousy in the minds of Mr. Pitt's followers; and when Mr. Pitt brought in a bill to amend the Acts for imposing a duty by excise on certain cotton manufacturers—Mr. Fox seconding the motion—an animated discussion sprang up, during which Mr. Pitt somewhat incautiously threw out an imputation on the evidence given before a committee of the House by some of the manufacturers. Mr. Sheridan warmly replied to him, "declaring that he had most unjustly aspersed those parties, whose conduct had been most laudable, and whose evidence was unquestionable." Upon this Mr. Rolle rose up, and with great warmth charged Sheridan with having made an inflammatory speech in the country, with a view to excite alarm and discontent. He said he would not mention the member who had gone down to Lancashire to stir up the manufacturers, to set them against the taxes, and to promote tumults and discontent; neither would he say who it was that distributed, or caused to be distributed, seditious and inflammatory handbills, and had them circulated all round the country; but the fact was so, and, if he could bring the proof home to the party, he would take the proper steps to have his head stuck upon Temple Bar. He went on in a similar strain, charging Fox and Sheridan with declaring in favour of Mr. Pitt, nay, even of seconding his motion and then voting against it, and stigmatised them as abandoning and deserting ground once taken in a most shameful manner. After Mr. Fox had replied to the empty threat of having heads stuck upon Temple Bar, and to the folly of supposing that circulating handbills was a capital offence, Mr. Sheridan rose and denied any participation in the handbills, but said he was not surprised at the soreness evinced by him about publications. The handbills were not the compositions that hurt him, but compositions less prosaic, but more popular, he was afraid, had made Mr. Rolle so sore. This allusion was quickly taken up by the House and received with loud laughter. He continued by saying that he was aware that the honourable gentleman had suspected that he was either the author of these compositions or in some other way concerned in them. He did assure him, upon his honour, he was not, nor had he ever seen a line of them till they were in print in the newspaper. Mr. Rolle was not very courteous upon this manly avowal, but continued his assertions of doing all within his power to punish the author of these seditious publications. With regard to the "Rolliad," he said that he held the author of those compositions in sovereign contempt as well as his works; but as the cap fitted the right honourable gentleman, he was welcome to wear it. Sheridan again replied, and in a firm and manly tone assured the right honourable gentleman that whilst he talked at random he should not notice him; but if he charged him with being concerned in circulating any seditious handbills, he would answer him both there and elsewhere very plainly and very coarsely. This language was of course unmistakable, and completely silenced Mr. Rolle, who bore it unmoved :—

> " Here to the ferule Rolle his hand resigned,
> Here to the rod he bared the parts behind,
> But him no strifes subdued—and him no fear
> Of menaced wrath, in future more severe."

Mr. Sheridan next distinguished himself in a speech of great vigour and power upon the propositions made by the Government to give commercial freedom to Ireland. Of the soundness of his views there must be considerable question; and although he was supported by the Liberal party in Ireland and by the English manufacturers, his opposition to the ministry, rather than his patriotism, must have led him to the expression of opinions which, however plausible, are inconsistent with the principles which regulate trade, and upon which the commercial prosperity of a nation must depend. Animated and forcible were the doctrines in the style of their delivery, but futile and inconsistent in themselves. The principal ground on which Sheridan rested his opposition to the measure brought forward was that the Parliament of Great Britain was about to extend its power and to legislate for Ireland ; that the Irish Parliament had neither hinted at, nor alluded to, a proposal that the laws for regulating trade and navigation should be the same in both countries.

In the following session Mr. Pitt introduced a measure for effectually providing for the security of his Majesty's dockyards at Plymouth and at Portsmouth by a permanent system of fortification, for enabling the fleet to act with full vigour and effect for the protection of commerce, the support of our distant possessions, and the prosecution of offensive operations. Mr. Sheridan, in opposing the motion, seized upon the argument that had been advanced, that a system of defence by fortification would diminish the number of troops, and therefore would give less cause for the constitutional jealousy of the power of the crown.

A question of a most extraordinary character now arose, which gave Sheridan an admirable opportunity of exhibiting to the whole empire the ability, the genius, and the eloquence which had already acquired for him a high reputation. The impeachment of Warren Hastings before the House of Lords afforded to his accusers an opportunity of appealing to the high sense of honour, to the feelings, to the judgment of the nation. It was neither to the political nor to the fashionable circles they had to address themselves, but to an enlightened people, who for the first time heard that the most distinguished rulers of nations could be brought, by legitimate authority, before the tribunal of public opinion, and could be subjected to bitter accusations and to the most inquisitorial treatment. They were astonished to behold a man, to whom power over nations had been delegated, arraigned as a culprit and denounced as a villain. That Warren Hastings had been guilty of the most daring acts of tyranny and of oppression there can be little doubt; but that the peculiarity of his position, the extraordinary nature of the government he held, the ignorance of those principles which are now the guides of our conduct, are in a great measure to plead as a justification, is almost as generally acknowledged. Like Pizarro in Peru, Cortes in Mexico, or his predecessor in India, Lord Clive, he was compelled to have recourse to measures as bold as they are dangerous, and which are incompatible with that state of civilisation best understood by European nations. Hurried onward by the anxious desire to retain power, he left the straightforward path that prudence keeps, and involved himself in mazes of deceit, which led to the grossest violations of national faith and honour. His delinquencies, however, would have most probably passed unknown, had they not been dragged into daylight by men who themselves were endowed with singular powers, and had the mightiest energies of mind to direct them. The grandeur of the question and the necessity for its solution seem to have acted on those who were engaged upon it, and urged them on with irresistible ardour in their attack. Posterity has derived a noble lesson from their labours. The delegated governors over a feeble people have learnt that they dare not trample upon the laws and the privileges which have existed; they have seen that the pride of an oppressor has been

humbled by individuals, and that, even where crimi-
nality cannot be proved, the suspicion of its existence
is sufficient to excite attention and to call for inquiry.

The good sense of the present age has taught us,
however, that it is altogether unfair to judge of a man,
filling a high position in former days, by the standard
which we now pronounce to be the guide of conduct.
The Governor-General of India was, at the period at
which Warren Hastings was called to the station, the
chief of a handful of conquerors over millions whom
he was led to consider of an inferior race. He fancied
that he should acquit himself of the charge committed to his care if he extended widely the dominion
of a company of merchants in England ; and that, if
he remitted wealth to them, he was at liberty to have
recourse to such means as the people over whom he
ruled had been accustomed to. He therefore employed
artifice to encounter artifice ; resolute boldness and
an arm of strength to dismay and overrule those who
had submitted to the first who dared to conquer.
He looked upon himself as a stranger suddenly introduced into the midst of nations timid and anxious to
be relieved from the last batch of tyrants who were
placed over them. The monarchs who nominally
ruled were shadows, under whose pretended sway
ministers, more powerful than themselves, exacted
all that they chose to demand, and whose despotism
none dared to resist. Warren Hastings was called upon
to divide and to conquer his enemies, to look upon the
whole system of government as a machine to be guided
by the will of the person who chose, either by daring or
by intrigue, to seize the helm ; and all those who held
power as tools which were to be used as best might
suit the views of the chief of the moment. It never

crossed the mind of Warren Hastings that England was anxious to bestow the blessings of a paternal government upon the nations of Asia, or that the time would ever arrive that she would seek to be beloved instead of feared; that she should ever dream of making the natives venerate, admire, and love her laws and her institutions. He sought to avail himself of the system he found in existence, not because it was contrary to the wishes of the mother country and opposed to the best interests of the people, but because it allowed no one but himself to exact and to enrich themselves. The only opposition he had to encounter was from the members of the Council: the stand they took was unfortunately upon personal, not upon moral, grounds. There was too much of bitterness in their animosity to act upon a mind constituted as his was, and too much of cabal to produce an influence upon the British residents in India.

The observations made by that great advocate, Erskine, are perhaps the best palliation for the line of conduct pursued by Hastings—they are founded upon the great truth that he who gives authority is responsible for its due exercise. Whilst the charges against Warren Hastings were published by the House of Commons, Mr. Logie, a clergyman of the Church of Scotland, wrote a pamphlet, in which they were investigated with considerable warmth and energy. On the 15th of February Mr. Fox moved in the House "that a pamphlet, entitled 'A Review of the Principal Charges against Warren Hastings,' contains matter disrespectful to his Majesty, and scandalous and indecent paragraphs reflecting on the motives which induced this House to impeach Warren Hastings, Esq., of high crimes and misdemeanours." The princi-

The Life of Sheridan

pal passage from which this charge sprang is : "Such
an exertion of public virtue (the impeachment of Mr.
Hastings)—if to public virtue it shall be referred—is,
indeed, above all Greek, all Roman fame, and will
furnish a memorable example to future times, that
no abilities, however splendid, no services, however
beneficial or meritorious, that not even the smile of
the sovereign, nor the voice of the people, can protect
a British subject from impeachment, and a public
delinquent from punishment, if found guilty. For
the future, when any officer shall return home from
a situation of responsibility, his only hope must be in
joining a powerful faction ; for his services, let them
be ever so high, or his loyalty, be it ever so exemplary,
would be insufficient for his security." Mr. Pitt
moved as an amendment that the words " his Majesty "
be omitted. Mr. Sheridan observed that the passage
insinuated that an impeachment was a mode of
prosecution which leaves the sovereign no power of
extending mercy after conviction, and in reply to an
observation of the chancellor of exchequer, who spoke
of Mr. Hastings' position as a person impeached as not
a very exalted one, remarked, that till he was convicted
the station of Mr. Hastings was not, in the eye of the
law, reason, or common sense, to be considered one
of degradation. Mr. Fox at length moved that " an
address be presented to his Majesty, most humbly to
desire that he will be graciously pleased to give directions to his Majesty's Attorney-General to prosecute."
The motion was unanimously agreed to. On the 9th
December 1789, Mr. John Stockdale, the printer, was
tried on a criminal information, filed by the Attorney-
General. It was the lot of Erskine, the noble defender
of the helpless, to plead for him. The speech is a

perfect model of eloquence, and exhibits that style of devotion to the cause of him whom he supported which gave such peculiar interest to all he said. He did not plead for another in the cold, dispassionate manner of the hireling; he rushed into the very midst of the peril which surrounded his client; he felt with him, he thought with him, he proclaimed that he acted as he himself would have done, and, with that generous zeal which belonged to his character, he would have shared in his punishment if despotism and tyranny would have dared to inflict it. Not content with clearly showing the innocence of Stockdale, he threw his shield over Hastings, and with impetuous ardour and elegant words he spoke of the charges against him. He boldly expatiated on the striking absurdity exhibited by a power, itself the author of all the rapine and the oppression, in presuming to sit in judgment upon those to whom it had delegated its authority, and by whom its own tyranny had been exercised. He dwelt upon the ridiculous conduct of the nation that proceeded onwards in the most iniquitous career of plunder and rapacity, and then suddenly saying to the subordinate instruments of its usurpation, "Thus far shalt thou go, and no farther." The nation was responsible for the violation of human happiness in the exercise of her Eastern dominion. With that happy power of seizing every incident that occurred, observing some slight appearance of approbation of what he had said in one or two of the jurymen, he concluded the topic thus : "Gentlemen, you are touched by the way of considering the subject, and I can account for it. I have been talking of man and his nature, not as they are seen through the cold medium of books, but as I have seen them in climes reluctantly submitting to our authority. I have seen an indignant savage chief surrounded by his subjects, and holding in his hand a bundle of sticks, the notes of his untutored eloquence. 'Who is it,' said the jealous ruler of the forest encroached upon by the restless foot of the English adventurer—'who is it that causes the mountains to lift up their lofty heads ? Who raises the winds of the winter and calms them again in the summer ? The same Being who gave to you a country on your side of the water, and ours to us on this.' " Of this, the most perfect speech ever pronounced by Erskine, the result was the triumph of Stockdale, of Warren Hastings, and of liberty over that party which ought to have disdained to prosecute for libel an individual who was nobly fighting intellectually against power, dominion, and a mighty array of talent.

Warren Hastings, as Governor of India, found from his masters at home that money was the chief object which they required from their delegate. He, too anxious to fulfil their commands, was regardless of the means he employed ; and, though he himself was neither sordid nor rapacious, he lent all the faculties of his mind to the plunder and the rapine which rendered India a scene of desolation and of misery. The iniquities of his government were excusable in his eyes, for they were the result of stern necessity ; there could be no check to his despotism, no limit to his avarice, but the helplessness to which he had reduced nations and the poverty to which he exposed them. Edmund Burke was the great leader who undertook to hold up to public detestation and to condign punishment the individual whom he believed to be guilty of the greatest enormities, and to have trampled with unscrupulous cruelty upon the helpless beings with whom he was thrown into contact. He was supported by Sheridan, by Wyndham, and men whose names belong to the history of their country ; but by no one more enthusiastically or more powerfully than by Sheridan.

It is deeply to be deplored that we possess such mutilated remains of his speech, which created throughout the whole of the country such an extraordinary sensation, that was listened to by the House with the most profound admiration, that elicited even from his adversaries expressions of their wonder at the mighty powers he displayed. Of the speech of February 7, 1787, before the House of Commons, a feeble outline only has been handed down to us. All the records of that day speak of it as one of the most magnificent displays of human intellect that had ever been exhibited. For five hours and a half he commanded the universal attention of a crowded House. When he had concluded a speech which had riveted his audience, a loud and long-continued burst of enthusiastic applause seemed to echo simultaneously from all quarters ; the usual decorum was forgotten, all seemed carried away by the impulse they had received. Burke declared it to be " the most astonishing burst of eloquence, argument, and wit united of which there was any record or tradition." Fox pronounced a eulogium, and declared "all that he ever heard, all that he had ever read, when compared with it dwindled into nothing, and vanished like vapour before the sun." The debate was suspended, and after a short expression of the opinion of several members, who declared that, though they came prepossessed in favour of Hastings, a miracle had been wrought upon their minds, whilst others wished time to cool before they were called to vote, the House adjourned, with the concurrence of Sheridan's great adversary, Pitt, who acknowledged that the speech surpassed all the eloquence of ancient or modern times, and possessed everything that genius or art could furnish to agitate and control the human mind.

Mr. Burke spoke of his address thus : " Of all the various speeches of oratory, of every kind of eloquence that had been heard either in ancient or modern times, whatever the acuteness of the bar, the dignity of the senate, or the morality of the pulpit could furnish, had not been equal to what that House had that day heard in Westminster Hall. No holy religionist, no man of any description as a literary character, could have come up in the one instance to the pure senti-ments of morality, or, in the other, to the variety of knowledge, force of imagination, propriety and viva-city of allusion, beauty and elegance of diction, and strength of expression to which they had that day listened. From poetry up to eloquence, there was not a species of composition of which a complete and perfect specimen might not have been culled from one part or other of the speech to which he alluded, and which he was persuaded had left too strong an im-pression on the minds of that House to be easily ob-literated." We learn from Moore, that there exists a copy of this speech, taken in shorthand by Mr. Gurney, which was sometime in the possession of the Duke of Norfolk, then in the hands of Sheridan, and afterwards in those of Moore himself. He has furnished us with some extracts, but it is a matter of regret that the public has not an opportunity of seeing it. We are now dependent upon that which has been published in the debates, from which, of course, we can form but a superficial idea of its merits. Sheridan commenced by showing that "in truth the prosecution was not begotten in prejudice or nursed in error. It was founded on the clearest conviction of the wrongs which the natives of Hindustan had suffered through the maladministration of those in whose hands the country had placed extensive powers, which ought to have been exercised for the benefit of the governed, but which had been used by the prisoner at the bar for the shameful purposes of oppression.

"To convince their lordships that the British government—which ought to have been a blessing to the powers in India connected with it—had been a scourge to the natives, and the cause of desolation to the most flourishing provinces in Hindustan, he had only to read a letter that had been received not long since from Lord Cornwallis, the present Governor-General of Bengal. In that letter the noble lord stated he had been received by the Nabob Vizier with every mark of friendship and respect; but the honours he received at the court of Lucknow had not prevented him from seeing the desolation that overspread the face of the country, the sight of which had shocked his very soul. He spoke to the nabob on the subject, and earnestly recommended it to him to adopt some system of government that might restore the prosperity of his kingdom, and make his people happy. The nabob's answer was strikingly remarkable. That degraded prince said to his lordship, that as long as the demands of the English Government upon the revenue of Oude should remain unlimited, he (the nabob) could have no interest in establishing any system of economy;

and, whilst the English should continue to interfere in
the internal government of his country, it would be
in vain for him to attempt any salutary reform ; for
his subjects knew he was only a cipher in his own
dominions, and therefore laughed at and despised his
authority and that of his ministers."

He then observes, that it ought to be shown that the
ruling powers at home will not countenance future
delinquents. "In looking round for an object fit to
be held out to the world as an example of national
justice, their lordships must necessarily fix their eyes
upon Mr. Hastings. He was the great cause of the
degradation of our character in India, and of the
oppression of its devoted inhabitants ; and he was
the only victim that could atone for the calamities
he had occasioned.

"But whilst he pointed out the prisoner at the bar
as a proper object of punishment, he begged leave to
observe that he did not wish to turn the sword of
justice against that man merely because an example
ought to be made ; such a wish was as far from his
heart as it was incompatible with equity and justice.
If he called for punishment upon Mr. Hastings, it was
because he thought him a great delinquent, and the
greatest of all those who, by their rapacity and oppression, had brought ruin on the natives of India and
disgrace upon the inhabitants of Great Britain.

"Whilst he called for justice upon the prisoner, he
could wish also to do him justice. He would be
sorry that the weight and consequence of the Commons of Great Britain, in whose name the prosecution
had been set on foot, should operate to his prejudice.
Indeed, whilst he had such upright judges as their
lordships, it was impossible that anything could injure

him but the clearest and most unequivocal proofs of guilt. . . . It is not the peering suspicion of apprehending guilt; it is not any popular abhorrence of its widespread consequences; it is not the secret consciousness in the bosom of the judge which can excite the vengeance of the law and authorise its infliction. No! in this good land, as high as it is happy, because as just as it is free, all is definite, equitable, and exact; the laws must be satisfied before infliction ensues, and ere a hair of the head can be plucked, LEGAL GUILT must be established by LEGAL PROOF!"

He dwelt upon the enormity of the attack upon the princesses. "Having alluded to the different defences made by the prisoner, Mr. Sheridan next adverted to the allegations in the second charge that had been supported in evidence. He said that the managers had proved the high birth and great rank of the Begums, or Princesses of Oude; they had also proved, from the evidence of Sir Elijah Impey, Mr. Middleton, Mr. Goring, and others, how sacred was the residence of women in India. A threat, therefore, to force that residence and violate its purity by sending armed men into it was a species of torture the cruelty of which could not be conceived by those who were unacquainted with the customs and notions of the inhabitants of Hindustan. A knowledge of the customs and manners of the Mussulmans of Turkey would not enable one to judge of those of Mussulmans in India. In the former, ladies went abroad veiled, and, though not so free as those in Christian countries, still they were not so closely shut up as were the ladies professing the same religion in Hindustan. The confinement of the Turkish ladies was in a great measure to be ascribed to the jealousy of their husbands; in Hindu-

stan the ladies were confined because they thought it
contrary to decorum that persons of their sex should
be seen abroad. They were not the victims of jealousy
in the men ; on the contrary, their sequestration from
the world was voluntary ; they liked retirement because
they thought it best suited to the dignity of their sex
and situation. They were shut up from liberty, it was
true, but liberty, so far from having any charms for
them, was derogatory to their feelings. They were
enshrined rather than immured. They professed a
greater purity of pious prejudice than the Mohammedan
ladies of Europe and other countries, and more zeal-
ously and religiously practised a more holy system of
superstition. Such was their sense of delicacy that
to them the sight of man was pollution, and the piety
of the nation rendered their residence a sanctuary.
What, then, would their lordships think of the tyranny
of the man who could act in open defiance of those
prejudices, which were so interwoven with the very
existence of ladies in that country that they could not
be removed but by death ? What, he asked, would
their lordships think of the man who could threaten
to profane and violate the sanctuary of the highest
description of ladies in Oude, by saying that he would
storm it with his troops, and remove the inhabitants
from it by force ?

"Mr. Sheridan showed next that there was a very
good ground for presuming that the treasures possessed
by the Begum were the property of that princess. She
had endeared herself to her husband, the late nabob,
by flying to him in the moment of his distress, after
his defeat at Buxar, and carrying with her to his relief
the jewels with which, in happier days, his fondness
for her had enriched her. Upon these she raised him

The Life of Sheridan

a large supply. When the political generosity of this country restored him afterwards to his throne, his gratitude to his wife knew no bounds; her ascendency over him was such that she prevailed upon him to appoint his son by her his successor.

"The present nabob, as had appeared from a passage in a letter written by Mr. Hastings to him, and since proved in evidence, owed to her, not only his birth and succession to the crown, but also the preservation of his life; for one day his savage father, in a rage, attempting to cut him down with his scimitar, the Begum rushed between her husband and her son, and saved the latter through the loss of some of her own blood, for she was wounded by the blow that was not aimed at her. A son so befriended and so preserved Mr. Hastings had armed against such a mother. He invaded the rights of that prince, that he might compel him to violate the laws of nature by plundering his parent; and he made him a slave, that he might afterwards make him a monster. Mr. Hastings was bound to be the protector of the Begum instead of her plunderer; for her husband on his deathbed bequeathed her to his friendship, and Mr. Hastings had always called that husband his brother; but no consideration could make him discharge the duties of any obligation that could set bounds to his rapacity."

He next adverts to the conduct of Sir Elijah Impey. "The transactions in which Sir Elijah Impey bore a share, and the tenor of his evidence, were the next objects of Mr. Sheridan's animadversion. The late Chief-Justice of Bengal, he remarked, had repeatedly stated that Mr. Hastings had left Calcutta with two resources in his view—those of Benares and of Oude. It appeared, however, from every circumstance, that the latter resource was never in his contemplation, until the insurrection in Benares, terminating in the capture of Bedjegur, had destroyed all his hopes in that province. At that instant the mind of Mr. Hastings, fertile in resources, fixed itself on the trea-sures of the Begums, and Sir Elijah Impey was despatched to collect materials for their crimination. 'But I have ever thought,' said Mr. Sheridan, 'the selection of such a personage, for such a purpose, one of the greatest aggravations of the guilt of Mr. Hastings.' That he, the purity of whose character should have influenced his conduct even in his most domestic retirements ; that he, who, if consulting the dignity of British justice, should have remained as stationary as his court in Calcutta—that such a man should be called to travel 500 miles for the transaction of such a business, was a deviation without a plea and a degradation without example. This, however, was in some degree a question to be abstracted for the consideration of those who adorned and illumined the seats of justice in Britain, and the purity of whose character precluded the necessity of any further obser-vations on so different a conduct.

" 'This giddy Chief-Justice,' said Mr. Sheridan, 'dis-regards business. He wants to see the country : like some innocent schoolboy, he takes the primrose path and amuses himself as he goes ; he thinks not that his errand is on danger and death, and that his party of pleasure ends in loading others with irons. When at Lucknow he never mentions the affidavits to the nabob —no, he is too polite ; he never talks of them to Mr. Hastings—out of politeness, too. A master of cere-monies in justice ! When examined at the bar, he said—he imagines there must have been a sworn interpreter, from the looks of the manager. How I looked, Heaven knows,' said Mr. Sheridan, 'but such a physiognomist there is no escaping. He sees a sworn interpreter in my looks; he sees the manner of taking an oath in my looks; he sees the Bason and the Ganges in my looks! As for himself, he only looks at the tops and bottoms of affidavits! In seven years he takes care never to look at these swearings, and then goes home one night and undoes the whole; though, when he has seen them, Sir Elijah seems to know less about them than when he had not.'"

The termination of this speech has been most admired. "But justice is not this halt and miserable object! it is not the ineffective bauble of an Indian pagod! it is not the portentous phantom of despair! it is not, like any fabled monster, formed in the eclipse of reason, and found in some unhallowed grove of superstitious darkness and political dismay! No, my lords!

"In the happy reverse of all these, I turn from this disgusting caricature to the real image! Justice I have now before me, august and pure, the abstract idea of all that would be perfect in the spirits and the aspirings of men!—where the mind rises, where the heart expands, where the countenance is ever placid and benign; where her favourite attitude is to stoop to the unfortunate, to hear their cry and to help them, to rescue and relieve, to succour and save; majestic from its mercy, venerable from its utility, uplifted without pride, firm without obduracy, beneficent in each preference, lovely though in her frown!

"On that justice I rely; deliberate and sure, abstracted from all party purpose and political speculations—not in words, but on facts! You, my lords, who hear me, I conjure by those rights it is your best privilege to preserve; by that fame it is your best pleasure to inherit; by all those feelings which refer to the first term in the series of existence, the original compact of our nature—our controlling rank in the creation. This is the call on all to administer to truth and equity, as they would satisfy the laws and satisfy themselves, with the most exalted bliss possible or conceivable for our nature—the self-approving consciousness of virtue, when the condemnation we look for will be one of the most ample mercies accomplished for mankind since the creation of the world.

" My lords, I have done."

On the following day the House of Commons resolved that a committee should be appointed to prepare articles of impeachment against Warren Hastings.

Edmund Burke.	Welbore Ellis, Esq.
Right Hon. C. J. Fox.	Right Hon. F. Montague.
R. B. Sheridan, Esq.	Sir Grey Cooper.
Sir James Erskine.	Philip Francis, Esq.
Right Hon. T. Pelham.	Sir Gilbert Elliott.
Right Hon. W. Wyndham.	Dudley Long, Esq.
Right Hon. And. St. John.	Viscount Maitland.
J. Anstruther, Esq.	Hon. G. A. North.
Wm. Adam, Esq.	General Burgoyne.
M. A. Taylor, Esq.	Charles Grey, Esq.

A division took place upon the nomination of Mr. Francis, who had been a member of Council in India, had fought a duel with Hastings, and had been personally at variance with Hastings. He was rejected by a majority of 96 to 44. On the 25th of April there were laid upon the table the articles of impeachment which had been prepared by the committee; they

The Life of Sheridan

were read a first time, and ordered to be taken into consideration on the 9th of May. On that day a division took place on the question whether the report should be received. Mr. Pitt, the prime minister, and his friends, either convinced of the necessity of yielding to the reiterated demands of the opposition, or unwilling to expose himself to the unpopularity of shielding Hastings, or, as it has been stated, jealous of the favour bestowed upon him by the king, joined the ranks of those to whom they were habitually opposed, and, by a majority of 175 to 89, the report was read a second time. Mr. Burke then rose and moved : " That Warren Hastings, Esq., be impeached of high crimes and misdemeanours upon the said articles." Mr. Frederic Montague next rose, and moved : " That Mr. Burke, in the name of the House of Commons and of all the Commons of England, do go to the bar of the House of Lords and impeach Warren Hastings, Esq., late Governor-General of Bengal, of high crimes and misdemeanours, and do acquaint the Lords that the Commons will, with all convenient speed, exhibit articles against him, and make good the same." The motion being agreed to, Mr. Burke, attended by the members of the House of Commons, appeared before the Lords at their bar, and solemnly impeached Mr. Hastings. A day was named, and, on Mr. Burke's report to the House of Commons, he moved that the committee already named be appointed managers of the trial, and that the House of Commons attend as a committee of the whole House. Assent to these motions was given, and each party prepared for the trial.

On the 13th of February commenced, in Westminster Hall, this remarkable trial. Macaulay has,

The Life of Sheridan

with singular felicity, given us a graphic sketch of the scene. He has associated with it the best historical recollections, and mingled them with the leading characters of the day. The author of "Evelina," who was present on the occasion, has described to us her own sensations, and furnished us even with the chit-chat of "the ingenious, the chivalrous, the high-souled" Wyndham, as well as of Burke, and of many principal actors in the scene. She has, in less poetic language, placed before our eyes all that struck her fancy. We find her shuddering and drawing involuntarily back, when Burke, the head of the committee, made his solemn entry, holding a scroll in his hands, walking alone, his brow knit with cor-roding care and deep-labouring thought; trembling when Hastings was brought to the bar, and summoned by a loud voice, "Warren Hastings, come forth; answer to the charges brought against you, save your bail, or forfeit your recognisances." There stood the late Governor-General of Bengal. He moved on slowly, he made a low bow to the chancellor and to the court, he bowed again, and then, advancing to the bar, he leant his hands upon it and dropped upon his knees; but a voice in the same moment proclaiming he had leave to rise, he stood up almost instan-taneously, and a third time profoundly bowed to the court. What an awful moment this for such a man— a man fallen from such height of power to a situation so humiliating; from the most unlimited command of so large a portion of the Eastern world, to be cast at the feet of his enemies, of the great tribunal of his country, and of the nation at large, assembled thus in a body to try and to judge him.

In the striking words of Macaulay, we may say "that

The Life of Sheridan

neither the culprit nor his advocates attracted so much attention as his accusers. In the midst of the blaze of red drapery a space had been fitted up with green benches and tables for the Commons. The managers, with Burke at their head, appeared in full dress. The collectors of gossip did not fail to remark that even Fox, generally so regardless of his appearance, had paid to the illustrious tribunal the compliment of wearing a bag and sword. The box in which the managers stood contained an array of speakers such as perhaps had not appeared together since the great age of Athenian eloquence. There were Fox and Sheridan, the English Demosthenes and the English Hyperides. There was Burke, ignorant indeed or negligent of the art of adapting his reasonings and his style to the capacity and taste of his hearers, but in amplitude of comprehension and richness of imagination superior to every orator ancient or modern."
He proceeds, in a splendid passage, which it would be criminal to mutilate by extracts, to delineate two of the master minds of their age, Wyndham and Earl Grey. The first day was passed in reading the charges against Hastings ; this was done in so monotonous a tone that little interest was taken in the proceedings. From Madame D'Arblay we may draw our conclusion that, amongst the auditory assembled, there were many who looked upon the accused with eyes of pity and of respect, and that at the commencement of the trial he was rather the object of commiseration than of dislike. It was on the third day that Burke opened the charges ; and during the four following days he occupied the attention of the House of Lords with what may be considered to be a general outline of the charges brought against Hastings. He delivered an eloquent

The Life of Sheridan

address, such as might be expected from one who had for months studied his subject with the utmost care; who had brooded over the wrongs which nations had endured; who deeply felt, and had ample means of giving expression to his feelings. He was listened to with the profoundest attention; and as he painted the manners, the habits, and the government of the nations of Asia, and portrayed the wrongs inflicted by Hastings, torrents of fervid eloquence were poured forth which touched the hearts of his enraptured auditory. "When he narrated, he was easy, flowing, natural; when he declaimed, energetic, warm, and brilliant. The sentiments he interspersed were as nobly conceived as they were highly coloured; the wild and sudden flights of his fancy burst forth from his creative imagination, fluent, forcible, and vivid."

Fox was the next of the accusers; his speech occupied a space of five hours. The impression produced by both these speeches upon Madame D'Arblay is worthy to be remembered, particularly as it is well known that her report was listened to with the deepest interest by the queen, and that, from that high quarter, it reached his Majesty, who, during the whole of the early portion of the trial, exhibited the greatest anxiety. She states "that Burke's opening struck me with the highest admiration of his powers, from the eloquence, the fire, the diversity of expression, and the ready flow of language with which he seemed gifted. When he came to his two narratives, when he related the particulars of those dreadful murders, he interested, he engaged, he at last overpowered me. I felt my cause lost. I could hardly keep my seat. My eyes dreaded a single glance towards so accused a man as Mr. Hastings; I wanted to sink on the floor, that they might be saved from so fearful a sight. I had no hope he could clear himself, not another wish in his favour remained ; but when, from this narration, Mr. Burke proceeded to his own comments and declamation, when the charges of rapacity, cruelty, and tyranny were general, and made with all the violence of personal detesta-tion, and continued and aggravated without any fur-ther fact or illustration, then there appeared more of study than of truth, more of invective than of justice, and, in short, so little of proof to so much of passion, that, in a very short time, I began to lift my head ; my seat was no longer uneasy, my eyes were indif-ferent which way they looked, or what object caught them, and before I was aware of the declension of Mr. Burke's power over my feelings, I found myself a mere spectator in a public place, and looking all around me, with my opera-glass in my hand."

She says, " Mr. Fox spoke with a violence which had a sort of monotony, that seemed to result from its being factitious ; he looked all good humour and negligent care the instant before he began a speech of uninterrupted passion and vehemence ; and he wore the same careless and disengaged air the very instant he had finished. A display of talents, in which the inward man took so little share, could have no powers of persuasion to those who saw them in that light ; and therefore, however brilliant they might be, they were useless to their cause, for they left the mind of the hearers in the same state that they found it."

The eagerness displayed by the public to hear Burke and Fox was even surpassed on the 3rd of June, when it was known that upon that day the task of continuing the accusation devolved upon Sheridan. His speech in the House of Commons still vibrated on

the ears of his audience ; and the press had been busy
in drawing comparisons between what had been heard
in the House of Commons and before the Lords.
Westminster Hall presented a most extraordinary
sight ; on no one day had there been such an array of
talent, of beauty, or of rank.   As early as eight o'clock
the avenues leading to the Hall were thronged ; the
passages through Old and New Palace Yard are described as having been crowded with persons of the
first distinction, many of them peeresses in full dress,
who stood in the open air upwards of an hour before
the gates were opened.   The exertions made in
pressing forward to get convenient seats had nearly
proved fatal to many.   It seemed as if the eyes of the
whole kingdom were on that day fixed on Sheridan.
The eager quidnuncs in the country, who were not so
speedily gratified with the intelligence of the day as
they now are, had made every exertion to obtain the
earliest report of the speech ; every printing press was
called into use, and every means used to forward it to
the country.   The usual forms of opening the business
of the day, even the procession of the Lords, previously so attractive, seemed tedious, and the impatient auditory could scarcely wait the hour of twelve,
when the peers took their places.   Large sums were
offered and declined for tickets or for privilege ; even
fifty guineas, it has been said, was refused.   When
Sheridan entered the manager's box every eye was
turned towards him.   When the Lord Chancellor
signified that the assembly was prepared to hear him,
he rose, and commenced a speech which was continued on four several occasions.   On one of these he
was so completely exhausted as to be compelled to
retire, and the House adjourned the court.   On his

recovery, three days afterwards, he again warmed into his subject, and completed his masterly address. With his great display of eloquence, it may be said that the interest of the drama ceased. The trial, it was true, proceeded, but it dragged slowly on ; all the enthusiasm which had been excited seemed, after Sheridan had delivered his address, to have died away. It was scarcely to be expected that a second speech would strike the minds of the public with the same success as the first. The freshness of the materials was over ; the feelings were not to be roused by a second edition, as they had been by the first impression. Fox, it has been said, strenuously recommended that the speech should only be the echo of the one that had excited such boundless admiration. This opinion was not in unison with that of Sheridan, who felt that he could draw upon his own genius for new resources. He boldly dared and succeeded. He was listened to with delight, and again won the applause of his country.

Sheridan appears to have made himself intimately acquainted with every fact that had occurred in India, and with every individual who had been in communication with Hastings. He had deeply studied the characters of all the parties implicated, had sought out the motives of their actions and commented upon them with masterly discrimination. He clearly saw that Warren Hastings, with a view of supplying the wants of the Indian treasury, had cast a longing eye upon the sacred city of Benares, and had marked it out as a legitimate object of plunder. Here he expected to draw resources for his army, and remittances for his employers at home. Cheyte Sing, the ruling prince, had annually paid a rich tribute ; but it was imagined that he had accumulated from his large revenues considerable treasures. Demand upon demand was made upon him. In order to soothe Hastings, a bribe of twenty thousand pounds was offered and received. The transaction was for a time concealed, but after some delay the money was paid over to the company; and then not only were the previous contributions required, but fines were demanded for the delay, and a requisition was made that the unfortunate ruler should keep a body of cavalry for the service of the company. After every species of humiliating treatment, Hastings went himself to Benares, and demanded half a million, "determined to make Cheyte Sing pay largely for his pardon, or to exact a severe vengeance for past delinquency." The prince, notwithstanding every attempt to conciliate the Governor, was made prisoner in his own capital; his subjects rushed to arms, released him, and so hemmed in Hastings that he was in the utmost peril. At one moment the people of the whole province were in commotion; an army was raised which almost threatened the annihilation of the English, but discipline and valour soon put it to the rout. Cheyte Sing fled; the dominions passed away from him. Hastings annexed them to the British possessions; but he was grievously disappointed, not only that the amount of the treasure was far inferior to the calculations that had been made, but that the army claimed it as conquerors. To Oude he next looked; but he was well aware that the reigning vizier was too poor to assist him; that from him he could not look for that money which became every moment of greater importance to him. The two chieftains, however, met, each having his own

The Life of Sheridan

views — Hastings desirous of some pretext to lay an impost, Asaph ul Dowlah ruminating how he was to avoid payment of what he already owed. In whose mind the tempter first created the suggestion of their uniting to pillage a third party we cannot surmise, but upon that point they both agreed, and the two sagacious statesmen, without appearing to have much repugnance, determined that they should confiscate the wealth of the mother and the grandmother of one of the parties. These two princesses, known under the title of the Begums of Oude, had succeeded to the revenues of the last nabob, and possessed his treasures, which were estimated at three millions. The son had at different periods made attacks upon his mother's property, and had extorted money from her. She had turned with the utmost anxiety to the English Government to protect her, and a treaty under its auspices had been drawn up, in which, under the condition of certain subsidies being paid to her son, he undertook never again to molest her.

Disgraceful as is the fact, the Government that had stood forward as a mediatory power and as a guarantee that no further extortions should occur, became a partner in an atrocious robbery ; and in the most discreditable manner plundered and abused the helpless princesses. Under the pretext that these aged ladies had instigated the rebellion at Benares, it was resolved that their entire possessions should be taken from them, and that this wholesale spoliation should be regarded as a set-off against the debt due from the vizier of Oude to Hastings. The palace in which these ladies resided was stormed. The company's troops took possession, and, shameful to relate, the princesses were almost starved into giving up twelve hundred thousand pounds; whilst two unfortunate beings, who acted as their prime ministers, were thrown into prison, and actually put to the torture. Of the influence of Hastings over the authorities in India there can be no stronger proof than that the chief judge, Sir Elijah Impey, anxious to partake the infamy of the deed, left his judicial seat at Calcutta to obtain anything in the shape of evidence by which to criminate the Begums, rushed to Lucknow, administered oaths to any one ready to swear, and tarnish the purity of his ermine. Here, then, was ample material for the impassioned eloquence of Sheridan. How much is it to be deplored that we have but a meagre outline of that splendid harangue which astonished his contemporaries. A few extracts will show the style in which he treated the subject.

Of the character of Hastings he spoke in the following words : " After having stated his complicated infamy in terms of the severest reprehension, Mr. Sheridan proceeded to observe that he recollected to have heard it advanced by some of those admirers of Mr. Hastings who were not so explicit as to give unqualified applause to his crimes, that they found an apology for the atrocity of them in the greatness of his mind. To estimate the solidity of such a defence, it would be sufficient merely to consider in what consisted this prepossessing distinction, this captivating characteristic of greatness of mind. Is it not solely to be traced in great actions directed to great ends ? In them, and them alone, we are to search for true estimable magnanimity. To them only can we justly affix the splendid title and honours of real greatness. There was indeed another species of greatness, which displayed itself in boldly con-

The Life of Sheridan

ceiving a bad measure, and undauntedly pursuing
it to its accomplishment. But had Mr. Hastings
the merit of exhibiting either of these descriptions
of greatness—even of the latter? He saw nothing
great, nothing magnanimous, nothing open, nothing
direct in his measures or in his mind; on the contrary, he had too often pursued the worst objects
by the worst means. His course was an eternal
deviation from rectitude. He either tyrannised or
deceived, and was by turns a Dionysius and a Scapin.
As well might the writhing obliquity of the serpent
be compared to the swift directness of the arrow, as
the duplicity of Mr. Hastings' ambition to the simple
steadiness of genuine magnanimity. In his mind all
was shuffling, ambiguous, dark, insidious, and little;
nothing simple, nothing unmixed, all affected plain-
ness and actual dissimulation, a heterogeneous mass
of contradictory qualities, with nothing great but his
crimes, and even those contrasted by the littleness
of his motives, which at once denoted both his baseness and his meanness, and marked him for a traitor
and a trickster. Nay, in his style and writing there
was the same mixture of vicious contrarieties—the
most grovelling ideas were conveyed in the most
inflated language, giving mock consequence to low
cavils, and uttering quibbles in heroics, so that his
compositions disgusted the mind's taste, as much as
his actions excited the soul's abhorrence. Indeed, this
mixture of character seemed by some unaccountable
but inherent quality to be appropriated, though in
inferior degrees, to everything that concerned his
employers. He remembered to have heard an honourable and learned gentleman (Mr. Dundas) remark that
there was something in the first frame and constitution

of the company, which extended the sordid principles of their origin over all their successive operations; connecting with their civil policy, and even with their boldest achievements, the meanness of a pedlar and the profligacy of pirates. Alike in the political and the military line could be observed auctioneering ambassadors and trading generals; and thus we saw a revolution brought about by affidavits, an army employed in executing an arrest, a town besieged on a note of hand, a prince dethroned for the balance of an account. Thus it was they exhibited a government which united the mock majesty of a bloody sceptre and the little traffic of a merchant's counting-house, wielding a truncheon with one hand and picking a pocket with the other."

The speech on the 2nd of April, on the acceptance of various bribes by Hastings, went to prove that corruption had been the leading principle of all his actions in India, and attempted to overthrow the prevailing opinion that, as he did not amass treasures for his own use, he was not corrupt for interested purposes—that he was not mercenary.

"Mr. Sheridan declared he had been among those who, at one time, conceived that Mr. Hastings was not stimulated in his conduct, as Governor-General, by any view to his own emolument, and that his fortune was trifling compared with the advantages which fell within his power. But the more close and minute investigation which it was his duty to apply to the facts contained in the charge had completely altered his opinion, and he scarcely harboured even the slightest doubt of being able to satisfy the committee that Mr. Hastings had all along governed his conduct by corruption as gross and determined as his oppression and injustice had proved severe and galling. In reviewing his conduct, he had found it to spring from a wild, eccentric, and irregular mind. He had been everything by fits and starts. Now proud and lofty, now mean and insidious, now generous, now just, now artful, now open, now deceitful, now decided — in pride, in passion, in everything changeable, except in corruption. In corruption he had proved uniform, systematic, and methodical; his revenge a tempest, a tornado, blackening, in gusts of pride, the horizon of his dominion, and carrying all before it."

It was on the fourth day that, in the presence of the great historian, Gibbon, he exclaimed, "I do say that if you search the history of the world you will not find an act of tyranny and fraud to surpass this! If you read all past histories, peruse the annals of Tacitus, read the luminous page of Gibbon, and all the ancient or modern writers that have searched into the depravity of former ages, to draw a lesson for the present, you will not find an act of treacherous, deliberate, cool cruelty that could exceed this!" Gibbon, delighted with this compliment, spoke of it in his memoirs. He says: " Before my departure from England I was present at the august spectacle of Mr. Hastings' trial in Westminster Hall. It is not my province to absolve or condemn the Governor of India, but Mr. Sheridan's eloquence demanded my applause; nor could I hear without emotion the personal compliment that he paid me in the presence of the British nation." Little did the innocent man dream that the ever-ready wit of Sheridan had neutralised this elegant encomium; for some one asking him how he could bestow the epithet luminous on

Gibbon's work, in a half-whisper, he said, "I called it voluminous."

It is true that Miss Sheridan's partiality for her brother may have given a bias to her judgment, but she has expressed herself on the occasion of having heard the principal speakers on the trial. "And last, not least," says she, "I heard my brother. I cannot express to you the sensation of pleasure and of pride that filled my heart the moment that he rose. Had I never seen or heard his name before, I should have conceived him the first man among them at once. There is a dignity and grace in his countenance and deportment very striking, at the same time that one cannot trace the smallest degree of coxcomb superiority in his manner. His voice, too, appeared to me extremely fine." There are letters, too, extant from Mrs. Sheridan, in which she speaks of her husband's success with all the natural triumph of an attached woman; her exultation springs from the heart. Burke seems occasionally to have written to her when he was anxious to have an impression made upon the memory of Sheridan. In a letter, he says to her : "I know that his mind is seldom unemployed, but then, like all such great and vigorous minds, it takes an eagle's flight by itself, and we can hardly bring it to rustle along the ground with us birds of meaner wing in covey. I only beg that you will prevail on Mr. Sheridan to be with us this day, at half after three, in the committee. Mr. Wombell, the paymaster of Oude, is to be examined there to-day. Oude is Mr. Sheridan's particular province, and I do most seriously ask that he would favour us with his assistance. What will come of the examination I know not, but without him I do not expect a great deal from it ; with him I fancy we may get out something material." It appears that this beautiful and highly-gifted woman rendered every assistance to her husband in his pursuit of information. Amongst his papers there exist ample proofs that she wrote out, with diligence and assiduity, pages of importance to him. She copied pamphlets and collected from various sources memorandums bearing upon any subject that occupied his attention ; these she pasted together, or by some contrivance of her own made easy of reference.

His triumph has been thus acknowledged by Lord Byron :—

> " When the loud cry of trampled Hindostan
> Arose to Heaven in her appeal to Man,
> His was the thunder, his the avenging rod,
> The wrath—the delegated voice of God,
> Which shook the nations through his lips, and blazed,
> Till vanquished senates trembled as they praised."

An event of a nature calculated to excite the most lively interest in the nation now occurred, and demanded from each individual taking a lead in the direction of the public mind the utmost anxiety and reflection. Early in the month of July 1788 a visible alteration took place in the health of the king. The physicians in attendance recommended that his Majesty should go to Cheltenham to try the effects of the mineral waters there, as some tendency to excitement had been observed. It was resolved that the journey should be taken without the usual pomp and ceremony. The party, therefore, was the smallest possible, without guards or state ; still the loyalty of the people would not allow the monarch to pass without exhibiting affectionate homage. "Every town seemed all face, filled with people as closely fastened to one another as they appear in the pit of the play-

The Life of Sheridan

house." To this journey, which was undertaken as a change from the monotony of Windsor and as likely to divert the attention of the king, and to the life at Cheltenham, has been ascribed the direction which this malady now took. Early in the month of October the royal household saw, with unspeakable alarm, the gradual advance of a mental disorder.

Amongst the most interesting narratives of the day is that which the authoress of our classic novels, " Cecilia " and " Evelina," has furnished us with in her memoirs, published not long since under the name of her diary and letters. Miss Burney was in immediate attendance on the queen, and hence has been enabled to describe to us with the utmost fidelity the commencement, progress, and termination of the disease. We are let into the inmost recesses of the royal palace; we have graphically described the state of alarm and anxiety felt by all, and are taught to look with veneration and admiration at the tenderness and solicitude of the afflicted queen. Such a work is invaluable ; and if it be not quite equal in interest to that melancholy but interesting narration which Clery has given us of his attendance upon Louis XVI. when in the Temple, it is only because, from the different catastrophes, our feelings are not so deeply impressed with sympathy and terror. No one could more faithfully delineate the first approach of one species of frenzy than Miss Burney has done. She thus speaks : " I had a sort of conference with his Majesty, or rather I was the object to whom he spoke, with a manner so uncommon that a high fever could alone account for it : a rapidity, a hoarseness of voice, a volubility, an earnestness, a vehemence rather—it startled me inexpressibly—yet with a graciousness exceeding even all I met with before—it was almost kindness. The following day," she goes on with her diary, telling us, " I met him in the passage from the queen's room ; he stopped me, and conversed upon his health near half-an-hour, still with the extreme quickness of speech and manner that belongs to fever, and he hardly sleeps, he tells me, one minute all night ; indeed, if he recovers not his rest, a most delirious fever seems to threaten him. He is all agitation, all emotion, yet all benevolence and goodness, even to a degree that makes it touching to hear him speak. He assures everybody of his health, he seems only fearful to give uneasiness to others." November 1st, we find her describing him with a hoarse and altered countenance: " Nor can I ever forget him in what passed this night ; when I came to the queen's dressing-room he was still with her. He was begging her not to speak to him when he got to his room, that he might fall asleep, as he felt great want of that refreshment. He repeated his desire at least a hundred times, though far enough from needing it—the poor queen never uttered one syllable. He then applied to me, saying he was really very well, except in that one particular, that he could not sleep."

As we peruse these and similar passages in her diary, we are strongly reminded of the interview between Hamlet and Ophelia in the play-scene, and are struck with admiration of the knowledge which Shakespeare must have possessed of the workings of the mind under the first approaches of mental derangement. She proceeds to describe the deep distress of the queen, her solitary anguish, overpowered with terror lest she should betray her feelings, and express the inevitable danger towards which she saw the king was gradually verging. Harassed by his state, believing it unknown to any but herself and her household, she at length found that a whispering of the infirmity of the king had commenced; and then read in the *Morning Herald* some anecdote which she was desirous that the editor should retract, and answer, at his peril, any further such treasonable paragraph. On the 5th of November a terrible scene occurred, which rendered all further hesitation as to the nature of his malady impossible. The king in the afternoon went out in his chaise with the princess royal for an airing; he was all smiling benignity, but gave so many orders to the postillions, and got in and out of the carriage twice, with such agitation, as to excite Miss Burney's alarm. Retiring in her own room, she was struck in the evening with the uncommon stillness that reigned throughout the palace; nobody stirred, not a voice was heard, not a step, not a motion—there seemed a strangeness in the house most extraordinary. The equerries then passed to and fro with unusual gravity, whisperings only were exchanged—all was mysterious horror. At length the news was told her, that the king at dinner had broken forth into positive delirium, which had long been apprehended by all who saw him most closely; the queen was so overpowered as to fall into violent hysterics; all the princesses were in misery, and the Prince of Wales burst into tears.

The night that followed was a fearful one. Miss Burney was called upon to attend her Majesty. "My poor royal mistress! never can I forget her countenance—pale, ghastly pale, she was seated to be undressed, and attended by Lady Elizabeth Waldegrave and Miss Goldsworthy; her whole frame was disordered, yet she was still and quiet. These two ladies

assisted me to undress her, or rather I assisted them,
for they were firmer from being longer present; my
shaking hands and blinded eyes could scarce be of
any use. The king, at the instance of Sir George
Baker, had consented to sleep in the next apartment;
in the middle of the night the king insisted upon
seeing if the queen was not removed from the house,
and he had come into the room with a candle in his
hand, and satisfied himself she was there; he stayed
a full half-hour, and the depth of that terror during
that time no words can paint." The confirmation
of the worst fears that had been apprehended gave
now no pretence for keeping from the nation the sad
change that had occurred in a monarch who had
gradually become popular, and for whom the tenderest
solicitude was from that period displayed. The earlier
days of the king's reign had not been propitious, and
he had incurred displeasure from his obstinate ad-
herence to his own preconceived views; but now all
was forgotten, all was anxious affection, and, amid
hopes and fears, the nation turned to Parliament to
learn from its deliberations what would be the steps
which, in consonance with the spirit of the constitution, would be taken. Various were the surmises which
were afloat, as to the placing the power in the hands
of the heir apparent to the throne, and to whose
custody would be committed the person of the afflicted
monarch. Upon the first assembling of Parliament,
it was resolved that an adjournment should take place
for a fortnight, and on the 4th of November a report
of the Privy Council was laid on the table, and another
adjournment took place till the 8th of December.

The Prince of Wales had, from the previous circumstances of his career, become the centre around

which the opposition of the time revolved; its members looked forward to the day when he should be in possession of power as that on which their triumph would be secured, and they therefore displayed the greatest anxiety that he should be proclaimed unrestricted regent; and the doctrines they upheld were that he at once had a right to assume the royal authority. To these pretensions the administration of the day, headed by Mr. Pitt, was strenuously opposed, and the feelings of the great mass of the people were also decidedly hostile to them. It unfortunately happened that the taste and morals of the party desirous of seeing his Royal Highness at the head of affairs were most questionable. Mr. Fox, its leader, however highly gifted with intellectual power, and loved for his generous and affectionate temper, was too much addicted to those social pleasures which border on folly to be generally esteemed. Sheridan's prudence had begun to be more than doubted, and reports were widely disseminated of the recklessness of those who frequented Carlton House. Hence the slow and protracted steps which were taken by the House of Commons, the caution exercised, and the apparent wisdom of deep reflection (whilst, in fact, intrigue of every description was going forward in various sections of the parties), were quite in consonance with public opinion.

Mr. Fox was sent for from Italy; and when Mr. Pitt came forward to propose that a committee be appointed to examine the journals of the House, and report precedents of such authority as may have been had in cases of the personal exercise of the royal authority being prevented or interrupted by infancy, sickness, infirmity, or otherwise, with a view

The Life of Sheridan

to provide for the same, Mr. Fox at once took up the position "that whenever the sovereign, from sickness, infirmity, or other incapacity, was unable to exercise the functions of his high office, the heir apparent, being of full age and capacity, had as clear and express a right to assume the reins of government and exercise the power of sovereignty as in the case of his Majesty's demise." Mr. Pitt's reply kindled a fire throughout the country. In the collection made of the works and the correspondence of Dr. Parr, is to be found a letter upon the subject of the king's illness from Mrs. Sheridan, in which she says: "An unlucky word about right, made use of by Charles Fox in the House, has made some little confusion in the heads of a few old Parliamentaries, who did not understand him, and Pitt has taken advantage of this and means to move a question about it on Tuesday, which our friends wish to avoid by moving the previous question, thinking Pitt's motion mischievous and quite unnecessary." Mr. Pitt said "that the very announcement of a claim of right rendered an inquiry into precedent and history of the greater consequence, for if such an authority should be discovered, all further debate in that House would be unnecessary; but he boldly said that the assertion of such a right in the Prince of Wales or any one else was little short of treason against the constitution of the country. He pledged himself to prove that in the case of the interruption of the personal exercise of the royal authority, without the existence of any lawful provision being previously made for carrying on the government, it belonged to the other branches of the nation at large to provide, according to their discretion, for the temporary exercise of the regal functions in the name and behalf of the sovereign, as they should deem requisite, and that the Prince of Wales had no more right of himself, without their decision, to assume the government than any other individual in the country." This great constitutional doctrine was generally assented to ; neither the replies of Mr. Fox nor the invectives of Mr Burke could shake it.

Upon the assertions of the two heads of parties, it was impossible for Sheridan, who was looked upon in the House as the personal friend of his Royal Highness, to be silent ; yet his situation was one of the utmost delicacy. He had, in a letter which still exists, given the most judicious advice to that illustrious personage. He had stated "that it would greatly advance his Royal Highness's credit, and lay the strongest grounds to baffle every attempt at opposition to what he considered the just claims and rights of his Royal Highness, that the language of those who may be in any sort suspected of knowing his wishes and feelings should be of great moderation in disclaiming all party views, and avowing the utmost readiness to acquiesce in any reasonable delay."

When Mr. Pitt moved that the House will, on Tuesday next, resolve itself into a committee to take into consideration the state of the nation, Sheridan began a temperate and cautious speech. He said "that he felt it his duty to contend against the propriety and expediency of putting the abstract proposition of the right of the Prince of Wales. It could not conciliate, but, on the contrary, it might create dissension and animosities, and therefore he insisted it would be unwise, as it was obviously unnecessary, to agitate it, or to press the House to come to any vote on it." The next sentence called down a long and continued " Hear ! hear !" from both sides of the House ; by both parties it was hailed as indiscreet at first, but after reflection it was considered to be called for by the circumstances of the case. " He begged leave to remind the right *honourable gentleman* of the danger of provoking that claim to be asserted—(a loud cry of " Hear ! hear !")—which he observed had not yet been preferred." (Another cry of " Hear ! hear !") He then repeated the words, and asked, " Would the right honourable gentleman choose to have his own proposition put upon the journals, to have it recorded as his opinion, that the Prince of Wales had no more right to exercise the royal authority during the incapacity of the king than any other individual ? " If he would not, why would he press an abstract proposition that must throw the nation into anarchy and confusion ? Mr. Pitt replied to this, somewhat insidiously, by saying " that he trusted the House would do their duty in spite of any threat, however high the authority from which it might proceed." Mr. Sheridan then denied that his language could be construed into a threat ; he had only spoken of the danger which might arise if the prince should be provoked to assert a claim which he had not yet preferred, and the discussion of which he must continue to think as mischievous in its tendency as it was absolutely unnecessary. Resolutions were carried on the 22nd December, on the motion of Mr. Pitt, which virtually brought the matter to a formal decision, taking from the Prince of Wales any claim, as a right, which he might wish to establish of acting as regent of the kingdom. The

House indeed divided, but the resolutions were carried by a majority of 93 : 158 voting on an amendment, 251 against it.

The readiness, the quickness with which Mr. Pitt seized every word uttered by his adversaries to aid his arguments, either by ridiculing any accidental blunder, exposing some doctrine incautiously advanced, or dexterously leading them into some glaring avowal of opinions inconsistent with the principles of Whiggery, have been generally acknowledged. When Mr. Fox used the rash and unadvised words to which we have alluded, a smile irradiated the usual gloomy and haughty face of the prime minister ; and when the sentence was concluded, he slapped his thigh with exultation, and turning to the member who was seated near him, triumphantly exclaimed, "I'll unwhig the gentleman for the rest of his life !" and certainly, during the whole of the debate that followed, he took up a doctrine before unknown to a party that asserted the right divine of kings, and laid down an axiom, somewhat inconsistent with their usual creed, that the voice and the sense of the people, through their constituents, were to be consulted in the choice of a substitute for kingly power. Having carried the essential point, that the Lords spiritual and temporal and the Commons of Great Britain now assembled, and lawfully, fully, and freely representing all the estates of the people of this realm, have the right, and are in duty bound, to provide the means of supplying the defect of the personal exercise of the royal authority arising from his Majesty's indisposition, Mr. Pitt, on the 16th of January, moved : "That it was expedient that his Royal Highness the Prince of Wales should be empowered

The Life of Sheridan

to exercise and administer the royal authority under the style and title of regent of the kingdom"; and then brought forward a series of resolutions as restrictions upon his power. A debate of great interest ensued, during which Sheridan exhibited considerable tact and readiness. Lord Belgrave having concluded a complimentary speech in favour of the minister, with a quotation from Demosthenes, Sheridan promptly rose and immediately pointed out the misapplication of the lines, and, in defence of his party, uttered a eulogium, certainly called for by the insinuations of his adversaries, that the prince would be surrounded by bad advisers.

"The right honourable gentleman had more than once wantonly attacked that side of the House as containing a political party. As for himself (Mr. Sheridan added), he made no scruple to declare he thought it the glory and honour of his life to belong to that party. He who knew the character of that party, knew it was an honour which any man might covet. Was it a disgrace to have been formed under the Marquis of Rockingham, and under his banners to have combated on behalf of the people with success? Was it a disgrace to be connected with the Duke of Portland, a nobleman who, swayed by no mean motives of interest, nor influenced by any ambitious designs to grasp at power, nor with a view to any other purpose than the welfare of the country, dedicated his mornings unremittingly to the promotion of the public good? Mr. Sheridan remarked, he could not advert to his right honourable friend (Mr. Fox) without declaring it was the characteristic distinction of his heart to compel the most submissive devotion of mind and affection from all those who came under

The Life of Sheridan

the observation of it, and force them, by the most powerful and amiable of all influences, to become the inseparable associates of his fortune. With respect to his talents, he would not speak of them; they would derive no support from any man's attestation, nor from the most flattering panegyric of the most enlightened of his friends. Thus much he would only observe, with regard to the abilities of his honourable friend, that it was the utmost effort of any other man's talents, and the best proof of their existence, that he was able to understand the extent and comprehend the superiority of them. It was the pride and glory of his life to enjoy the happiness and honour of his friendship; and he desired to be told whether the Duke of Portland and Mr. Fox were less worthy of the confidence of their country, or more unfit to become ministers, because an arrogant individual chose presumptuously to load them with calumny? Were he an independent man, standing aloof from party, and wholly unconnected with it, he could not with patience hear the right honourable gentleman's insulting language; but as a party man, boasting himself to be one, how did the right honourable gentleman imagine he should receive his reflections but with that scorn and disdain which became a man conscious of the worth and value of those with whom he was connected?"

His observations on the patronage reserved were: "He reprobated the idea of reserving the patronage of the royal household, and adverted to the right honourable gentleman's having charged his right honourable friend (when on a former occasion he quitted office) with having left a fortress behind him. The charge was true; he admitted that his right honourable friend had done so; but then, like a coarse, clumsy workman, he had built his plan in open day, and retired with his friends, who served without pay, though their services had been long continued. Not so the right honourable gentleman over the way; like a more crafty mason, he had collected his materials with greater caution, and worked them up with abundantly more art. Perhaps he had taken the advice of the noble duke, famous for fortification, and, with the aid of that able engineer, had provided a corps of royal military artificers, and thrown up impregnable ramparts to secure himself and his garrison. Upon this occasion the king's arms doubtless might be seen flying as a banner on the top of his fortress, and powerful indeed must prove the effect of the right honourable gentleman's thundering eloquence from without, and the support of the royal artificers from within, against his political adversaries. Mr. Sheridan reprobated the person, whoever it might be, that advised her Majesty to lend her name to such a proposition as that which was then made to the committee; and declared that were the one ground of suspicion of the bad advisers of the regent to be taken away, the right honourable gentleman could not be said to have produced a single argument in support of his system. He described the power that the ex-minister would derive from retaining the patronage of the king's household; and contended that the pretext that his Majesty's feelings would be shocked when he recovered and found his household changed, was ridiculous." He then added, "To talk, therefore, of his Majesty's feelings, when he should recover and find his household changed, was to suppose that he would be less shocked to learn

The Life of Sheridan

that the constitution of his country was changed, part of his dominions ceded to foreign potentates, and other essential and important calamities and disgraces entailed on his country; which was like a man who, having been entrusted with the mansion-house of a person during his incapacity to take care of it, should suffer it to go to ruin, and the winds of heaven to blow through almost every part of it, the enclosures to be broken down, the flocks of sheep to be shorn and exposed to the storms, and all left to ruin and decay, except a few looking-glasses and old worthless gilt lumber that were locked up in an old-fashioned drawing-room. Mr. Sheridan represented the ex-minister coming down to the House in state, with the cap of liberty on the end of a white staff, a retinue of black and white sticks attending him, and an army of beef-eaters (whom the master of the horse, the lord steward, and lord chamberlain were to be employed in marshalling) to clear his way through the lobby."

During the long, protracted debates Mr. Sheridan assiduously attended the House, and made many useful observations upon the various stages of the Restriction Bill. The occasions on which he distinguished himself were many, evincing throughout a great anxiety to serve his Royal Highness, and to preserve the royal prerogative intact.

That which most tended to give the public a bad opinion of Fox, of Burke, and even of Sheridan, was the somewhat indecorous manner in which they treated the malady of the king; the too visible worship of the rising sun, and, above all, the party spirit with which they treated all public questions. Even the physicians were treated as partisans; their evidence handled with levity, sarcasm, or flat denial, just as it pleased those

who addressed the House. The admirable prognostics
of Dr. Willis, who was thoroughly conversant with
mental maladies, were made the theme of abuse; whilst
the attainments of Dr. Warren (whose practical skill,
notwithstanding his reputation as a scholar, was
generally questioned) were lauded to the skies; because the one was ready and somewhat talkative,
whereas the other, a slow-thinking man, was silent,
reserved, and only expressed his opinions when called
upon to do so. That Dr. Warren's hastily-formed
judgment should have been put into competition with
Dr. Willis's long-continued study is to be regretted,
because it misled the party, and induced Sheridan to
make a most unsuitable speech in the House, and to
boldly accuse Dr. Willis of prevarication and evasion,
to call him a hasty decider and a random speaker; to
say that the physic he administered "reminded him of
those nostrums which were to cure this and that
malady, and also disappointments in love, and long
sea voyages."

Of the letter which was addressed to Mr. Pitt, and
attributed to Mr. Sheridan, so widely circulated and
generally admired, the evidence of Sir James Mackin-
tosh has settled the doubted question of its authorship;
and to Mr. Burke is due whatever of merit it may
exhibit. The rumour that was so generally prevalent
that Sheridan had written it plainly shows that every
literary production of merit was supposed to be derived
from his pen. It is unnecessary to pursue the course
which was followed by Sheridan throughout the long
discussions which this interesting subject provoked.
Whatever of good feeling he may have gained in the
bosom of the prince and his royal brothers, he must
have offended the queen by the whole drift of his

The Life of Sheridan

arguments on the clauses which gave her Majesty the custody of the royal sufferer.

Among the thirty-two clauses which constituted the Regency Bill, was a clause that provided against the regent marrying a Papist. Mr. Rolle, with considerable indelicacy, renewed the discussion which had once been opened on the subject of the supposed alliance of the Prince of Wales with Mrs. Fitzherbert by moving that the words " or who is or should be married in law or in fact to a Papist," be inserted. Lord North, Mr. Grey, and Mr. Courtenay replied in somewhat strong language. In the course of the debate Sheridan alluded to Mr. Pitt having on several occasions signified his departure from office.

" Mr. Pitt said the honourable gentleman had indulged himself in imputing words to him which he had never spoken, and applying arguments which he had never uttered. The honourable gentleman contended that he had not signified his departure from office. Surely the honourable gentleman had a perverse memory. His successors had been named to him, but he had never yet heard of the least circumstance which authorised him to declare that he was about to quit his place. When he did hear anything like it, he should have much to say to that House, to express his acknowledgments for the support he had received, to confess his obligations to them, and to declare his hopes that he should not quit his situation avowing principles less worthy of their regard and esteem than he brought with him into office.

" Mr. Sheridan observed that the right honourable gentleman, he did not doubt, would make a fine speech at his exit from office ; or, according to the vulgar

The Life of Sheridan

expression, an excellent delivery of his last dying words and confession."

These lengthened debates were drawn to a conclusion by the announcement that his Majesty was restored to his usual state. The news was received with unbounded joy by the people, who were thoroughly wearied of the procrastination of the Ministry. Tedious, however, as may have been the discussions, they have been of deep value, and have furnished us with one of the landmarks by which the nature of the British constitution may be judged of.

The health of his father, Thomas Sheridan, had gradually declined. He for some time resided at Margate, and from thence, if he should find no amendment, he intended to proceed to Lisbon. His complaints, however, did not diminish, and on the 14th of August 1788 he expired. He had for some short time retired from the stage, and had given public readings at Freemasons' Hall, at Hickford's Rooms, and Coachmakers' Hall. His works, with the exception of the "Loyal Subject," "Romeo and Juliet," and "Coriolanus," which he altered and produced whilst manager of the Dublin stage, and a Life of Dean Swift, were principally devoted to the elements of language. They are : "A Discourse delivered in the Theatre at Oxford, and in the Senate House at Cambridge ; " "A Dissertation on the Causes of the Difficulties which occur in learning the English Language ; " "A Course of Lectures on Elocution ; " "A Plan of Education for the Young Nobility and Gentry of Great Britain ; " "Lectures on the Art of Reading ; " "A General Dictionary of the English Language ; " "Elements of English." A likeness, said to be exceedingly good, is prefixed to the second edition of his Dictionary.

The Life of Sheridan

Although at one period of his life the father was estranged from the son, and always seemed to give a preference to the elder brother, a reconciliation had taken place, in consequence of efforts repeatedly made and oftentimes spurned by the father. Sheridan, however, paid unremitting attention to him in his last illness, and evinced for him the sincerest filial affection. His eldest sister, referring to the existence of those differences, which she lamented, says in a letter, "and yet it was that son, and not the object of his partial fondness, who at last closed his eyes." Dr. Parr wrote, at the request of Sheridan, a tribute to his memory, which, however, was not inscribed upon the cenotaph intended by the son for St. Peter's Church, Margate. It is, however, worthy to be recorded. "This monument, A.D. 1824, was, by subscription, erected to the memory of Thomas Sheridan, Esq., who died in the neighbouring parish of St. John, August 14, 1788, in the 69th year of his age, and according to his own request was there buried. He was grandson to Dr. Thomas Sheridan, the brother of Dr. William, a conscientious nonjuror, who in 1691 was deprived of the bishopric of Kilmore. He was the son of Dr. Thomas Sheridan, a profound scholar and eminent schoolmaster, intimately connected with Dean Swift and other illustrious writers in the reign of Queen Anne. He was husband to the ingenious and amiable author of 'Sidney Biddulph' and several dramatic pieces favourably received. He was the father of the celebrated orator and dramatist, Richard Brinsley Sheridan. He had been the schoolfellow, and through life was the companion of the amiable Archbishop of Markham. He was the friend of the learned Dr. Sumner, master of Harrow School, and the well-known Dr. Parr. He took his first academical degree in the University of Dublin about 1736. He was honoured in the University of Oxford with the degree of A.M. in 1758, and in 1759 he obtained the same distinction at Cambridge. He for many years presided over the theatre of Dublin and at Drury Lane; he in public estimation stood next to David Garrick. In the literary world he was distinguished by numerous and useful writings on the pronunciation of the English language. Through some of his opinions ran a vein of singularity mingled with the rich ore of genius. In his manners there was dignified ease, in his spirit invincible firmness, and in his habits and principles unsullied integrity."

This elegant summary of the principal characteristics of the life of a man who had used indefatigable exertions, but unsuccessfully, to promote the cause of education, is one of those productions of the classic pen whose judgment in the selection of ideas and of words to express them has been unequalled. There now is a plain monument raised to the memory of Mr. Thomas Sheridan in St. Peter's, Margate, by a friend of Mr. Jarvis, who attended him professionally during his illness.

The great movements which occurred in France began to excite the attention of the people of England, and caused them to watch each event which sprang up, and to turn with anxious eye to the views taken of them by the parties who most deeply interested themselves in the direction of the public mind. The great Revolution of France, it must ever be borne in recollection, commenced with moderation, displaying only a determination to obtain by simple means a constitution worthy a free people, but innumerable difficulties

presented themselves. A disastrous series of occurrences led to the ruin of all established forms ; unquiet
and ambitious minds were opposed to capriciousness
and to feebleness ; horror followed upon horror, until
Europe, dismayed with the frightful scenes enacted
upon the stage, shrank back with loathing from the
contemplation. All at first was anticipation of good,
but the end was shame and destruction. It first appeared as the gentle breeze which refreshes as it passes
along, but soon became the whirlwind, destroying as
it swept by. Many of those who at first beheld a
nation attempting to contribute to the increase of the
happiness of human nature by the establishment of a
government which should lead to freedom, to public
order and security, were pleased to see the overthrow
of a tyranny which arbitrarily pressed upon the
humbler classes of society. They were prepared for
a bold struggle, carried on by daring and determined
innovators ; but they did not expect the eccentric
course which they took. They did not anticipate the
violence that arose, nor the murders that were
committed ; the transition state is always one of
prodigious effort, during which none can foresee its
results. For those who had to encounter the dreadful
position of society consequent upon the thorough
overthrow of all that existed in royalty and in aristocracy, it must indeed have been fearful ; but that
which has been obtained from the rude shocks is
liberty, social order, and contentment. The perils
that have been gone through could only have been
borne and supported by the insane ; but another race
enjoys the benefits, and feels the harmony that has
arisen out of discord, the mildness which was wrung
from tyranny and oppression.

The Life of Sheridan

Sheridan was amongst those who gazed with unspeakable satisfaction at the earliest struggles of the manacled slave to unbind his fetters, to raise himself from the ground, and draw in the free breath of heaven. With him were associated men who were deeply imbued with the love of a pure, free, and mild constitution, who saw in the Government of France corruption, imbecility, cupidity, and all those crimes which a long indulgence in despotism engenders and fosters. They were delighted to find a people rousing themselves from their slumber, proclaiming their rights with an irresistible and omnipotent voice, seeking that which justice entitled them to, and determined to obtain it. They could not foresee all that arose out of this patriotic energy; and, as events occurred, their minds were often reconciled to circumstances which cooler reflection might not have sanctioned. The distrust which those who governed in France brought upon themselves shook the loyalty of those who would have supported them, and eventually led to their own destruction. It is impossible for those who merely read the page of history to form any just idea of the impressions produced by these events upon the people of England. The changes were so various, they followed so rapidly one upon the other, that all reasoning was set at defiance. The fears of men were so worked upon, too, that no one became a dispassionate witness of the occurrences. Rank and power were annihilated in one country, and those who possessed them in England began to dread that their time was fully come; they prepared themselves for the struggle, and the champion of free institutions had but little chance against odds most discouraging. Sheridan, and those with whom he acted, boldly proclaimed opinions unpalatable to them, and a war of words, mingled with hatred and with fear, soon sprang up.

At this period Sheridan gave incessant labour to the duties of the House ; he was a frequent speaker, selected points of interest to the community, and brought assiduity and labour to assist his natural abilities. Had the indefatigable industry with which he pursued the various subjects of discussion been exhibited by an individual connected with the administration, he would soon have filled a most distinguished post ; but all his zeal, all his efforts, were directed against the system pursued by Mr. Pitt. His investigations of the public revenue, his statement of the resources and of the expenditure of the empire, led him to perceive many of the fallacious views, to combat, expose, and ridicule them. His lengthened speeches on the appointment of a committee of finance upon the Tobacco Regulation Bills proved to the country that he was neither indolent nor superficial ; but that he diligently inquired, and clothed the result of his examination in eloquence such as rendered abstruse questions interesting and intelligible. He sometimes met with abuse from the press ; but what man who stands prominently before the public can escape the calumnies, the gibes, and the scoffs of those who are opposed to him ? And if on the one side he is loaded with censure, he is certain on the other to meet with flattery and adulation. On one occasion he was rather carried away by too anxious a desire to defend himself, and he introduced a notice of the feelings that some entertained towards himself. He said that "uncommon pains had been taken in the public prints to defame all those who had taken any part in endeavouring to procure a repeal of the Tobacco Act; and no one had been more distinguished on the occasion than himself. He begged leave to apologise for speaking concerning himself; he at all times disliked egotisms, and more so on the present occasion when the attention of the committee was to be taken up with the consideration of important subjects; but still, as it was the part which he had taken in this business that had drawn upon him the ill-will of those who had traduced him, and as they had connected his personal character with the important business in which he was then engaged, he hoped that the committee would suffer him to trespass for some few minutes on their patience, whilst he should proceed to a few remarks upon the attacks that had been made upon him. Those who made those attacks had gone out of the common path, and instead of pursuing the old sober staple of abuse, had descended to the lowest scurrilities, and fallen without mercy, not only upon his public conduct, but also on his private life. They had made charges of a singular nature, and endeavoured to rob him of the esteem and friendship of those whom he valued most in society. Fortunately, however, their charges were as void of truth as they were fraught with malice. He had hitherto treated them with contemptuous silence, and would have continued in this disposition to the present day, if he had not felt some reason to think—which reason he had not heard till a few hours ago—that some of those charges were considered as founded on truth. What he more particularly alluded to were whispers or reports of jealousies among some of his dearest friends, and of a certain opposition affirmed to have been made by

The Life of Sheridan

a noble duke (Portland) against some views or expectations which he (Mr. Sheridan) was said to have entertained; concerning such whispers and reports, he could truly declare that there was not in them one grain of truth. The opinion which they ascribed to the noble duke had never been entertained by him. Mr. Sheridan observed that he would not venture to state to the committee the opinion that the noble duke was pleased to entertain of him, lest he should be accused of vanity in publishing what he might deem highly flattering. All, therefore, that he would assert on this occasion was, that if he had it in his power to make the man whose good opinion he should most highly prize think flatteringly of him, he would have that man to think of him precisely as the noble duke did, and then his wish on that subject would be most amply gratified.

"The jealousies to which he was described as having given occasion existed only in the brain of the traducers; they did not, they could not, exist anywhere else. He was, therefore, perfectly at his ease whilst the traducers were propagating their calumnies. He defied any man to charge him with any one act which could be tortured into a violation of any engagement founded on honour and integrity. If he could be charged, in truth, with any dishonourable, mean, or unmanly act, he should feel very differently indeed; his mind in that case would sting him more than the most bitter reproaches of his most calumniating enemies. As to any pretensions which might be ascribed to him, to situations far beyond his natural weight in the community, he would only observe that it was the peculiar excellence of the British constitution that a man could push forward into notice and distinction the talents or abilities, whatever they might be, with which Providence had endowed him."

Occasionally happy thoughts, sparkling allusions, and playful raillery enliven his dullest speeches, but it would be the height of injustice to quote them, for they are so incorporated with the rest of the matter that they would lose all their value were they to be extracted and placed alone before the reader's eye. When the session terminated, which it did amidst the complaints of Sheridan of the procrastination of public business, the Parliament was dissolved; he hastened down to Stafford and secured his election, but not without difficulty and expense. He then returned to London to lend his aid to Charles Fox, who stood for Westminster. Here he had to meet one of the most unflinching politicians of the day, Horne Tooke. No one dared to express his sentiments more freely, no one had more sarcastic power; no man better understood the art of carrying with him the working classes and the humbler orders of society. Ready in wit, quick in apprehension, his sallies, his repartees, neither delicate nor fashioned to any but those he addressed, were listened to with delight. As a candidate for Westminster, no one but the great and good Sir Francis Burdett better knew his supporters. It was understood that Sheridan had been anxious to try his power in Westminster, and in a letter from Mrs. Sheridan to him, whilst on his canvass at Stafford, this passage occurs: "I am half sorry you have anything to do with them, and more than ever regret you did not stand for Westminster with Charles."

Horne Tooke, instead of finding a proposer and seconder, boldly came forward and put himself in nomination; and — saying that the two candidates should have been ashamed to have sat and heard such ill-deserved praise bestowed upon them by their respective proposers and seconders—offered himself. He told the crowd that, as so many of these fine qualities and virtues had never done them the least good, they might as well now choose a candidate without them."

Various are the sallies which are recorded as marking the sarcastic vein of the man, but there was one so personal to Sheridan that he never forgave it, and, although at one period some degree of intimacy had existed between them, it ceased. Charles Fox, who was seldom listened to with patience by the surrounding crowd, left the hustings, while Sheridan, whose good-humoured stories and lively wit were rather in favour, remained. Tooke observed upon this, " that it was usual with the quack doctor, when he quitted the stage, to leave his jack-pudding behind him." His ready answer to a partisan of Charles Fox has been recorded ; who, addressing him, said, " Well, Mr. Tooke, as this is Monday, you are sure to have all the blackguards with you." " I am delighted to hear it, sir," was the reply, " more especially when it comes from such good authority." Sheridan found himself quite unequal to cope with his virulent antagonist ; the personalities, the invectives he had to encounter were not at all to his taste. He winced under the merciless infliction of the scourge ; he felt how much more potent was his adversary, and was not sorry when Tooke was defeated.

The first session of the new Parliament saw Sheridan an active opponent of the administration. Little, however, is worthy of notice, except the still further widening of the breach between Burke on the one side

The Life of Sheridan

and Fox and Sheridan on the other. Mr. Burke's
work, "Reflections on the French Revolution," had
attracted the deepest attention; it had produced an
effect upon the followers of the Whig school, though
the great leaders remained unchanged and unchange-
able. The party was nearly broken up. The spirit of
loyalty which was maintained throughout the work,
overpowered, in many instances, the newly-awakened
feeling for liberty. The doctrines of equality, of
fraternisation, had alarmed the privileged classes;
and they hailed the book as the manifesto of those
who loved royalty, and would uphold the church in
opposition to that which they so much dreaded. On
the 6th of May, the House of Commons was witness
to an unequalled display of passion on one side, and
tenderness on another. Burke, with violence and
impetuosity, severed the ties of friendship that so long
had bound the two great men together. Burke's
warning voice against the danger of trying new
theories, his wish to cherish the British constitution,
and to save it from the influence of French philosophy,
passed by unheeded; but when Fox whispered that
there would be no loss of friendship, Burke repudiated
the idea: "Yes, there was a loss of friendship; he knew
the price of his conduct; he had done his duty at the
price of his friend—their friendship was at an end."
Here Fox betrayed an amiable weakness; tears coursed
each other down his cheek as he rose to reply. The
House was visibly affected; not a sound was heard.
It was felt that men of noble nature, long deeply
attached, were torn from each other by a high sense
of honour, by a sacred feeling of duty, and the love
of their native land. Although the greater part of
those with whom Sheridan usually acted saw without

The Life of Sheridan

apprehension the commencement of the conflict in France, there was one master-spirit of the age who feared danger in the struggle, and left the old companions of his political views. Burke, with whom Sheridan had lived on terms of intimacy, who had fought the battle against Hastings so nobly with him, who had cheered him on, and who had received him fainting in his arms, after his great effort in the House of Lords, from the earliest moment expressed his dissent from his former friend, and by his writings and speeches attempted to counteract his opinions. On the 9th of February came on the discussion on the Army Estimates; the session had been opened on the 1st of February, and as early as the 5th Mr. Fox had taken an opportunity, whilst discussing the reduction of the army, to observe that the army in Paris had, by its refusal to obey the court, set a glorious example, and shown that men by becoming soldiers had not ceased to be citizens; and therefore one of his great objections to a standing army had been removed. Mr. Burke, after some eloquently expressed compliments on Mr. Fox, deprecated the effects which such language was likely to produce; and said "that so strongly was he opposed to any the least tendency towards the means of introducing a democracy like that of the French, as well as to the end itself, that, much as it would afflict him if such a thing should be attempted, and that any friend of his should concur in such measures—he was far, very far, from believing they could — he would abandon his best friends, and join with his worst enemies to oppose either the means or the end." This declaration called forth from Fox one of the most beautiful eulogiums ever pronounced by one friend upon

The Life of Sheridan

another. After stating the value he placed upon his
friendship, he thus spoke of the splendid powers of
that great orator : " If he were to put all the political
information which he had learned from books, all
which he had gained from science, and all which any
knowledge of the world and in affairs, into one scale,
and the improvement which he had derived from his
right honourable friend's instruction and conversation
were placed in the other, he should be at a loss to
decide to which to give the preference." Burke was
evidently pleased with these explanations, and rose
to express his satisfaction ; but Sheridan was not so
easily acted upon. He uttered " some warm compliments to Mr. Burke's general principles ; but said that
he could not conceive how it was possible for a person
of such principles, or for any man who valued our
own constitution and revered the Revolution that obtained it for us, to unite with such feelings an indignant and unqualified abhorrence of all the proceedings
of the patriotic party in France.

" He conceived theirs to be as just a Revolution as
our own, proceeding upon as sound a principle and
a greater provocation. He vehemently defended the
general views and conduct of the National Assembly.
He could not even understand what was meant by the
charge against them of having overturned the laws,
the justice, and the revenues of their country. What
were their laws ? The arbitrary mandates of capricious
despotism. What their justice ? The partial adjudica-
tions of venal magistrates. What their revenues ?
National bankruptcy. This he thought the funda-
mental error of the right honourable gentleman's
argument, that he accused the National Assembly of
creating the evils which they had found existing in

The Life of Sheridan

full deformity at the first hour of their meeting. The public creditor had been defrauded; the manufacturer was out of employ; trade was languishing; famine clung upon the poor; despair on all. In this situation, the wisdom and feelings of the nation were appealed to by the Government; and was it to be wondered at by *Englishmen*, that a people so circumstanced should search for the cause and source of all their calamities; or that they should find them in the arbitrary constitution of their government, and in the prodigal and corrupt administration of their revenues? For such an evil, when proved, what remedy could be resorted to but a radical amendment of the frame and fabric of the constitution itself? This change was not the object and wish of the National Assembly only; it was the claim and cry of all France, united as one man for one purpose. He joined with Mr. Burke in abhorring the cruelties that had been committed; but what was the striking lesson, the awful moral, that was to be gathered from the outrages of the populace? What but a superior abhorrence of that accursed system of despotic government which had so deformed and corrupted human nature as to make its subjects capable of such acts—a government that sets at nought the property, the liberty, and lives of the subjects; a government that deals in extortion, dungeons, and tortures; sets an example of depravity to the slaves it rules over; and, if a day of power comes to the wretched populace, it is not to be wondered at, however it is to be regretted, that they act without those feelings of justice and humanity which the principles and the practice of their governors have stripped them of. At the same time, if there were any persons who, for the purposes of their own private and per-

The Life of Sheridan

sonal ambition, had instigated those outrages, they, whatever their rank, birth, or fortune, deserved the execration of mankind. Justice, however, required that no credit should be given to mere rumours on such a subject."

Mr. Burke replied that he most sincerely lamented over the inevitable necessity of now publicly declaring that, henceforth, he and his honourable friend were separated in politics. He complained "that he had not represented his arguments fairly; it was not what he expected in the moment of departed friendship. On the contrary, was it not evident that the honourable gentleman had made a sacrifice of his friendship for the sake of catching some momentary popularity?—all the applause which he could gain from clubs was scarcely worthy the sacrifice which he had chosen to make for such an acquisition." Attempts were in vain made to heal the breach thus made between two men who had so often fought together mighty battles against power, against corruption and tyranny. A meeting took place at Burlington House, according to a previous arrangement; it lasted from ten o'clock at night until three in the morning, and never was there a more remarkable display of talent on both sides. Burke was, however, implacable; all communication ceased between them; and though Sheridan spoke of him, in the House of Commons, as one for whose talents and personal virtue he had the highest esteem, veneration, and regard, all was in vain. Burke spoke of him with asperity from that time forward, and attributed to his unwarrantable interference his own secession from his former party.

It was alleged that Sheridan had hastened on this

separation by his imprudent speeches, and that this was the result of jealousy, and an anxious desire to fill the place in Charles Fox's esteem that for a quarter of a century Burke had enjoyed. Of the littleness that could invent this calumny we may speak with contempt, but of the eagerness to diffuse the venom we think with disgust. It is not unlikely that Sheridan should have urged on this explanation of the differences which existed in that great party, whose chief end and aim was declared to be the love of a pure and well-defined constitution, which, whilst it guarded the liberties of a people, acknowledged frankly the great principles of royalty and of a House of Lords.

A speech made by Sheridan on a motion of Mr. Grey, against any interference in the war between Russia and the Porte, is well worthy of perusal, as illustrating the information, and likewise the discretion and tact with which he could handle a subject of difficulty. It is remarkable for the avowal of a doctrine that the prerogative of the crown to declare war might prove obnoxious to the House, and that there existed an ancient, constitutional, and most useful function of a British House of Commons to advise the crown, and by a due application of their preventive wisdom to save the country from that expense and calamity into which they might otherwise be plunged, either by the terror of ministers, their imprudence, their neglect, or their corruption.

Mr. Sheridan retired in the month of April from the business of the House ; during this period there are no records of speeches to be met with, no traces of his occupation. In fact, his mind was harassed by many conflicting thoughts. Mrs. Sheridan's state of health excited the deepest apprehension. She was compelled to seek change of air at Clifton. The state of Drury Lane Theatre, too, was such as to be a source of much anxiety to him; it had been pronounced by competent persons to be unfit to receive large audiences, and that it was necessary that it should be rebuilt. The circumstances attending such a determination could not fail to require all the attention of Mr. Sheridan. His time and mind were devoted to the completion of the plans that were now devised, and from which hopes were entertained that ultimate advantages would accrue. These hopes were not destined to be fulfilled; and we may look to this period of this great man's life as the one from which sprang all the ultimate misfortunes that gradually overpowered him. He had now attained the zenith of his reputation. His popularity, his talents, and his exertions were all the theme of general eulogy. Though some slight embarrassments had occurred, they had passed away like the fleeting clouds across the summer sun; but he was now destined to fall from the giddy height, and to feel how transitory are all the gifts of fortune. He had, it would seem, three establishments, and his style of living was such as became a man mingling in the richer class of society and enjoying all that luxury can give. To build the theatre seemed an easy task; all that was required was one hundred and fifty thousand pounds. This was raised with the utmost facility in three hundred debentures of five hundred pounds each; but the difficulty of paying the interest on that large sum was scarcely calculated upon. Three instalments were to be paid up, and as soon as one was paid all was prepared. On the 4th of June, his Majesty's birthday, Old Drury Lane, the scene of so many extraordinary circumstances, closed for ever. The company went to the Opera House, and from thence, when the musical season commenced, to the Haymarket, where they played at advanced prices. On the 4th of September the first stone of the new theatre was laid. Unforeseen difficulties, fresh expenses, vexatious negotiations, combined to retard the completion of the new theatre ; and during this interval a sad calamity occurred.

It was in the year 1792 that Sheridan had to mourn over the grave of his beautiful and affectionate wife. She was only thirty-eight years of age, when a pulmonary disease bereft him of the cherished partner of his happiest days. From that moment a blight fell upon him — he soon became an altered man. There was no one who was ever admitted into her presence that did not feel there was a divinity about her. Jackson, the great composer, said "that to see her, as she stood singing beside him at the pianoforte, was like looking into the face of an angel." The Bishop of Norwich was wont to say that she seemed to him "the connecting link between woman and angel." Even the licentious and coarse John Wilkes was fascinated into respect and admiration ; he pronounced her the most beautiful flower that ever grew in nature's garden. "This beautiful mother of a beautiful race" united so many charms, was so gifted by art as well as by nature, as to surpass the ordinary beings of the earth. The incense that was offered at her shrine doubtless produced some influence upon her mind, which from her earliest years had been accustomed to the sweetest sounds of flattery. She was taught by a host of admirers that she was the theme of general adora-

The Life of Sheridan

tion; she listened to the voice of the charmer, and
the ill-nature of the world, which never brooks
superiority in an individual, accused her of coquetry,
of levity, nay, of forgetfulness of the high duties
which women are called upon to perform when
they would be held up as examples to their sex.
Still she was a ministering angel to Sheridan; and
whatever may have been the occasional sources of
their disunion, she entered into all his cares and
anxieties with the devotion of an attached and affectionate woman. Her letters breathe a spirit of tender
love, of pride in the man of her choice, of deep
anxiety and solicitude for his success in each of his
undertakings. She assisted him in all the varieties
of public character he was called on to assume; the
dramatist, the manager of a playhouse, the statesman, found in her one fully capable of appreciating
his powers, of embellishing them, of drawing them
out. She was an admirable judge of poesy—herself
a poet; she was a useful critic of the drama; she
was skilled in electioneering; and everything that to
him was an object of importance became for her a
source of inquiry. Probably most of the readers of
Moore's " Life of Sheridan" have felt that the chap-
ter dedicated to the death of Mrs. Sheridan is one of
the most perfect of all that have appeared, and to
that we must refer for an insight into the character
of this most interesting woman. He has collected
together a number of letters that exhibit, in their
full charms, all the bright virtues with which she was
adorned, and sufficiently account for the deep grief
which her loss inflicted upon her husband. Whatever may have been those imperfections which she,
in common with the rest of mankind, inherited, they

of course were forgotten and quickly buried in oblivion; whilst memory loved to cherish the remembrance of those fascinations which charmed all who
approached her. Sheridan mourned over his sad loss,
and turned with hope to a child in whom he thought,
perhaps, he might see her mother's virtues and her
mother's charms reflected. Of this consolation, however, he was deprived; she died under circumstances
which must have poignantly added to his grief. "A
large party was assembled at Sheridan's to spend a
joyous evening in dancing; all were in the height
of merriment; he himself remarkably cheerful, and
partaking of the amusement, when the alarm was
given that the dear little angel was dying. It is
impossible to describe the confusion and horror of
the scene." His affliction was severe. The child,
in death, was so like her mother that every one was
struck with the resemblance. For four or five days
Sheridan lingered over the remains. His sense then
taught him to bear up against the affliction which
had bent him down, and he became resigned to the
loss of his cherished hopes.

Kelly says: "I never beheld more poignant grief
than Mr. Sheridan felt for the loss of his beloved
wife; and, although the world, which knew him only
as a public man, will perhaps scarcely credit the fact, I
have seen him night after night sit and cry like a
child, while I sang to him, at his desire, a pathetic
little song of my composition:—

"'They bore her to a grassy grave.'"

On the 13th of December the House assembled;
during the vacation the aspect of affairs had gradually
become more serious. The speech from the throne

announced the necessity of calling out the militia; that there existed a design to attempt the overthrow of the constitution, evidently pursued in connection and concert with persons in foreign countries; that the utmost efforts had been made to observe a strict neutrality in the war on the Continent, and to avoid any interference in the internal affairs of France. But there existed strong and increasing indications there of a determination to excite disturbance in other countries, to disregard the rights of neutral nations, to extend its limits by conquest, as well as to adopt, towards other states, general measures not conformable with the laws of nations or existing treaties. It was incumbent on Parliament to take steps to augment the naval and military force and to maintain internal tranquillity. The speech concluded.

The address was moved by Sir James Sanderson, the Lord Mayor of London, and seconded by Mr. Wallace. An amendment was moved by Mr. Fox, who, looking upon it as the production of the Ministry, felt that he had a right to deny the assertions contained in the speech. He did not believe in the existence of an insurrection, nor any desire to excite one; that the alarm only existed in the artful designs and practices of the Ministry; there never was at home a greater spirit of loyalty; and as for those who were fighting for liberty in France, he wished them success. His amendment was, "That the House should enter into an immediate examination of the facts which were stated in the speech, and had been the cause of thus summoning Parliament." An animated debate ensued, in which, on one side, the opinions of Burke, of Wyndham, and of Dundas were given; on the other, those of Grey, of Erskine, and of Sheridan.

Wyndham expressed his regret that he was compelled to oppose his former friends, but was satisfied that the nation was in peril; and though there might be tranquillity on the surface, there was beneath confusion and tumult.

Sheridan's speech was concise, but admirably to the point. "He believed the formidable band of republicans which had been mentioned to exist in this country to be men in buckram. . . . Such was his idea of the character of Englishmen, that he would take upon him to assert that were but one French soldier to land upon our coast, under the idea of effecting any change in our government, every hand and heart in the country would be roused by the indignity and unite to oppose so insulting an attempt. . . . As to the question of war, he should vote that English ministers be impeached who should enter into a war for the purpose of re-establishing the former despotism in France; who should dare in such a cause to spend one guinea, or shed one drop of blood."

The amendment was negatived. The majority of the minister had, by the desertion of so many from the Whig party, largely increased; 290 voted with him, 50 against him. Mr. Fox, still desirous that peace should be maintained, moved, on the following day, an amendment: "Trusting that your Majesty will employ every species of negotiation, to prevent the calamities of war, that may be deemed consistent with the honour and dignity of the British nation." He was seconded by Sheridan. "Peace he wished for, by all means peace; but," he added, "if it could

The Life of Sheridan

not be obtained, he should vote for vigorous war—
not a war of shifts and scraps, of timid operation or
protracted effort, but a war conducted with such
energy as shall evince to the world that the nation
was fighting for its dearest and most invaluable privileges." The motion was negatived; but undismayed
by defeat, desirous that the nation should not plunge
into that long and fearful train of calamities which
war brings with it, Fox, even on the following day,
proposed that a minister should be sent to France to
treat with the provisional committee. Burke observed
"that he thought the debate should not proceed
during the unavoidable absence of Mr. Pitt, who was
absent at Cambridge, for the university of which he
was canvassing." Sheridan replied, "He must be
excused for paying no respect whatever to the observation of a right honourable gentleman (Mr. Burke)
that it was improper to bring forward these discussions
in the absence of his Majesty's first minister! This
was a tender respect to the dignity of office in that
right honourable gentleman; but he must be permitted to say that the representation of the country
was indeed placed in a degraded light, if it was to be
maintained that the great council of the nation was
not, in this momentous crisis, a competent court to
discuss the dearest interests of the people, unless the
presence of a certain minister of the crown sanctioned
their deliberations. But on what ground did they
regret the absence of the treasury leader? Had
there appeared any want of numbers or ability to
compensate for this loss? What exertion that he
could have furnished had been unsupplied? Had
there been any want of splendid and sonorous
declamation to cover a meagreness of argument?

[216]

Any want of virulence of invective to supply the place of proof in accusation? Any want of inflammatory appeals to the passions where reason and judgment were unsafe to be resorted to? Unquestionably, in all these respects, the chancellor of the exchequer had not been missed; in one article indeed they might be justified in regretting his absence. They had been pressed to prove the facts asserted in the king's speech and in the proclamation. Not an atom of information could any present member of the Government furnish; doubtless, therefore, the insurrection was a secret deposited in the breast of the chancellor of the exchequer; and he had taken in his pocket all the proofs of the plot to assist his election at Cambridge." He then touched upon what is now universally acknowledged, that the French nation was maddened by the interference of foreign powers; that to them all the horrors that stained that glorious desire to be free, which marked the first onset of the Revolution, are owing. He asked, "Were the free and generous people of England ready to subscribe to the Duke of Brunswick's manifesto?—that hateful outrage on the rights and feelings of human nature; that wretched tissue of impotent pride, folly, and inhumanity; that proclamation which had steeled the heart and maddened the brain of all France; which had provoked those it had devoted to practise all the cruelties it had impotently threatened to inflict; which had sharpened the daggers of the assassins of the 2nd of September; which had whetted the axe now suspended over the unfortunate monarch—was the nation ready to subscribe to this absurd and detestable rhapsody? An honourable officer (Sir James Murray) had attempted to defend his performance—but how? By denying that it intended what it professed and threatened. From a British officer of his character and understanding a different defence might be expected. The honourable baronet had given instances where the conduct of the Prussian army contradicted the spirit of their manifesto; what instances on the contrary side might be adduced he would not then discuss. One case alone had been sufficient to decide him as to the true spirit of the league—the brutal rigour with which La Fayette had been treated. Whatever else he was, he was a brave man, and he was in their power. The use they had made of that power sufficiently showed how they would have treated others whom they might well consider as entitled to tenfold enmity." This speech was indeed worthy the occasion, and was amongst his happiest efforts in defence of his feelings and his opinions.

Goaded on to madness by the injudicious interference of foreign powers, feeling that they could place no reliance on royal promises, that all was hollowness and subterfuge, the French nation committed a mighty crime, which separated it from the rest of Europe. A feeble yet good king—the very original from whom Shakespeare might have drawn his Henry the Sixth—was sacrificed; the apprehension of such a catastrophe had for some time haunted the imagination of those who were most eager for that temperate reform of abuses to which they trusted that the French Revolution would have gradually led. No one can read the speech which Sheridan next made in the House, whilst yet the fearful tribunal was sitting which might commit an act of inhuman cruelty, without feeling that he was actuated by the

The Life of Sheridan

sincerest love of his country, and the hope that the furious spirit raging in Paris might be allayed. It was on the 20th of December, when Mr. Hobart brought up a report from the committee of supply granting 25,000 men for the service of the year, that he expressed sentiments which even his adversaries, with the exception of him who was called "the Renegade" Burke, applauded. He stated "that he was most willing, should the hateful necessity arise, to join in the unanimous support of the House to every proposition tending to give vigour and effect to the war; still he thought that there existed in France a sincere disposition to listen to and respect the opinion of the British nation; he in his soul and conscience believed that there was not one man of any party or description who did not deprecate, and who would not deplore the fate of those persecuted and unfortunate victims, should the apprehended catastrophe take place; amongst those whose hearts would be most revolted and disgusted would be those who had been foremost in rejoicing at the destruction of the old despotism in France, and who had eagerly hoped that, to whatever extremes, as to principles of government, a momentary enthusiasm might lead a people new to the light of liberty, that however wild their theories might be, yet there would have appeared in the quiet, deliberate acts of their conduct those inseparable characteristics of real liberty and of true valour, justice, magnanimity, and mercy." Burke rose and reprobated the use of such words. "The truth was the king was in the hands of assassins, who were both his accusers and his judges, and his destruction was inevitable." He launched out into misrepresentations, to which Sheridan replied, observing,

The Life of Sheridan

" he would not attribute them to any ill-purpose, or any ill-motive, but to ill-temper that had so run away with him that he scarcely knew what he meant or what he said." Events rapidly succeeded each other, scarcely a day intervened without some new shock to public feeling by the impetuous progress of the Revolution. The execution of the king decided many who had previously wavered in their opinions; the Whig party in Parliament dwindled to the smallest span, the great mass of the people were awe-struck by the daring act, and listened to the approach of war with less repugnance than was expected; nay, they even doubted the sagacity of Pitt, who seemed to hesitate, until he was urged on by his new associates. At length, on the 12th of February, the message came from the throne, announcing that a declaration of war had been made; an address was moved, assuring his Majesty that he might rely on the firm and effectual support of the representatives of the people in the prosecution of a just and necessary war. Mr. Fox's amendment still led to the expression of a hope that a pacification should be the means followed. Burke opposed him in language totally uncalled for; he laid great stress upon the fact that the healths of Fox and of Sheridan had been received with great enthusiasm in Paris. He dwelt upon the impiety of the French, their open avowal of Atheism, and was bitter upon his former friends, exulting at the diminution of their numbers, and designating them as a phalanx.

Sheridan greatly distinguished himself by his memorable reply; he brought the full force of his eloquence into play, mingling retort, ridicule, and argument in the most forcible manner. He said that he was provoked to rise by the insinuations and

The Life of Sheridan

charges of Mr. Burke against his honourable friend
Fox. Never before had he indulged himself in such
a latitude of ungoverned bitterness and spleen towards
the man he still occasionally professed to respect.
His ridicule of the smallness of the number of friends
left to the object of his persecution ill became him,
of all mankind ; but he trusted, however small that
number was, there ever would be found among them
men not afraid, upon such a subject, to oppose
truth and temper to passion and declamation, however eloquently urged or clamorously applauded. He
made a bold attack on the different set of principles
he had at different times urged, and taunted him with
his own changes of views, which ought to forbid
his allusion to the change of opinion in others. "A
book was produced, and he was proceeding to read
a former speech of his (Mr. Fox's), as if he had ever
once retracted his opinion on this subject. When the
Speaker called him to order, the honourable gentleman did not seem to take the interruption kindly,
though certainly he ought to have been grateful for
it ; for never, sure, was there a man who had a
greater interest in discouraging the practice of con-
trasting the past and present speeches, principles, and
professions of any public man. Was the honourable
gentleman ready to invite such a discussion respecting himself ? If he were, and his consistency could
be matter of regular question in that House, he did
not scruple to assert that there was scarcely an iota
of his new principles to which there was not a
recorded contradiction in his former professions.
Let a set of his works be produced, one member
might read, paragraph by paragraph, his present
doctrines, and another should refute every syllable of

The Life of Sheridan

them out of the preceding ones. It was a consolation to those who differed from his new principles to know where to resort for the best antidote to them."

His invectives against Burke were concluded by a bitter attack upon the Allies then marching on France; he preferred seeing England fight single-handed against France. He feared the enemy less than the ally; he disliked the cause of war, but abhorred the company we were to fight in still more. He denounced the conduct of the Allies in the Polish Revolution, as having massacred the fairest offspring of virtue — truth and valour. "Could the right honourable gentleman palliate these things? No! But had he ever arraigned them? Why had he never come to brandish in that House a Russian dagger, red in the heart's blood of the free constitution of Poland? No; not a word, not a sigh, not an ejacula-tion for the destruction of all he had held up to the world as a model for reverence and imitation! In his heart is a record of brass for every error and excess of liberty, but on his tongue a sponge to blot out the foulest crimes and blackest treacheries of despotism." This allusion to the fact that on one occasion Burke went to the House of Commons, and, with prodigious attempt at stage effect, brandished a dagger which his fancy or bewildered imagination led him to believe was precisely similar to one which must be used in the French Revolution, told with great effect upon the House.

Mr. Sheridan gave notice of his intention to bring forward a motion relative to the existence of seditious practices in the country; and, with a view of obtaining a full attendance, a call of the House was ordered for the 4th of March, but when the

The Life of Sheridan

motion was to be brought forward after the ordinary business, no Mr. Sheridan made his appearance. Mr. Lambton apologised ; Mr. Thornton moved an adjournment ; Mr. Fox hoped everybody would be punctual ; Sir Henry Houghton thought that a minister ought to be waited for ; Mr. Pitt said he was always anxious to be punctual — and everything was said that could be said to gain time and to allay the murmurs which began to rise, and the many little anecdotes which were whispered about Sheridan never being punctual, when at last he appeared, with a very proper apology in his mouth and one of his best speeches. He laughed at the supposed sedition, the lurking treason, and the panic ; of the latter he gave a good picture, and placed his late friends, Wyndham and Burke, in the foreground. "This panic had already had a great effect, and, indeed, it was much too general an impression to proceed from real danger ; a general panic was always created by phantoms and imaginary evils. It had been always so in the panics of armies ; for instance, he believed that there was not once to be found in history an instance in which the panic of an army had proceeded from real danger ; it always proceeded either from accident or some stratagem of the enemy. Indeed, the thing bore evidence for itself ; had the danger been real, there must have been a difference of opinion as to the amount of it, for while there was a difference in the size and character of the understandings of men, there must be a difference in their opinions ; but those who believed anything upon the tales of sedition, which he had before alluded to, believed everything that was said about it, and that of itself proved its fallacy. There were numerous instances recorded, both in prose and verse, where nations had been misled, and had acted upon such false alarms. There were many instances in which a panic had been communicated by one class of men to the other.

> ' Sic quisque pavendo
> Dat vires famæ : nulloque auctore malorum,
> Quæ finxere timent.   Nec solum vulgus inani
> Percussum terrore pavet : Sed curia, et ipsi
> Sedibus exiluere patres, invisaque belli
> Consulibus fugiens mandat decreta senatus.'

"His friend (Mr. Wyndham) had been panic-struck, and now strengthened the hand of Government, who, last session, agreeable to a vulgar adage, ' Rolled his Majesty's ministers in the dirt.' At that period he pulled off the mask of perfidy, and declaimed loudly against that implicit confidence which some had argued ought to be placed in ministers. He now thought such arguments were impolitic, and no man was more strenuous for that confidence which he had before with so much warmth reprobated. Another friend (Mr. Burke), to whose doctrines Mr. Wyndham had become a convert, had also been panic-struck. He had been so affected that he saw nothing but a black and clouded sky—a bleak opposition, where there was not a shrub or bush to shelter him from the gloomy aspect of public affairs ; but he had taken refuge in the ministerial gaberdine, where he hoped for security from the approaching storm."

It was in this speech that the motto of the *Sun* newspaper afforded him one of his happiest hits. The lines selected by the original proprietor of the journal were :—

> "Solem quis dicere falsum
> Audeat ?"

The Life of Sheridan

It was also on this occasion that he taunted Burke as having quitted the camp, but of returning to it as a spy.

A few nights afterwards Pitt took the House by surprise by a most eloquent speech, when stating the ways and means for the ensuing year; he recommended unanimity and liberality in the supplies, but at the same time to watch with vigilance and even jealousy. Sheridan spoke in reply with great readiness. "He said he gave the minister credit for the fairness of some of his observations, but he must frankly say he had felt the jealousy recommended much awakened by the very extraordinary and sudden appeal to the passions of the House. There was little novelty in it, excepting the novelty of introducing, in a day devoted to figures, all the arts of declamation. He had suddenly laid down his pencil and slate, as it were, and grasping the truncheon, had finished with an harangue, more calculated for the general of an army going to storm a French redoubt than a minister of finance discussing accounts in a sober hour of calculation with the stewards and attorneys of a burdened people."

The debates on the Traitorous Correspondence Bill furnished him with several opportunities of expressing his opinion upon the fallacious views entertained of the existence of treason. Lord Auckland's memorial to the States General and the Sheffield Petition for Parliamentary Reform both engaged his attention. He had several opportunities of coming into collision with Burke, and seemed rather to court them; he contrived to praise his eloquence, but to stigmatise his opinions. On one occasion, after his usual compliments to his wit, mirth, and humour, he said he

The Life of Sheridan

generally employed them on subjects which did not
call for either ; but wars, treasons, murders, or mas-
sacres. In alluding to Burke's praise of the King of
Prussia, he compared the king's conduct in Dantzic
with that of France—no act of hers was more desperate or more infamous. The party robbed cared
not whether he was plundered by a man with a white
feather or one with a nightcap on his head ; but a
head with a crown and a head with a nightcap totally
altered the moral quality of the action—death inflicted
by a hand wielding a pike was murder, swaying a
sceptre was innocent.

The session of this year was opened on the 24th of
January. The address from the throne stated that
upon the issue of the contest in which the nation was
engaged depended the maintenance of the constitution, laws, religion, and the security of civil society ;
it dwelt upon the advantages obtained by the allied
forces and the necessity of prosecuting the war with
energy and vigour ; it stated that the internal discontent and confusion in France were produced by
a system which violated every restraint of justice,
humanity, and religion ; that the principles which
were promulgated in France tended to destroy all
property, to subvert the laws and the religion of
every civilised nation, and to introduce universally
that wild and destructive system of rapine, anarchy,
and impiety—the effects of which, as manifested in
France, furnished a dreadful but useful lesson to the
present age and posterity. The speech was of considerable length, and called upon the nation, in what
is now considered a hackneyed style, though then
admired as original, to exert itself to pay for all the
expenses of the war.

The Life of Sheridan

Lord Mornington, after the mover and the seconder had gone through the usual routine of saying a vast deal about nothing in the ordinary form of eloquence, commenced an elaborate speech to prove that as long as the French maintained the principles they had adopted, the war should not be relinquished. "Mr. Sheridan began with observing that the noble lord who had just sat down had divided a speech, more remarkable for its ability than its brevity, into two parts : the first, a detail of all the atrocities that had been committed during the whole course of the Revolution in France ; the second, a kind of posthumous arraignment of the offences of Brissot and his associates. As he did not perceive any noble or learned member inclined to rise on behalf of the accused, so he conceived the pleadings on the part of the prosecution to be closed ; and as the Speaker was evidently not proceeding to sum up the evidence, he hoped he might be permitted to recall the attention of the House to the real object of that day's consideration. He admired the emphasis of the noble lord in reading his voluminous extracts from his various French documents ; he admired, too, the ingenuity he had displayed in his observations upon those extracts ; but he could not help further expressing his admiration that the noble lord should have thought proper to have taken up so many hours in quoting passages in which not one word in ten was to the purpose, and often where they did apply to the question, they directly overset the principles they were brought forward to support." He then delivered a speech, which has been handed down to us corrected by himself ; hence are we enabled to form some opinion of the readiness with which he could answer an opponent, the immense mass of matter connected with the politics of Europe that he had thoroughly digested, and the soundness of the views of the party he represented. Had this speech only remained for the judgment of posterity of the general principles maintained and the soundness of the policy pursued by the advocates for peace, it would have been enough. The frenzy, folly, and rashness of individuals in France had been roused by the surrounding nations, their fears had been excited, great and dreadful enormities had been committed at which the heart shuddered, and which not merely wounded every feeling of humanity, but disgusted and sickened the soul—all this was most true ; but what did it prove ? —what but that eternal and unalterable truth which had always presented itself to his mind. A few days afterwards Sheridan took occasion to explain to the minister, who in his simplicity and innocence seemed to be ignorant of its meaning, the nature of a ministerial job ; and he gave a curious list of persons who had received money for services not performed, observing that he was only influenced by motives of goodwill to the persons. Mr. Pitt very injudiciously asked, if he made that assertion, could any member of the House credit it ? Mr. Sheridan was about to rise, when he was interrupted by Mr. Fox declaring that in his opinion, founded upon experience, Mr. Sheridan had as much personal credit in that House as Mr. Pitt. Sheridan rose : "Whether," said he, "if I repeat my assertion, any member of the House will doubt it or not, I cannot say ; but I believe that it is in this House alone that the right honourable gentleman will venture to tell me so." The subject, however, dropped, after some remarks from Mr.

The Life of Sheridan

Hanley and Mr. Yorke on the impropriety of personalities during the serious business of the House. Mr. Sheridan spoke this session ably on several subjects which have now lost their interest, such as on the naval force at that period, on the defensive state of Halifax, on a petition from Fysche Palmer suffering from imprisonment, on a judgment of the Court of Session in Scotland upon the introduction of foreign troops into the country, on voluntary aid for raising troops without the consent of Parliament, and on taxing placemen upon the suspension of the Habeas Corpus Act.

At length Drury Lane was rebuilt. Heavy had been the expenses and the disappointments; and, above all, the law had been appealed to. On the 10th of March a grand concert, formed of selections from Handel, collected together a large audience, and on the 21st of April the first dramatic performance took place. The play was "Macbeth"; the afterpiece, "The Virgin Unmasked." The prologue on the occasion was by General Fitzpatrick. The house was found generally well adapted for performances, and gave great satisfaction. There was a tribute to the memory of the old house which was universally approved of; a plank of the stage which Garrick had so often trod was preserved, and formed a part of the new flooring. In a short time a little piece was brought out by Sheridan in honour of Lord Howe's victory; it was called the "First of June."

On the 30th of December Parliament met for the despatch of business. Sheridan was at his post, still maintaining the same opinions, still fighting against his great adversary. A speech of his upon the repeal of the Bill for suspending the Habeas Corpus Act gave him an opportunity, of which he fully availed himself, of showing that it was uncalled for by the state of the country; he expatiated on the detestable system of spies and informers, of the charges of sedition, of levying war, of trials, and solemnly asked Mr. Pitt what would be the state of the country which would restore to British freemen the most glorious bulwark of their freedom. Upon Mr. Fox's motion for a committee on the state of the nation he spoke with great ability; the two friends, backed by a small minority, still continued to express with freedom those opinions which were entertained by a large body of men in England, who, satisfied with the security which the laws gave them, wished for no other change but such as would give to the people at large more ample opportunity of expressing their wishes through their representatives, and whose desire was such a reform in the House of Commons as might take from the proprietors of boroughs the preponderating influence they held.

On the 1st of June, Mr. Anstruther, Solicitor-General to the Prince of Wales, as Duke of Cornwall, acquainted the House that his Royal Highness had authorised him to assure the House that he was anxious that some regulation should be adopted for the purpose of establishing order and regularity in the expenditure of his income, and to prevent the incurring of debt in future, and further, to appropriate such a part of his income for the liquidation of his debts as might seem proper to the House. The prince was no longer on terms of intimacy with the leading Whigs, nor did they feel any wish to renew their homage to him. Mr. Grey, although he would vote for his having an income sufficient to support him in his position, would not pay his debts from the money of the people. Mr. Fox asked if he was well advised to apply to the House after the promise in 1787. Mr. Sheridan thought the prince's debts ought to be paid, but his Majesty should set the example. He accused those who had given him advice. By the plan now proposed, the prince had not the grace of suggesting retrenchments, nor the checks upon his future conduct. His past misconduct was exhibited in the harshest point of view ; he was set in a gilded pillory, sent to do public penance in an embroidered sheet. He was left in possession of too much income to exempt him from envy and too little to exempt him from scorn. To pay the debts something ought to be given by the king. He afterwards proposed that the estates belonging to the Duchy of Cornwall should be sold to assist in the liquidation of the debts. Mr. Sheridan continued to make remarks on the king. In the course of the debates he repudiated having received any reward, as had been insinuated, from the Prince of Wales, and positively asserted, in the face of the Parliament and the country, that he had not even been presented with a horse or a picture, and that he was independent in his views and opinions of the royal prince.

Whenever the opportunity presented itself, Sheridan pursued his former friend, Burke, with the same determination he had done in the previous session ; but some of the allusions are now almost unintelligible sarcasms. Ill-natured observations abounded on both sides. A quotation from a convivial writer of the day, Captain Morris, whose songs are almost now forgotten, was hailed from Burke with great cheers by his party, and responded to by Sheridan's friends, when he had with great felicity quoted also from the same author. On the occasion of the Volunteer Bill, Mr. Francis expressed his regret that all freedom of debate was lost by confining every discussion to three or four persons. That if it were the object of eloquence to weary and deaden the attention of an unhappy audience, to exhaust all patience, to stupefy rather than convince, then, indeed, the gentlemen he alluded to were supremely eloquent. Mr. Burke said he should take the hint which was drawn from a writer of very high authority with the gentleman opposite :—

> "Solid men of Boston, make no long potations,
> Solid men of Boston, make no long orations,
>   Bow, wow, wow."

Sheridan observed that the injunction against long orations was not the only moral precept in that system of ethics alluded to. He would remind him of another passage :—

> "He went to Daddy Jenky, by Trimmer Hall attended ;
> In such good company ! good lack ! how his morals must be mended !"

Mr. Burke complained of the attack upon his morals. Sheridan answered : "He had supposed him to have a superabundance, and he might spare some to the gentlemen that surrounded him." Once again was Sheridan called upon to appear in Westminster Hall as an accuser of Warren Hastings. On the 14th of May he replied to the evidence and arguments offered by the counsel for Mr. Hastings in answer to the Begum charge. It was customary for a brother manager to accompany the manager who was to speak, with a bag containing whatever minutes might be referred to. Michael Angelo Taylor was the individual upon whom this duty devolved; and he requested Sheridan to give him the bag and papers. Sheridan's answer was, " He had none, and he must get on as well as he could without them. . . . He would abuse Ned Law, afterwards Lord Ellenborough, ridicule Plumer's long speech, make the court laugh, please the women, and, in short, with Taylor's aid, would get triumphantly through his task." The case was opened, and he got on very well for some time, but the chancellor asked for a minute to which he was referring; Sheridan said his friend Taylor would read it. Mr. Taylor despatched a messenger for the bag, whilst Sheridan requested permission in the meantime to proceed. But soon again the chancellor wished to see the minutes; a great outcry was raised for the bag; the blame was laid on the solicitor's clerk; another messenger was sent off to Sheridan's house. On went Sheridan brilliantly and cleverly; and when the chancellor a third time anxiously required the minute, Sheridan, with great coolness and dignity, said : "On the part of the Commons, and as a manager of the impeachment, I shall conduct my case as I think proper. I mean to be correct, and your lordships, having the printed minutes before you, will afterwards see whether I am right or wrong." Fox, who was in the manager's room, ran eagerly to the Hall, and fearing that Sheridan would suffer inconvenience from the want of the bag, asked Taylor what could be done; he, hiding his mouth with his hand, whispered him, as Moore says, in a tone of which they alone who have heard the gentleman relate the anecdote can feel the full humour, "The man has no bag." The speech itself is so poor, when contrasted with his former efforts upon the same subject, that it is not surprising that it has been univer-

The Life of Sheridan

sally condemned; and the introduction of some observations on woman, her fortitude, her power of bearing suffering, which have been much applauded, was altogether in worse taste than Sheridan usually exhibited. He had, however, upon the two former occasions, exhausted every source of interest, and spoke unprepared and almost forgetful of the subject of his former triumphs.

The session of 1795 commenced untowardly. The people of the humbler class in London were doubtless much irritated at the constant suspicions of disloyalty which the ministers so loudly proclaimed; their irritation was excessive; they disliked the repeal of the Habeas Corpus Act, which they had been taught to believe was the palladium of their liberty. The line of conduct pursued by Mr. Pitt was too evidently in favour of rank and wealth, and of those classes that enjoyed privileges which were denied to them. There was no outlet for the expression of their feelings. The press was gagged; for prosecutions for libel, whilst they only pretended to prevent sedition, were most unwisely urged against the free expression of thoughts very generally entertained by those whom neither corruption nor power could intimidate. The hatred of the system showed itself on the occasion of his Majesty's progress to Parliament for the purpose of opening the session.

On the 29th of October the king went, with the usual pomp, to the House of Peers, an opportunity which the people of London usually embrace to receive the monarch with the expression of the loyalty which animates their hearts. It is not only curiosity which collects so many together, but there is always an anxiety to know how the sovereign will be received.

The Life of Sheridan

The park was on this day thronged, but instead of loud acclamations from a contented people, there were loud murmurs, groans, and threatening words. The carriage was surrounded by persons loudly demanding "the dismissal of Mr. Pitt"; "Peace"; and even the expression "Down with the king!" was heard. As it approached the Horse Guards, stones were thrown at the king's carriage. In passing through Palace Yard a window was broken, and it was asserted that this had been done by an air-gun. His Majesty, with great calmness and composure, proceeded to execute the function for which the day was to be remarked, the delivery of the speech from the throne, and then returned to Buckingham Palace. But the infuriated populace had increased in numbers, in daring, and in violence; and with considerable difficulty did the royal cortège proceed from St. James's to Buckingham Palace. The speech was in every sense of the word unsatisfactory. Sheridan was exceedingly happy in his comments upon it. It commenced with, "It is a great satisfaction to me to reflect that, notwithstanding the many unfavourable events:" he observed, "He would venture to say, if any person could have previously known the speech, and had written to any part of England or Scotland, they would not have found a single man who would not have been surprised at the first noun substantive being 'satisfaction,' or at that substantive being used in any other part of the speech. It was said to be the mark of a resigned and religious temper to be easily satisfied. If that were true, there never were ministers of more meek and primitive piety than the present; for what they had been satisfied he knew not." He then took a view of affairs foreign and domestic, and expressed

The Life of Sheridan

his astonishment that ministers could suffer the king,
when he passed through his starving and oppressed
people — and, sorry was he to hear, irritated and
clamorous people—to come down to the House and
express his satisfaction. He spoke of the wretched
and miserable expedition to Quiberon, where, it was
true, the blood of French emigrants only had flowed.
It was not British blood but British honour that
bled at every vein. He believed that all the efforts
made were to restore the House of Bourbon, a race
always inimical to England as far as he could judge
of the spirit of their intentions. From their prevarica-
tions he thought they were simply watching for an
opportunity of effecting a counter-revolution for the
establishment of monarchy, and placing Louis XVIII.
upon the throne.

The violent conduct of the people had now given
to the administration the pretence which they had so
long wanted. They could no longer be told that dis-
affection existed in their own imaginations, that the
plots were of their own begetting, that their spies and
their informers had concocted the tales which alarmed
the timid and imposed upon the credulous. "The
King of England had," said they, "encountered a
reception such as the regicides of Paris had given to
their king." The Lords and the Commons addressed
the king after evidence had been taken of the outrage of
the day. A bill was brought into the House of Commons for securing the king's person and Government
against treasonable and seditious practices, and several
days were occupied in its consideration. Sheridan
took a prominent part in the discussion, and his
speeches were full of vigour, thought, and wit. During one of the debates he related a curious anecdote

respecting himself, in consequence of some observations of Mr. Hardinge on the licence of the stage, showing that the restrictions were in principle moral and not political. "The origin of the licence was in order to repress indecencies and abuses, such as a man must want common decorum to introduce. As a proof that the licence was sometimes abused, on the night before the first appearance of the 'School for Scandal,' he was informed that it could not be performed, as a licence was refused. It happened at this time there was the famous city contest between Wilkes and Hopkins. The latter had been charged with some practices, similar to those of Moses the Jew, in lending money to young men under age, and it was supposed that the character of the play was levelled at him in order to injure him in his contest, in which he was supported by the ministerial interest. In the warmth of a contested election, the piece was represented as a factious and seditious opposition to a court candidate. Sheridan, however, went to Lord Hertford, then lord chamberlain, who laughed at the affair, and gave the licence. For his own part he deemed a theatre no fit place for politics, nor would he think much of the principles or taste of the man who should wish to introduce them into stage representation." On the 23rd of November Mr. Stuart brought up a petition against the Bill from the London Corresponding Society. He produced a work attributed to Mr. Reeves, the framer and president of several associations against republicans and levellers, in which a doctrine was asserted "that the government of England was a monarchy; but the monarch was the ancient stock from which have sprung those goodly branches of the legislature, the Lords and

The Life of Sheridan

Commons. That these, however, were still only branches, and that they might be lopped off, and the tree be a tree still, shorn, indeed, of its honours, but not, like them, cast into the fire." The pamphlet was read. Sheridan moved "that the said pamphlet is a malicious, scandalous, and seditious libel, containing matter tending to create jealousies and divisions amongst his Majesty's subjects; to alienate the affection from our present form of government, and subvert the true principles of our free constitution, and that the said pamphlet is a high breach of the privileges of this House." He made several speeches, and concluded by moving "that the books be burnt by the common hangman." This punishment was all he proposed. He peremptorily objected to a prosecution. Ministers, however, preferred a trial, as they thought some of its odium would naturally fall on the Whigs, and they did not object to their willingness to increase the list of libellers. Sheridan said that he never recommended prosecutions for libels, because ministers had taken such matters into their own hands. He read a list of fifty or sixty persons who in the last three years had been prosecuted. He knew that if Mr. Reeves were found guilty, he would be called a convicted innocent, as others had been called acquitted felons. The trial, however, was resolved on. Sheridan having been induced no longer to oppose it, of course an acquittal took place, in a case where neither party took any interest in the trial.

The incidents attendant upon Sheridan's first marriage excited some surprise, and if those which marked the second hymen are not altogether as wondrous, they are sufficient to show that he had not forgotten his power over the female heart, and that when he

The Life of Sheridan

chose he could successfully exert it. He was at the mature age of forty-four when the charms of Miss Esther Jane Ogle, daughter of the Dean of Winchester, and grand-daughter of the former Bishop of Winchester, by the mother's side, appeared so irresistible that he was determined, in spite of any obstacle, to become her affianced husband. The first interview of the two personages was anything but flattering to the vanity of Sheridan, and leads us to form an inference that nothing but his determination to conquer, and his firm reliance upon his own resolves, would have ultimately led to a consummation of his hopes. At a fête given at Devonshire House sat Miss Ogle, where Sheridan for the first time saw her. He was walking before her. He heard her exclamation, "Fright! terrible creature!" and other names of similar unmistakable import applied to himself; for this elegant young lady, it seems, with bewitching frankness, was in the habit of openly giving epithets which she thought appropriate to men and things. Sheridan's countenance had, at this period of his life, lost much of the manly beauty it might once have had. Little remained but the brilliancy of his eye. Intemperance had stamped her marks upon his features in legible characters; the purple cheek, the fiery nose, its common offsprings, were too strongly developed not to be discerned by the quick glance of woman; indeed they had already begun to be subjects of public comment, and served for the merriment of a hustings mob, where allusions often, in his latter days more especially, were made to his being able to light a fire by the glare of his nose. Whether Sheridan felt that the young lady's reproach might be true or not, he was at any rate determined that, notwithstanding the visible

The Life of Sheridan

defects of his outward form, he would, by the fascinations of his mind, efface the first impression. Certain it is that he exerted himself to please and succeeded. Even his first advances produced some slight civility, the next meeting a little attention, another a declaration from her that although he was a monster he was very clever ; she subsequently found that though he was very ugly he was very agreeable. Gradually there was a little emotion experienced at his presence ; at length her heart was irresistibly attracted and then altogether lost. He was, indeed, the only man with whom she could live. Mutual vows of love and fidelity were exchanged. The dean, her father, was consulted. Any hint from him at the disparity of their years was unheeded. He in vain hesitated— they urged. He learnt enough of the private affairs of Sheridan to convince him that it would be what the world terms a bad match. He thought that he had found out a decent excuse to prevent the ill-assorted marriage, which was to say that he would not give his consent to his daughter's union with any man who could not put down fifteen thousand pounds in addition to five which he himself would give for a settlement upon his daughter. This, he flattered himself, would bring the affair to a conclusion, for where Sheridan was to find such a sum no ordinary mind could have imagined. But such were the admirable financial contrivances of his future son-in-law, that the dean found the money safely lodged in the banker's hands, to his own confusion, and the astonishment even of the most enthusiastic admirer of the skill of Sheridan. There was no deceit about it ; shares were sold in Drury Lane Theatre, an estate called Polesden, at Leatherhead in Surrey, was purchased ; it was care-

The Life of Sheridan

fully settled upon Mrs. Sheridan and her children, the trustees to this settlement being the late Lord Grey and Mr. Whitbread. The young lady, charming and desperately in love, was quickly united to the man of her choice, and they went to Southampton to enjoy the honeymoon, enraptured in each other's society. Such was the progress of the love-match.

Sheridan of course reflected that he must take an early opportunity of imparting the information of his intended marriage to his son Tom, who was at that moment supposed to be deeply immersed in study, under the care of his tutor, Mr. Smyth, at Bognor, where they had been staying for two or three months without having received the slightest communication. The long silence was at length interrupted by the arrival of a letter whilst they were at the breakfast table.

" MY DEAR TOM,—Meet me at dinner, at six o'clock on Wednesday next, at Guildford; I forget the inn. I want to see you.—Ever your affectionate father,

"R. B. S."

This note startled Tom, who marvelled what his father could have to say; a discussion sprang up between pupil and tutor as to the possible cause of this sudden invitation. Was it to propose a seat in Parliament? could it be to point out a good marriage? was it anything to do with Drury Lane Theatre? Sundry conjectures occupied their minds until the eventful Wednesday arrived, when, followed by his groom, off rode Tom. Mr. Smyth was left alone to ruminate until his pupil's return, which he naturally must have expected on the following day; but the Thursday rolled on without his appearance; Friday,

VOL. I. [241] Q

Saturday, and Sunday—not a line from either father or son. At length, on Monday, came a letter to this effect :—

"MY DEAR MR. SMYTH,—Here I am, have been, and am likely to be. My father I have never seen, and all that I can hear of him is, that instead of dining with me on Wednesday last, he passed through Guildford on his way to town, with four horses and lamps, about 12. I have written to him letter after letter to beg he will send me his orders, and at all events some money, for I have only a few shillings, having paid the turnpikes faithfully, and I am so bored and wearied out with waiting here, and seeing neither father nor money, nor anything but the stable and the street, that I almost begin to wish myself with you and the books again.—Your dutiful pupil,

"T. S."

It must at any rate have been some relief to Mr. Smyth's mind to have read a note acknowledging his pupil's whereabouts ; but what must have been the state of nervous anxiety in which he was kept for the next ten or twelve weeks, during which he had to pace the beach at Bognor, hoping that every succeeding day might bring with it some solution to this strange enigma ? At length came a frank from Sheridan, enclosing an epistle from Tom, which, in some measure, threw a light upon the mysterious occurrences which had naturally excited such singular conduct both from father and son. He learned from it the step, which he characterises as one of extreme folly and vanity on both sides, which Sheridan and Miss Ogle were about to take. He could find some excuse for the lady, who was doubtless dazzled by the reputation and fascinated by the conversation of the man, but none for one who had arrived at a period of life when prudence, if he ever possessed any, was called for, and the exertion of his intellect for more useful purposes in life. The answer was to this effect :—

"MY DEAR MR. SMYTH,—It is not I that am to be married, nor you. Set your heart at rest, it is my father himself; the lady, a Miss Ogle, who lives at Winchester; and that is the history of the Guildford business. About my own age—better me to marry her, you will say. I am not of that opinion. My father talked to me two hours last night, and made out to me that it was the most sensible thing he could do. Was not this very clever of him? Well, my dear Mr. S——, you should have been tutor to him, you see. I am incomparably the most rational of the two, and now and ever, yours very truly and affectionately,   T. S."

Sheridan, who wanted Wanstead "for his hymeneal doves," was desirous to drive thence his volatile son and his amiable tutor, and determined that they should go to Cambridge. Mr. Smyth, who had received for his attention to Tom nothing in the shape of salary, and who saw that, though treated personally with the greatest respect and attention, he was left on every occasion to shift for himself, wrote a strong letter to Sheridan; receiving no answer, he posted to town, determined to tender his resignation. "Never did minister," says he, "enter a royal apartment more full of rage and indignation at the abominable behaviour of his sovereign master than I did the drawing-room of Mr. Sheridan. I have since often thought of the interview that passed, of the skill with which Sheridan conducted himself, the patience with which he listened to my complaints, and the concern which he seemed to express by his countenance when I intimated to him that though I had rather serve him for nothing than the best nobleman in the land for the best salary he could give me, still that my family were in ruin about me, and that it was impossible——; and that he had used me, since his intended marriage, so unceremoniously, and outraged me in a variety of ways so intolerably, that neither with proper prudence nor proper pride could I continue with him any longer; nor would I sanction, by staying with his son, any measure so contrary to my opinion and so pregnant with ruin, as the one now resolved upon, his going to Cambridge." Sheridan listened with great attention, offering little or no resistance. At last he began : "All this ruin and folly, which I entirely confess," said he, "originates in this one source, this marriage of mine with Miss Ogle ; but you know, my dear Smyth," patting him on the shoulder, "no one is very wise on such subjects. I have no place to put her in but Wanstead. I did not consult you about Tom's going to Cambridge, for I knew you would be quite against it. The boy is totally ruined if you do not accompany him. It will be impossible for any one else to have any chance with him, nor should I be satisfied with any one else. I cannot put him in the army, as you suppose ; the ministers really make such blundering expeditions. To crown all, the theatre is out of order ; our last new piece, the 'Iron Chest,' that should have been a golden one, is really iron. And the result of my folly—my madness, if you please—is that I am

worried and tormented to death; and if you, at this
moment, desert me and join this general combination of circumstances against me, I know not what
is to become of me; and, in short, you must give
me further trial, and let me see if I cannot redeem
myself and make you some amends for your kindness and consideration for me. I do not deserve it,
I fully admit."

It may well be imagined that a young and confiding spirit, such as that possessed by Mr. Smyth, was
soon soothed and flattered by similar expressions of
confidence and regard from a man whose genius had
been his charm and delight, and who was looked to,
even then, with all his faults, as one of the greatest
men of the day. He gradually yielded, and, "at
last, like the month of March in the calendar," says
he, "I came into the room like a lion, and went
out like a lamb. I recovered myself," continues he,
"a little as I went downstairs. What a clever
fellow this is, I thought to myself as I went out of
the door; and, after a few paces down the street
I made one discovery more — what a fool am I!"
But the most characteristic incident occurred just
at the conclusion of the interview. "I wrote you a
letter," said Smyth; "it was but an angry one; you
will be so good as to think no more of it." "Oh,
certainly not, my dear Smyth!" replied Sheridan;
"I shall never think of what you have said in it, be
assured." Putting his hand in his pocket, "Here it
is," giving it up to Smyth, who was glad enough to
get hold of it, and throw it into the fire. "Lo and
behold, I saw that it had never been opened!" The
attachment of Sheridan to his son was of the most
affectionate character; his anxiety was constantly

shown at school and whilst he was under the tuition of Mr. Smyth. On one occasion Sheridan sent for him in the greatest haste from Warwickshire, where he was under the tuition of Dr. Parr, having dreamt that he had seen Tom fall from a high tree, the consequence of which had been a broken neck. It is singular that a man of so much common sense should have been so superstitious, but to his dreams he was wont to give implicit confidence ; and another curious fact is that he would neither travel on a Friday nor allow a new play to be brought out upon that, which he considered an unlucky day. If Tom was upon the ice on a frosty day, if he were out shooting, if he were doing anything that Sheridan considered to be attended with danger, there was no peace until he had abandoned it. So much tenderness seems hardly reconcilable with the general conduct of Sheridan ; such, however, was it that it could not but tend to render Mr. Smyth's charge by no means a pleasant one. Attached, however, to the public character of the father, and pleased with the frank, genuine disposition of the son, he seems to have borne, with true philosophy, the awkward position in which he was placed, until no longer human nature could endure it. The younger Sheridan seems to have possessed social qualities of a high order, and to have been endowed with many excellent intellectual qualifications. He had naturally a good voice and a taste for music. Though he returned his father's affection, he was not blind to his faults. He used frequently to lament his indolence and want of regularity, and at times, though proud of his great abilities, was unable to refrain from indulging in sarcasm at his father's expense.

The Life of Sheridan

Tom Sheridan was the idol of the young men at Cambridge, who pronounced him the cleverest fellow in the place, as in point of humour and fun he certainly was. His father once said to him, what really was the case, "Tom, you have genius enough to get a dinner every day in the week at the first tables in London, and that is something, but that is all, you can go no further." They thoroughly understood each other ; the son was equally complimentary to the father, as many well-known anecdotes testify. On one occasion Tom Sheridan complained, over the bottle, to him that his pockets were empty. "Try the highway," was the father's answer. "I have," said Tom, "but I made a bad hit. I stopped a caravan full of passengers, who assured me they had not a farthing, for they all belonged to Drury Lane Theatre and could not get a single penny of their salary." Kelly tells a somewhat similar story. He says that father and son were supping with him one night after the Opera, at a period when Tom expected to get into Parliament. "I think, father," says he, "that many men who are called great patriots in the House of Commons are great humbugs. For my own part, if I get into Parliament I will pledge myself to no party, but write upon my forehead, in legible characters, 'To be let.'" "And under that, Tom," said his father, "'Unfurnished.'" Tom took the joke, but was even with him upon another occasion. Mr. Sheridan had a cottage, about half a mile from Hounslow Heath. Tom, being very short of cash, asked his father to let him have some money. "I have none," was the reply. "Be the consequence what it may, money I must have," said Tom. "If that is the case," said the affectionate parent, "you will find a case of

The Life of Sheridan

loaded pistols upstairs and a horse ready saddled in the stable; the night is dark, and you are within half a mile of Hounslow Heath." "I understand what you mean," said Tom, "but I tried that last night; I unluckily stopped Peake, your treasurer, who told me that you had been beforehand with him, and had robbed him of every sixpence in the world."

The session of this year was not distinguished at its commencement by any striking feature. Sheridan had manfully expressed his opinions and his feelings upon the great points which had been agitated. The minor questions which were now brought forward, and were principally to enable the Government to carry on the war into which they had entered, engrossed but little of his attention. He carefully abstained from throwing any impediments in the way; he simply pointed out the steps which he thought should be pursued, and supported Mr. Fox on every occasion when he thought that support necessary. After a very brilliant speech from that gentleman, on a motion which he made to censure the ministers for advancing money to the Emperor of Austria without the consent of Parliament, Sheridan made an admirable address to the House, which concluded with a contest between Lord Chatham and Mr. Pitt. A motion made by General Fitzpatrick, to obtain the release of La Fayette, through the intercession of his Majesty with the Emperor of Germany, called forth from Sheridan some well-expressed opinions on the infamy of the detention of that great man in the prison of Olmutz. He expressed the highest veneration for his character, and believed that he might vie with the brightest characters in

The Life of Sheridan

English history. To the spirit of a Hampden he united the loyalty of a Falkland.

On the 26th of February, the Ministry was compelled to take a step which alarmed the times and seemed to hold forth the dread of an impending calamity. An order was issued by the Privy Council prohibiting the directors of the Bank of England from issuing any cash payments till the sense of Parliament could be taken, and proper measures adopted to support the public and commercial credit of the kingdom. On the following day a message was sent to the House of Commons, recommending the subject to their immediate and serious attention. The debates were long and arduous, they were frequent and monotonous, yet did Sheridan give unwearying attention to them, and night after night exhibit the same energy and industry of which his adversaries have doubted. The annals of the country show how well he fought her battles, and how sincere he then was, in his bold attacks upon the corruption and profligacy of the system he opposed; occasionally he introduced some happy hits, even upon the driest subjects. Thus, during the debate on the stoppage of cash payments, he made a fanciful allusion to the Bank. "An elderly lady in the city, of great credit and long standing, who had lately made a *faux pas*, which was not altogether inexcusable. She had unfortunately fallen into bad company, and contracted too great an intimacy and connection at the St. James's end of the town. The young gentleman, however, who had employed all his arts of soft persuasion to seduce the old lady, had so far shown his designs, that by timely cutting and breaking off the connection there might be hopes of the old gentlewoman once more regaining her credit and injured reputation." Mr. Harrison's motion for the reduction of useless places gave him an opportunity of making a short but useful appeal to those who were at that time battening upon the public spoil. He more particularly alluded to Mr. Rose, whose name he publicly gave, as one holding several sinecures and situations which amounted to £10,000 annually, so that he did not spare those whom he condemned, and pointed out those whom he accused of corruption. If during the early part of the spring the nation had been somewhat alarmed at the state of its credit, it had now reason to feel the utmost anxiety. A mutiny was announced to have broken out in the Channel fleet; the dismay with which the intelligence was received was unequalled by any terror which the disasters of those times had occasioned. The stoutest hearts quailed, the kingdom was agitated from one end to the other, men looked at each other, as they dreaded that there was something more to be told, and that at last the downfall of the British empire was at hand.

The particular subjects to which Sheridan devoted his attention during the remainder of the session were an expedition to the West Indies, and that to Quiberon Bay. He still continued to enliven the House by his reading, and his sallies of wit and his humour. There are several speeches extant, from which extracts unfortunately cannot be made, which show that he possessed that readiness of reply and quickness of thought which some have denied to him. The dissolution of Parliament, which took place on the 20th of May, sent him back to his constituents at Stafford, who welcomed him there with every mark of respect, and returned him unopposed to the next Parliament.

The Life of Sheridan

Mr. Sheridan now became mixed up in one of those singular literary disputes which at the time of their occurrence excite the deepest interest, but are soon consigned, like every other marvel, to oblivion, excepting amongst those who love the curiosities of literature. William John Ireland was the son of a gentleman well known amongst the well-informed writers of the day. He had published some illustrations of Hogarth which had pleased the public, and he had likewise given to the world other works—"A Picturesque Tour through Holland;" "Picturesque Views on the Rivers Thames and Medway." Young Ireland had received a good education, had early imbibed a love of the drama, and one of his earliest recollections was that he had been delighted by a private play performed at Sheridan's residence in Bruton Street. At the early age of eighteen he wrote a tragedy, but instead of bringing it before the public under his own name, he conceived the singular idea of producing it as a work of Shakespeare's which had accidentally come to light after a long lapse of years. He told his father that a grand discovery had accidentally been made at the house of a gentleman of property; that among a quantity of family papers the contracts between Lowin, Condell, and Shakespeare, and the lease granted by him and Herring to Michael Fraser, had been found; that soon afterwards the deed of gift to William Henry Ireland, described as the friend of Shakespeare, in consequence of having saved his life on the Thames when in extreme danger of being drowned, and also the deed of trust to John Heminge, had been discovered; that in pursuing the search he had been so fortunate as to find some deeds establishing beyond all controversy the title of this gentleman to a considerable property, deeds of which the gentleman was as ignorant as of his having in possession any of the MS. of Shakespeare; that in return for this service, in addition to the remarkable circumstance of the young man bearing the same name and arms with the person who saved Shakespeare's life, the gentleman promised him everything relative to the subject which had been or should be found either in town or at his house in the country. He then produced some MS. It is singular that the father should have lent so credulous an ear to the tale of his son, and should have become his tool; still more so, that so many men of high character and acknowledged talent should not have been able to discover the deception. It seems, from the young man's confession after the discovery, that he learnt to imitate the signature of Shakespeare from the facsimile in Steevens' edition, and by the assistance of a book written in the days of Elizabeth he was enabled to produce something which bore the resemblance to a play written about that period. It is to be regretted that he did not bestow his ingenuity and his assiduity upon a better cause. Had he done so, he would not have been characterised as a forger, but as a man of high talent. A worthy magistrate for London had once said that hanging a man for forgery is an infringement of the privilege of writing; Ireland thought the privilege of writing in imitation of those who are dead was no infringement upon the rights of any one. Men of the highest condition crowded to Norfolk Street; all were in raptures at what they saw; Dr. Parr fell on his knees to thank Heaven he had lived to see the autograph of Shakespeare,

The Life of Sheridan

Dr. Warton and others were equally pleased. The commentators on the great bard, however, were not so easily duped—Malone, Steevens, and Boaden pronounced the documents forgeries.

A goodly folio appeared at the price of £4, 4s., containing miscellaneous papers and legal instruments, under the hand and seal of William Shakespeare, including the tragedy of "King Lear," and a small fragment of "Hamlet," from the original MS. Malone wrote a letter to Lord Charlemont, proclaiming these forgeries. An original play, entitled "Vortigern," was taken to Sheridan, who, like the late Lord Byron, was not so enthusiastic in his admiration of the great dramatist as have been all the leading men of literature for the last two centuries; that, however, he was well acquainted with the writings of the bard, may be judged by an observation which he made whilst perusing it, upon coming to one line : "This is strange, for, though you are acquainted with my opinion of Shakespeare, he always wrote poetry." On reading a little further he laid down the play, observing, "There are certainly some bold ideas, but they are crude and undigested. It is very odd, one would think that Shakespeare must have been very young when he wrote the play. As to the doubting whether it be really his or not, who can possibly look at the papers and not believe them ancient?" The general excitement on the subject fully justified Sheridan in determining to bring out the play at Drury Lane ; and a negotiation was entered into for its purchase, which was at length concluded by the payment to Ireland of three hundred pounds, and an agreement to divide the profits of the performances for sixty nights. An immense assemblage was col-

lected on the 2nd of April, expectation was on the tip-
toe, a handbill was circulated at the entrance doors
complaining of a violent and malevolent attack upon
the MS., promising to produce an answer to the most
illiberal and unfounded assertions in Malone's Inquiry, and "requesting that the play of 'Vortigern'
may be heard with that candour that has ever distinguished a British audience." The appeal was not
in vain. The prologue, which gave Shakespeare as
the author of the play, was read by Mr. Whitfield,
who was too flurried to speak it. Kemble appeared
anything but satisfied with his part ; he, however,
went through it until the audience, provoked by the
poverty of the play, began to express loudly its
dissatisfaction. Kemble came forward, about the
beginning of the fourth act, begging for a candid
hearing. This was granted, until he pronounced
some bombastic lines, which he seemed himself to
feel to be ludicrous. The house bore it no longer ;
Mr. Barrymore attempted in vain to give "Vortigern"
out for repetition ; its fate was sealed, and the stamp
of ridicule was attached to all those who had signed
a document expressive of their confidence in the
genuineness of the forgery, at the head and front of
which stood forth the name of Samuel Parr.

During the greater part of this session the leaders
of the Liberal party took little or no interest in the
proceedings of the House of Commons. They found
that with their small minority it was useless to attempt
to oppose the ministerial measures, and that the
country was sufficiently alive to passing events without having their attention directed to them. On the
14th of December Sheridan and Fox were for the
first time present, and were received with an ironical

The Life of Sheridan

speech from Mr. Yorke. It was briefly noticed by Sheridan, in a speech in opposition to a motion of Mr. Pitt's that the bill for raising a sum for the supplies of the year by an increased assessment of taxes be read a second time. Finding the minority only 50, and the majority 175, he retired from further discussion for the session.

The following session was not allowed to pass by without the display of his varied knowledge and of his political principles. On the 4th of January he delivered an address worthy his great talents. It is ingenious, classical, worthy a statesman. The views on the condition of France and of England show that he had allowed none of the great occurrences of the day to pass without anxious examination and reflection. Some observations on libels were delivered by him on the 4th of April which breathe much sound constitutional doctrine, and in which he states that the rights and liberties of the people owed more to Erskine than any lawyer; but on the 24th of April he made a great impression by the avowal of his dread of French ambition, by an eager desire to show that he was no longer an advocate of that government. A message was brought down from his Majesty stating that he had received information that great preparations were making for the invasion of England, and that the enemy was encouraged by correspondence and communication with traitorous and disaffected persons. He dwelt upon the dangers which threatened the country as of no ordinary magnitude, and wished to rouse and stimulate the nation into exertion, to provide every means of resistance to the insolent menaces and attempts of the enemy. The same evening he expressed his entire disapprobation of a bill, brought into the House by Mr. Pitt, to suspend again the Habeas Corpus Act. He considered the nation's great and best privilege was trial by jury. Any successful attempt to check its attributes or diminish its virtues he regarded as the death-blow to the vitality of constitutional liberty.

No one who reads these speeches can for a moment doubt the genuine patriotism which animated the speaker. It is manly, just, and virtuous, when danger from a foreign foe threaten the subversion of our native land, to forget how great may be the differences of opinion which may exist between parties; to think only of opposing peril, but not wantonly to suspend the liberties of the people, because suspicion is engendered and doubts as to the honesty of some few may exist. Sheridan's opinions were hailed with delight by the great mass, and though amongst those with whom he acted the doctrines he promulgated were not so favourably received, and, indeed, shook his influence with many, he gained a higher degree of popularity than he had ever reached. He had carefully watched the tide of events, and had trimmed his bark in so skilful a manner as to have escaped the rocks and quicksands which threatened his brother Whigs. On the 18th of June he again made a brilliant speech. The subject was one admirably adapted to his powers—"The state of Ireland." With this concluded his efforts during this exciting period. The following year he principally devoted his energies to oppose the means which were taken to bring about the abolition of the Irish Parliament under the specious name of a Union. His principal object was to have the free consent and approbation of the two Parliaments then sitting, and to prevent the Government using either corruption or intimidation to obtain its appearance. Vain were his efforts ; and nearly half a century's experience has shown to us how fallacious were the hopes and promises held out. The evils that then afflicted Ireland have not diminished, and Sheridan's arguments are to this day unanswered—unanswerable. His absence from the general business of the House drew down upon him some censure on occasion of his seconding a motion of Sir Francis Burdett, relative to the state of Cold Bath Fields Prison. He observed, in reply, that nothing would satisfy gentlemen with regard to him ; they blamed him for absenting himself, and took care never to bid him welcome when he came ; but whenever he saw public principle abandoned or humanity outraged, and especially when he saw iniquity protected by the names and authority of members of that House, and the House called upon to give its sanction to such conduct, he would come forward. He then ably supported the liberal baronet, whose noble conduct on the occasion of the disclosures at the prison gained for him that public respect which he enjoyed to the last hour of his highly valuable life.

He made an elaborate speech this session on the failure of the expedition to Holland, and others of some historical interest on the overtures made by Napoleon Bonaparte for peace ; but it began to be evident that he was more careless both in the matter and the manner of his speeches, and in 1801 he spoke but once, and that somewhat feebly.

The session of 1802 was commenced with an incident which excited considerable amusement. The prime minister and Mr. Sheridan, entering the House at the same moment, walked up to the table and

The Life of Sheridan

took the oath at the same time. The premier, who was almost as careless in pecuniary matters as his great opponent, fumbled about in his pockets for two shillings, usually paid, but found nothing. He turned round to Sheridan, who by some extraordinary freak of fortune had money, and was actually able to be a lender and not a borrower. This gave rise to many witticisms. One of the morning papers contained the following paragraph : " Something is certainly on the carpet at present between the ministry and opposition, for we assert, from undoubted authority, that yesterday a loan was negotiated between Mr. Pitt and Mr. Sheridan." On the 14th of May he showed that, however careless he might have grown, he still retained a vigorous fancy, power of sarcasm, and consummate skill in party politics. Mr. Pitt had ceased to be minister of Great Britain ; he had allowed Mr. Addington to seize the reins of government until it might suit him to resume them, and Sheridan took the occasion to speak of the state of parties.

December the 8th he made an admirable speech which separated him still further from Fox, who, having been nobly received by Bonaparte, had conceived a high opinion of him, and designated him as an instrument in the hands of Providence to restore Switzerland to happiness, and to elevate Italy to splendour and importance ; whilst Sheridan pronounced him " an instrument in the hands of Providence to make the English love their constitution better, to cling to it with more fondness, to hang round it with true tenderness." It is impossible by means of extracts to do justice to the beauties contained in this admirable specimen of parliamentary

The Life of Sheridan

eloquence. It made a deep and lasting impression on the country, and did more to urge the nation on to resist the power of the ruler of France than any of the laboured harangues of any of the statesmen of the day.

An offer of the place of registrar to the High Court of Malta was offered for the acceptance of Tom Sheridan by Lord St. Vincent, but was with a high tone of feeling declined by his father, who, determined to avoid giving to his enemies any opportunity of assailing his political character, preferred making a pecuniary sacrifice of no little importance. The subject of the Prince of Wales's establishment was the only one on which he exerted his talents— a humorous description of what majesty would be without its externals, exemplified in the appearance that would be presented were the Speaker and the House to be deprived of their trappings, was the only feature worthy recording. A report was prevalent that Sheridan was prepared to form a coalition with Mr. Addington—his defence of Lord St. Vincent rather led to this idea—but the return of Mr. Pitt to power put a stop to any further thought of this alliance. Sheridan resumed his position. Some speeches made by him on the increase of the military establishments of the country will be perused, even now that the circumstances with which they were accompanied have lost their interest, with the best results, giving as they do incontestable proofs of his parliamentary ability, and his knowledge of the true principles upon which the freedom of a nation is based. Sheridan was now gratified by the recollection of the services which he had rendered the Prince of Wales. He was installed in the office of

The Life of Sheridan

Receiver-General of the Duchy of Cornwall, the noble-man holding that position being in India. He was to fill it until his return in the year 1808; however, it became permanently his own, in consequence of the death of Lord Lake. Upon the death of Mr. Pitt, and the formation of a short-lived administration of the Whig party, Sheridan was appointed Treasurer of the Navy, a situation far beneath his expectation and the talent he had displayed. His want of industry, his known habits of life, took from him the chance of a higher post; nor whilst he filled the one for which he was selected did he show any of his usual ability. The death of Mr. Fox soon drove him from the brief taste of the sweets of office. From that period the instances of his parliamentary exertions are but rare.

On the 24th February occurred the most serious calamity which could have befallen Sheridan—the Theatre Royal, Drury Lane, whose erection had so lately as 1794 been accomplished at so vast expense, was on that day totally destroyed by fire. It happened that there was no performance on that evening : that whilst Sheridan was in attendance in the House of Commons, on the occasion of Mr. Ponsonby's motion on the conduct of the war in Spain, the principal actors and officers of the theatre were enjoying the hospitality of Mr. Richard Wilson at his house in Lincoln's Inn Fields. All was mirth and glee there; a bumper, "Success and prosperity to Drury Lane Theatre," was just pledged around, and the glass raised to the lips, when the youngest daughter of the host rushed into the room, screaming out that Drury Lane Theatre was on fire. All rushed into the square. The fire raged with tremendous fury; the whole horizon was illuminated; no doubt could exist as to the sad truth. Messrs. Peake and Dunn, the treasurers, and Kelly, the acting manager, rushed to the spot, dashed upstairs, and at the hazard of their lives succeeded in saving the iron chest, which contained documents of great importance. The House of Commons was speedily made acquainted with the fearful event—indeed the interior of the House was illuminated by such blazes of light that there could be no doubt that some catastrophe was taking place. Every eye was turned to Sheridan, who sat in respectful silence, whilst that assembly, with due regard to its accomplished member, entertained a motion that the House should be adjourned; but with great composure he said "that whatever might be the extent of the private calamity, he hoped it would not interfere with the public business of the country." Kelly, the acting manager, states that with Roman fortitude he remained at his post whilst his playhouse was burning, and this really appears to have been the case. The ordinary version, as told by Moore, is not only that he left the House, proceeded to Drury Lane, witnessed with a fortitude which strongly interested all who observed him the entire destruction of his property, but gives currency to an anecdote which he does not evidently believe. " It is said that as he sat at the Piazza Coffee-House during the fire, taking some refreshment, a friend of his having remarked on the philosophic calmness with which he bore his misfortune, Sheridan answered, 'A man may surely be allowed to take a glass of wine by his own fireside.' Without vouching for the authenticity or novelty of this anecdote," adds Moore, " which may have been, for aught I know, like the Wandering Jew, a regular attendant upon

The Life of Sheridan

all fires since the time of Hierocles, I give it as I heard it."

The following day the actors assembled to dine with Mr. Wroughton, the stage manager, and Sheridan was requested to meet them, which he did with unusual punctuality. He spoke after dinner in a most feeling and honourable manner, gaining the approbation of all who heard him by the soundness of his advice, and the good taste with which it was given. He strongly inculcated upon the minds of the leading actors the necessity of adhering to each other. He said that he was aware that many of the principal performers might get profitable engagements at the different provincial theatres, but what would then become of the inferior ones, some of whom had large families? "Heaven forbid," he added, "that they should be deserted. No! I most earnestly recommend and entreat that every individual belonging to the concern should be taken care of. Elect yourselves into a committee, but keep in your remembrance even the poor sweepers of the stage, who with their children must starve, if not protected by your fostering care." Such were the sentiments of one who himself stood in the greatest need of consolation, who lost everything, even the pianoforte that belonged to her whom most he had loved to hear sing in harmony to its notes. It was a most embarrassing position in which to be placed, all hopes of rebuilding the house seemed to be at an end. A casual conversation which Sheridan held with Mr. Whitbread led to an arrangement by which an Act of Parliament was obtained for reconstructing it by subscription. It was agreed on that Sheridan was to receive £24,000 for his moiety of the property, £4000 for the property of the fruit offices and reversion of boxes and shares, and that Thomas, his son, was to receive for his quarter £12,000 ; but he was to have no concern or connection of any kind whatever with the new undertaking, nor was he to be paid until the theatre was built. Cruel, bitterly cruel were these stipulations, harshly were they enforced by Whitbread ; and those who read the agonising letters of Sheridan, and the matter-of-fact ones of Whitbread as given by Moore, will readily see that the eclipse of the greatest genius of England is to be attributed to his coming into contact with one of the coldest pieces of organisation that ever moved in any orbit. Sheridan had no money to secure his re-election at Stafford. He was now a broken man, left to the mercy of strangers—a melancholy example of the vanity of trusting to those who usurp the name of friends.

In 1812, for the last time, was heard in the House of Commons that voice which had so frequently been listened to with respect and admiration. Its richness was somewhat diminished, its tones were not so musical, nor was there any attempt to dazzle or to delight. The younger members looked upon George Canning as having already surpassed the favourite of their predecessors. Sheridan seemed conscious that his opponents and his former friends paid less attention to him ; and one evening, in somewhat of a splenetic mood, he observed, " I am now run over by these young ones. I am like an old clock thrust behind the door." "Very true," said a brother wit, Dudley North, "it's all tick, tick, tick with you now." He, however, closed his career with a speech worthy of his mighty talent, on the overtures made by France for peace. He characterised Napoleon as rapacious, insatiable, and treacherous, as one with whom it was

The Life of Sheridan

impossible to negotiate on an honourable basis. He concluded an animated address thus : " If after the general subjugation and ruin of Europe there should ever exist an impartial historian to record the awful events that produced this universal calamity, let that historian have to say Britain fell, and with her fell all the best securities for the charities of human life, for the power, the honour, the fame, the glory, and the liberties, not only of herself, but of the whole civilised world." This speech was in opposition to the opinions of those with whom he usually acted, for they would have unhesitatingly accepted the propositions which were made ; whilst he, firmly believing that no faith was to be kept with Napoleon, protested against them, and declared them to be a wretched manœuvre to cloak his designs upon Russia. Whatever may have been the views of his party, Sheridan's were the most popular with the nation. Happily for the repose of mankind, his voice was listened to amidst the many who thought with him. He must be looked upon as a true patriot, who, laying aside all party considerations and preferring the interests of his country to all others, boldly proclaims his opinions when founded upon honest conviction. Sheridan had the gratification of seeing the overthrow of the man whom he had ever held up to light as an enemy to true freedom, and of seeing the realisation of his long entertained hopes. His political career was now closed. On a dissolution of Parliament he found that Stafford was not prepared to return him ; he had no money ; he had no offices to give to the independent electors. They had not the noble spirit to recollect that he had been the ornament of the country, and that he conferred honour upon them, of which their children

The Life of Sheridan

might be proud to the latest generation, by accepting the post of their representative.

Sheridan usually held his levee in a most extraordinary manner. His visitors were distributed in various rooms according to their station, their intimacy, or their business with him. Some had access to his private room, others lounged about in the library, looking at the paintings, which had the appearance of being covered with dust and dirt; another party occupied the well-worn chairs of the parlours. Up and down paced, with fury in his eye, a determination to speak his mind, and no longer to be wheedled out of his money, some infuriated creditor who for days had in vain beset the avenues of Drury Lane Theatre with the hope of seeing the deeply indebted proprietor. In the butler's room were the equally anxious tradespeople ; there was a vast deal of grumbling everywhere ; each person had some want which must be instantaneously supplied. At every sound each eye was directed to a particular door from which it was expected that, unless the great man stole out quietly and unnoticed, he would at one time or other make his appearance. At length it was opened ; a sweet-toned voice was heard uttering something which seemed to please the listener, if a gentle laugh could enable the stander-by to form a judgment. Sheridan then came out. There was something in his appearance that, even in the days of his intemperance, at once captivated all who saw him. There was in the shape and form of his head, as John Kemble was wont to say, something eminently Shakspearian ; at any rate, the prints of the immortal bard bore some resemblance. His eye was strikingly brilliant ; his hair, powdered in the fashion of the day, softened

The Life of Sheridan

a letter to Sheridan, telling him the situation he had been placed in by the forgetfulness on his part to make the payment at the proper time, and giving him a full, true, and particular account of the unhandsome treatment to which he had been subjected. Sheridan, with great promptitude, sent for the hard-hearted creditor, Henderson, remonstrated with him on the great cruelty of which he had been guilty, reasoned with him on the hardship of the law of imprisonment for debt, made him feel that shutting a man up in a prison was a most unchristian deed, pointed out to him that he had acted arbitrarily, unjustly, until the heart of this most determined creditor was not only thoroughly softened, but his mind led to the conviction that he had done very wrong, and at last his purse was actually offered to Mr. Sheridan, from which, after much unwillingness and decent hesitation on his side and great perseverance on the other, he consented, with considerable reluctance, to draw a sum. Before the interview was concluded, Sheridan had contrived to borrow two hundred pounds from Henderson, and to render him the happiest man alive by condescending to accept such a loan. All, it is true, were not equally fortunate in gaining an interview with him. A gentleman who was one day waiting, as he had been the day before, by appointment in the parlour, observed a gentleman walking about, and in a sort of attempt to be civil to him, unfortunately said to him : "A fine day this. I had the pleasure of seeing you here yesterday." "Yesterday, sir ! Yes, sir, and so you might the day before, and any day for the last six weeks ; and if I have walked one yard, I have walked fifty miles on this damned carpet." This he said, grinding his teeth, his fist clenched, and pacing to and fro with much the appearance of a maniac.

On the first election at Stafford the general voice was all in Sheridan's favour ; his manners were so elegant, his liberality so unbounded, his promises so free, and what was more rare, they were uniformly kept. Each voter who wanted a place, to his great delight, had one given to him ; not one who asked it but was gratified with an offer either at Drury Lane Theatre or the Opera House, to which he immediately repaired and found that he was unhesitatingly installed in his new berth. This generosity gained Sheridan his election ; his return was triumphant; and he had the good fortune always to be enabled to oblige new friends, for most of those who occupied posts quickly resigned them, as their salaries were only promises to pay, which were realised, if at all, at such a distance of time as to wear out the patience of ordinary men. Much of the inconvenience to which Sheridan was subjected arose from his procrastination : whether it was a deed that he had to sign or a letter to frank, he would still put off doing it. Nothing was ever done in time or place. Letters containing money or bearing intelligence of importance remained unopened. Whether private or official business demanded his attention, still was there the same indolence, the same unwillingness to apply, which eventually led to the most serious results.

Professor Smyth was waiting one morning for him in his ante-room, and happened to cast his eyes on a table that stood in the middle of the room covered with manuscripts, plays, pamphlets, and papers of every description. As he proceeded to tumble them over and look at their superscriptions, he observed

letter from Hudson, from whom I have great resources coming. There are *political* events (*home*)
brewing. One letter more will catch me here. Ever
yours,   R. B. S.

"CHARLES WARD, Esq.,
   "Secretary's Office, Theatre, Drury Lane."

Although no man ever made a greater impression
in a social circle in his better days than did
Sheridan, yet, in the later period of his life, he was
generally taciturn for the greater part of the evening,
and towards its close he not unfrequently annoyed the
party by a species of raillery which was sometimes
not at all understood, and was even occasionally
offensive. He would, after playing the accomplished
listener with the utmost deference to each individual,
begin recapitulating all that had passed, repeating,
with sundry observations interspersed with his own
anecdotes, every remark that had been made, exhibiting great shrewdness and a wit of a peculiar
character. He was very fond of a butt, and nobody
ever came in his way of whom he made a better
use than the good-hearted Michael Kelly, a warm
Irishman, whom he loved to represent as an eternal
maker of genuine newly imported blunders. No
man had in those days furnished the stage with
more popular songs than Michael Kelly, but they
all had the reputation of being plagiarisms from the
continental composers. Kelly, finding the world wag
slowly on with him, had an idea of adding to his
occupations as stage-manager and music-seller that
of wine-merchant, in consequence of there being
such good vaults at the Opera House, close to his
warehouse. He consulted Sheridan, who said, "My

dear fellow, write over your door, 'Michael Kelly, composer of wines and importer of music.'" Kelly has, in his "Reminiscences," a version of his own, and adds, as his own repartee, "I will take the hint, Sir, and be a composer of all wines except old Sherry; for that is so notorious for its intoxicating and pernicious qualities, that I should be afraid of poisoning my customers."

Kelly, on another occasion, said a very happy thing to him, according to his own account. One evening that their Majesties honoured Drury Lane with their presence, the play, by royal command, was the "School for Scandal." When Mr. Sheridan was in attendance to light their Majesties to their carriage, the king said to him, "I am much pleased with your comedy of the 'School for Scandal,' but I am still more so with your play of the 'Rivals'; that is my favourite, and I will never give it up." His Majesty at the same time said, "When, Mr. Sheridan, shall we have another play from your masterly pen?" He replied that he was writing a comedy, which he expected very shortly to finish. "I was told of this," says Kelly, "and the next day, walking along Piccadilly, I asked him if he had told the queen that he was writing a play. He said he had, and he was actually about one. 'Not you,' said I to him, 'you will never write again; you are afraid to write.' 'Of whom am I afraid?' said he, fixing his penetrating eye on me. I said, 'You are afraid of the author of the School for Scandal.'" There is an anecdote of this sort that has been ascribed to Garrick, when he heard that Sheridan would bring out the "School for Scandal." "He has," said he, "great things against pleasing the town." "What are they?" was the

The Life of Sheridan

question. "His powerful 'Rivals.'" One of Sheridan's jests against Kelly was that on arriving together at Kemble's house on one occasion, Kelly went up the steps of the house, and begged Sheridan, who was scraping his own shoes, to scrape for him whilst he would knock at the door.

Another blunder, which Sheridan vouched for with perfect gravity, was that Kelly, on peeping through the hole in the stage curtain, exclaimed, "By Jasus, you can't stick a pin's head into any part of the house, it is literally choke-full; but how much fuller will it be to-morrow night when the king comes!" Some of these, although told by Michael Kelly with great good humour, are a little too bad of their kind, such as that on the first night when "Lodoiska" was got up, with great attention to the scenery; but during the storming of the castle, in the last scene, an accident occurred which might have proved fatal to Kelly and to Mrs. Crouch. Sheridan related all the circumstances, in his usual style, to the Duchess of Devonshire, and concluded by saying that Kelly had put a very puzzling question to him, which was— "Suppose, Mr. Sheridan, I had been killed by the fall, who would have maintained me for the rest of my life?"

But certainly the best practical joke that Sheridan played upon Kelly was told by him with the greatest naïveté. On the 2nd of July, a musical piece, called the "Glorious First of June," was brought out with unusual pomp. There was a prologue spoken by John Kemble himself, a grand sea-fight, a splendid fête, and everything was done to give it effect, as it was for the benefit of the widows of those who fell on that memorable occasion. It was brought out in three days; Kelly had been active in getting up the music, and had little time for the study of a part; he therefore went to Sheridan, and entreated him to make his speeches as short as possible, and to give him as little as he could to do. Sheridan received the request with his usual benignity of manner, and gave Kelly his assurance that he would comply with his wish. Kelly had to come on early in the piece to sing a song—"When in war on the ocean we meet the proud foe." There was a cottage in the distance, and Frederic (Kelly) was desired by the stage directions to look earnestly for a moment or two at the cottage and to exclaim, "There stands my Louisa's cottage, she must be either in it or out of it;" he then was to begin his song, and not one other word was there in the whole part. The audience quickly took up the joke, and this sublime and solitary speech produced the loudest laughter. At the conclusion of the entertainment Sheridan went into the green-room, and with the most perfect gravity complimented Kelly on the quickness he had displayed, and at his being so very perfect in the part which he had taken so much pains to write for him; and, considering the short time he had to study it, it was truly astonishing. All these jokes only served to amuse; for, as Kelly himself has said, during the five-and-twenty years through which he enjoyed his friendship, he never heard him say a single word that could wound the feelings of a single individual.

The new theatre at Drury Lane was at length finished, and under the direction of a committee it was opened on the 10th of October with "Hamlet" and the "Devil to Pay," but Sheridan was not present;

and although a resolution had been passed by the committee,[1] offering the use of a box to Mrs. Sheridan, as a gratifying mark of attention to him through her, and the offer had been twice announced by letter from Mr. Whitbread, he studiously avoided entering it for three years. At the end of that time he was persuaded by that excellent-hearted nobleman, the Earl of Essex, to dine with him and accompany him to see Kean, whom he had once only heard in private read Othello, and of whom he had formed a very high opinion. Once there, he found again the spirit of the past. He had left the box, as Lord Essex imagined, to return home, but he found him in the old classic haunt, the green-room, where, surrounded by a happy group of those who under his banners had reaped many a glorious laurel, he was welcomed to a festive scene with the warmest rejoicings; and as they filled bumpers to his health, he once again felt his hopes revive within him and the remembrance of the days that were past, nor did he forget his conversational talent when occasion presented itself to display it.

When dining at the house of Mr. Rogers, with Lord Byron and Moore, the conversation turned upon the addresses which had been sent to the committee of Drury Lane Theatre for selection.

[1] There was something irresistibly ludicrous in the first step taken by this body; "with due modesty and with the true spirit of tradesmen they advertised for the best poetical addresses, to be sealed and delivered within a certain number of days, folded and directed in a given form —in short, like the tender of a public contract." Forty-three persons contended for the prize, but all were rejected, and a composition of Lord Byron's was substituted; the only advantage which the public derived was the publication of one of the most successful series of parodies, under the name of the "Rejected Addresses," that has ever appeared.

The Life of Sheridan

Amongst others who had become competitors was Mr. Whitbread ; his, like the others, in allusion to the New Drury rising out of the fire, had some verses about the phœnix ; but Sheridan said that Whitbread made more of this bird than any of them —he entered into particulars, and described its wings, beak, tail—in short, it was a poulterer's description of a phœnix.

Misery now rapidly accumulated on him ; his creditors hoped, by cruelty exercised on his person, to draw from the pockets of his family and his friends the money which they held dearer than those virtues which Christian charity teaches. At length they seized him, after having taken possession of all that he had ; his books, his jewels, his pictures, even that of his first wife, were become the property of others. He was taken to a spunging-house ! So much was he affected, that upon his release bitter tears flowed rapidly down his cheek ; sensitive of personal honour, he deeply felt the humiliation to which he had been exposed, and ever afterwards spoke with bitterness of that which he called the profanation of his person.

Whatever may have been his distresses owing to his recklessness and his carelessness, both friends and enemies have expressed their belief that Sheridan possessed as anxious a desire to do his duty to his creditors as any man of the nicest sense of honour could do ; but that the untoward events which crowded on him—the fire at Drury Lane, the loss of his seat in Parliament—prevented his carrying out his views. The struggles he had to encounter were those of an honest man hoping to be able to pay, not of a dishonest one anxious to evade his just debts. Had he lived in these more commercial days, he would have escaped much of the obloquy that was heaped upon him.

So much has been urged against his Majesty George the Fourth for his desertion of Sheridan—so anxiously has it been attempted to impress upon the public mind that, forgetful of the earnest devotion, of the unceasing exercise of his talents in behalf of his royal master, he was allowed to linger on in penury and embarrassment without obtaining the slightest notice—that it has become a byword and a blot upon the memory of the monarch. The pen of Moore was dipped in the bitterest gall when he wrote his well-known "Lines on the Death of Sheridan," which hand down to posterity the opinions of Sheridan's friends on the conduct of the sovereign.

Still it would be unjust to pass over in silence those circumstances which, though derived from private sources, deserve to be known, and tend to rescue the character of the king from the charges of neglect and ingratitude. There is no one who does not admit one fact, that when Sheridan lost his seat for Stafford, when "he was excluded both from the theatre and from Parliament, the two anchors by which he held in life were gone, and he was left a lonely and helpless wreck upon the waves," that his Royal Highness offered, at his own expense, to find a seat for him in the House of Commons, that he stepped forward to shield him from the threats of arrest and imprisonment which began to harass him. Writers in the *Westminster* and *Quarterly Reviews* have stated that he actually presented him with £4000 for this purpose. From this statement Mr. Moore withheld his

The Life of Sheridan

belief; but the *Edinburgh Review*, in its admirable discussion of that author's "Life of Sheridan," thus gives the actual case: "With regard to the alleged gift of £4000 by his Majesty, we have the most sincere pleasure in saying that we have every reason to believe that the illustrious person is fully entitled to the credit of that act of munificence, though, according to our information, its unhappy object did not derive from it the benefit which was intended. The sum, which we have heard was about £3000, was by his Royal Highness's order placed in the hands of an attorney for Sheridan's benefit, but was there either attached by his creditors, or otherwise dissipated in such a manner that very little of it actually reached its destination. Nor is it to be forgotten that, however desirous his Royal Highness might have been to assist Sheridan, he was himself an embarrassed man; he had been careless of his own expenditure, and there was not in his treasury the means adequate to afford the relief he might have felt an inclination to give. Every portion of the prince's revenue was apportioned long before it was received, and though there was a sum annually devoted to objects of charity, and to works of benevolence, there was little left for the casual instances which presented themselves. But it was not royal munificence that was required, it was the assistance of his own immediate family that was denied him; the whole of his debts did not amount to £5000, and Mrs. Sheridan's settlement had been £15,000, and, however kind her conduct was towards him from the first moment of his malady, she does not seem to have influenced her friends to step forward to his pecuniary relief. All that has been affirmed of his forlorn situation at the hour of his death is borne out by the testimony of those who saw the utter destitution in which he was. A neglected house, the most deplorable want of the common necessaries of life, of decent control over the servants, whose carelessness, even of the physician's prescriptions, was remarked, do not speak of a wife's domestic management, however pure and sincere may have been her affection."

Professor Smyth has most graphically described what he observed on the melancholy occasion. He was in Kent when he heard that Sheridan was dangerously ill. He immediately went to his house in Saville Row; he was told by one of the old servants that his master was upon his deathbed. Nothing could be more deplorable than the appearance of everything: there were strange-looking people in the hall, the parlour seemed dismantled; on the table lay a bit of paper, thrown carelessly and neglected— it was a prescription—it was a strong cordial. He sent up his card to Mrs. Sheridan, to whose room he was summoned. Collecting all the firmness he could, for he was unprepared for such a meeting, he found Mrs. Sheridan displaying the virtues of her sex with a greater dignity and calmness than he had expected from her. She went to Sheridan for him, who sent by her a kind message to say, if he would wait, he would get ready and see him; but, after waiting, a bell was rung, and an announcement came to say that he was unequal to the interview. "You have come from the country," said Mrs. Sheridan; "you must have something to eat." On his declining it, "You think," said she, "that our poor house can furnish nothing. I do believe we can; let me try," and she rang the bell. He thanked her, but excused himself, telling her he would return the next day. The next day, however, Sheridan was no better; he talked with his wife, but his sensibility prevented his speaking much; she told him that she had sent for her friend, Dr. Howley, the Bishop of London, who had instantly come up from Oxfordshire to pray by him. On Mr. Smyth's venturing to ask after Mr. Sheridan, her reply was, " I never saw such awe as there was painted in his countenance—I shall never forget it." Thus passed away this great man, to whom was entrusted one of the finest minds and originally one of the best hearts.

Melancholy was the close of his existence. Early in the year 1816, symptoms of severe illness gradually exhibited themselves; his habits of life enfeebled his powers of digestion, his anxieties preyed upon his mind, until at length he sank beneath a load of misery. A diseased state of the stomach developed itself, with symptoms of a harassing nature. There was, however, in him a natural tone and vigour of constitution which would have enabled him, with adequate attention to himself, to have withstood the inroads that were making upon his constitution; but he had throughout life suffered but little, and therefore had not a monitor within him to advise a total change of his habits of life, nor to point out the necessity of obtaining medical aid, until at length Dr. Bain, to whose professional assistance his family usually had recourse, felt it his duty to warn him that his life was in danger. The first public notice of his illness was his absence from a dinner in honour of St. Patrick's Day, on which occasion the Duke of

Kent presided, and announced the afflicting cause
of Sheridan's absence. The intelligence was received
with marks of sympathy and affection, but these
were but empty tokens of respect, which, too, would
speedily have been forgotten had not an article
appeared in the *Morning Post* calculated to rouse his
friends from their apathy, and to point out the state in
which he, who was once a public favourite, was now
situated. "Oh, delay not to draw aside the curtain
within which that proud spirit hides its suffering.
Prefer ministering in the chamber of sickness to
mustering at the splendid sorrows that adorn the
hearse. I say, 'Life and succour' against 'Westminster Abbey and a funeral.'" This appeal, which
was made without the name of the sufferer being
mentioned, is ascribed by Moore to one who, though
on no very cordial terms with him, forgot every other
feeling in a generous pity for his fate, and in honest
indignation against those who now deserted him. It
was quickly responded to; at his door the names of
those who stand high in the ranks of the aristocracy,
who had been the friends of his prosperity, were left
as visitors. This was mockery. These great and rich
personages came too late. They should have shown
their feeling for him before. Already had his deathbed been brutally and shamefully outraged; a sheriff's
officer had arrested him—such were the laws of England—even in those fearful agonies when the soul
is about to quit this mortal frame, had prepared to
carry him in his blankets to a vile spunging-house,
and would have perpetrated the horrid act which
would have disgraced the country, had not his physician threatened the man of law with the responsibility which he would incur if the prisoner died

The Life of Sheridan

upon his road—an event of which there was every probability.

On Sunday, July 7, 1816, Sheridan expired. He was then in the sixty-fifth year of his age. The feelings of the public received a shock from an unfounded report that even his corpse was dishonoured, and that it had been arrested. Such an insult upon the morals of a people, such an abuse of the laws of the country, fortunately did not occur, and the rumour has been traced to have arisen out of the circumstance of the body being removed to the house of his attached friend, Mr. Peter Moore, in Great George Street, Westminster, from the residence of Sheridan, in Saville Row, as the distance to the Abbey would render a walking funeral from the shorter distance more convenient. On the following Saturday the last tribute of respect, empty as it was, was paid him by a royal and noble train, who followed the funeral pomp with the usual trappings of outward woe. There were two royal brothers, the Duke of York and the Duke of Sussex. There were noble pall-bearers—the Duke of Bedford, the Earl of Lauderdale, Earl Mulgrave, the Lord Bishop of London, Lord Holland, and Lord Spencer. Mr. Charles Brinsley Sheridan was the chief mourner. Amongst the titled phalanx was the Duke of Argyle, the Marquises of Anglesey and of Tavistock, several earls, lords, viscounts; amongst the least were the two men, "walking humbly side by side," who were the only real friends who soothed his dying hours, the author of the "Pleasures of Memory," Samuel Rogers, and the excellent physician, Dr. Bain. It was with great difficulty that an unoccupied spot could be found in the Poets' Corner for the remains; but at last, close to his great patron and attached

The Life of Sheridan

friend, the immortal Garrick, they found their resting-place, and a plain, flat stone tells the passer-by that there is to be found—

RICHARD BRINSLEY SHERIDAN

BORN 1751

DIED 7TH JULY 1816

THIS MARBLE IS THE TRIBUTE OF AN ATTACHED FRIEND

PETER MOORE.

DRAMATIC WORKS

Sheridan's Dramatic Works

I need scarcely add that the circumstance alluded to was the withdrawing of the piece to remove those imperfections in the first representation which were too obvious to escape reprehension, and too numerous to admit of a hasty correction. There are few writers, I believe, who, even in the fullest consciousness of error, do not wish to palliate the faults which they acknowledge ; and, however trifling the performance, to second their confession of its deficiencies by whatever plea seems least disgraceful to their ability. In the present instance it cannot be said to amount either to candour or modesty in me to acknowledge an extreme inexperience and want of judgment on matters in which, without guidance from practice or spur from success, a young man should scarcely boast of being an adept. If it be said that under such disadvantages no one should attempt to write a play, I must beg leave to dissent from the position, while the first point of experience that I have gained on the subject is a knowledge of the candour and judgment with which an impartial public distinguishes between the errors of inexperience and incapacity, and the indulgence which it shows even to a disposition to remedy the defects of either.

It were unnecessary to enter into any further extenuation of what was thought exceptionable in this play, but that it has been said that the managers should have prevented some of the defects before its appearance to the public, and in particular the uncommon length of the piece as represented the first night. It were an ill return for the most liberal and gentlemanly conduct on their side to suffer any censure to rest where none was deserved. Hurry in writing has long been exploded as an excuse for an

The Rivals

author. However, in the dramatic line it may happen that both an author and a manager may wish to fill a chasm in the entertainment of the public with a hastiness not altogether culpable. The season was advanced when I first put the play into Mr. Harris's hands. It was at that time at least double the length of any acting comedy. I profited by his judgment and experience in the curtailing of it, till I believe his feeling for the vanity of a young author got the better of his desire for correctness, and he left many excrescences remaining, because he had assisted in pruning so many more. Hence, though I was not uninformed that the acts were still too long, I flattered myself that, after the first trial, I might with safer judgment proceed to remove what should appear to have been most dissatisfactory. Many other errors there were which might in part have arisen from my being by no means conversant with plays in general, either in reading or at the theatre. Yet I own that, in one respect, I did not regret my ignorance ; for as my first wish in attempting a play was to avoid every appearance of plagiary, I thought I should stand a better chance of effecting this from being in a walk which I had not frequented, and where, consequently, the progress of invention was less likely to be inter-rupted by starts of recollection : for on subjects on which the mind has been much informed, invention is slow of exerting itself. Faded ideas float in the fancy like half-forgotten dreams, and the imagination in its fullest enjoyments becomes suspicious of its offspring, and doubts whether it has created or adopted.

With regard to some particular passages which on the first night's representation seemed generally dis-

Sheridan's Dramatic Works

liked, I confess that if I felt any emotion of surprise at the disapprobation, it was not that they were disapproved of, but that I had not before perceived that they deserved it. As some part of the attack on the piece was begun too early to pass for the sentence of *judgment*, which is ever tardy in condemning, it has been suggested to me that much of the disapprobation must have arisen from virulence of malice rather than severity of criticism ; but as I was more apprehensive of there being just grounds to excite the latter than conscious of having deserved the former, I continue not to believe that probable which I am sure must have been unprovoked. However, if it was so, and I could even mark the quarter from whence it came, it would be ungenerous to retort, for no passion suffers more than malice from disappointment. For my own part, I see no reason why the author of a play should not regard a first night's audience as a candid and judicious friend attending in behalf of the public at his last rehearsal. If he can dispense with flattery, he is sure at least of sincerity, and even though the annotation be rude, he may rely upon the justness of the comment. Considered in this light, that audience whose *fiat* is essential to the poet's claim, whether his object be fame or profit, has surely a right to expect some deference to its opinion, from principles of politeness at least, if not from gratitude.

As for the little puny critics who scatter their peevish strictures in private circles, and scribble at every author who has the eminence of being unconnected with them, as they are usually spleen-swoln from a vain idea of increasing their consequence, there will always be found a petulance and illiberality in their remarks which should place them as far

The Rivals

beneath the notice of a gentleman as their original dulness had sunk them from the level of the most unsuccessful author.

It is not without pleasure that I catch at an opportunity of justifying myself from the charge of intending any national reflection in the character of Sir Lucius O'Trigger. If any gentlemen opposed the piece from that idea, I thank them sincerely for their opposition ; and if the condemnation of this comedy (however misconceived the provocation) could have added one spark to the decaying flame of national attachment to the country supposed to be reflected on, I should have been happy in its fate, and might with truth have boasted that it had done more real service in its failure than the successful morality of a thousand stage-novels will ever effect.

It is usual, I believe, to thank the performers in a new play for the exertion of their several abilities. But where (as in this instance) their merit has been so striking and uncontroverted as to call for the warmest and truest applause from a number of judicious audiences, the poet's after-praise comes like the feeble acclamation of a child to close the shouts of a multitude. The conduct, however, of the principals in a theatre cannot be so apparent to the public. I think it therefore but justice to declare that from this theatre (the only one I can speak of from experience) those writers who wish to try the dramatic line will meet with that candour and liberal attention, which are generally allowed to be better calculated to lead genius into excellence, than either the precepts of judgment, or the guidance of experience.

THE AUTHOR.

DRAMATIS PERSONÆ

*(As originally acted at Covent Garden Theatre
in 1775)*

Sir Anthony Absolute	Mr. Shuter.
Captain Absolute	Mr. Woodward.
Faulkland	Mr. Lewis.
Acres	Mr. Quick.
Sir Lucius O'Trigger . . .	Mr. Lee.
Fag	Mr. Lee Lewes.
David	Mr. Dunstal.
Thomas	Mr. Fearon.
Mrs. Malaprop	Mrs. Green.
Lydia Languish	Miss Barsanti.
Julia	Mrs. Bulkley.
Lucy	Mrs. Lessingham.

Maid, Boy, Servants, &c.

SCENE—*Bath.*

TIME OF ACTION—*Five Hours.*

The Rivals

PROLOGUE

BY THE AUTHOR

Spoken by Mr. Woodward and Mr. Quick

Enter Serjeant-at-Law, *and* Attorney *following,
and giving a paper.*

Serj. What's here !—a vile cramp hand ! I cannot
see
Without my spectacles.
    Att.   He means his fee.
Nay, Mr. Serjeant, good sir, try again.   [*Gives money.*
    Serj. The scrawl improves ! [*more*] O come, 'tis
pretty plain.
Hey ! how's this ?   Dibble !—sure it cannot be !
A poet's brief ! a poet and a fee !
    Att. Yes, sir ! though you without reward, I know,
Would gladly plead the Muse's cause.
    Serj.   So !—so !
    Att. And if the fee offends, your wrath should fall
On me.
    Serj. Dear Dibble, no offence at all.
    Att. Some sons of Phœbus in the courts we meet,
    Serj. And fifty sons of Phœbus in the Fleet !
    Att. Nor pleads he worse, who with a decent sprig
Of bays adorns his legal waste of wig.
    Serj. Full-bottom'd heroes thus, on signs, unfurl
A leaf of laurel in a grove of curl !
Yet tell your client, that, in adverse days,
This wig is warmer than a bush of bays.
    Att. Do you, then, sir, my client's place supply,
Profuse of robe, and prodigal of tie——

Do you, with all those blushing powers of face,
And wonted bashful hesitating grace,
Rise in the court, and flourish on the case.   [*Exit.*
  Serj. For practice then suppose—this brief will
    show it,—
Me, Serjeant Woodward,—counsel for the poet.
Used to the ground, I know 'tis hard to deal
With this dread court, from whence there's no appeal ;
No tricking here, to blunt the edge of law,
Or, damn'd in equity, escape by flaw :
But judgment given, your sentence must remain ;
No writ of error lies—to Drury Lane !
  Yet when so kind you seem, 'tis past dispute
We gain some favour, if not costs of suit.
No spleen is here ! I see no hoarded fury ;—
I think I never faced a milder jury !
Sad else our plight ! where frowns are transportation,
A hiss the gallows, and a groan damnation !
But such the public candour, without fear
My client waives all right of challenge here.
No newsman from our session is dismiss'd,
Nor wit nor critic we scratch off the list ;
His faults can never hurt another's ease,
His crime, at worst, a bad attempt to please :
Thus, all respecting, he appeals to all,
And by the general voice will stand or fall.

The Rivals

PROLOGUE

BY THE AUTHOR

SPOKEN ON THE TENTH NIGHT BY MRS. BULKLEY

GRANTED our cause, our suit and trial o'er,
The worthy serjeant need appear no more :
In pleasing I a different client choose,
He served the Poet—I would serve the Muse ;
Like him, I'll try to merit your applause,
A female counsel in a female's cause.

    Look on this form,[1]—where humour, quaint and
       sly,
Dimples the cheek, and points the beaming eye ;
Where gay invention seems to boast its wiles
In amorous hint, and half-triumphant smiles ;
While her light mask or covers satire's strokes,
Or hides the conscious blush her wit provokes.
Look on her well—does she seem form'd to teach ?
Should you expect to hear this lady preach ?
Is grey experience suited to her youth ?
Do solemn sentiments become that mouth ?
Bid her be grave, those lips should rebel prove
To every theme that slanders mirth or love.

    Yet, thus adorn'd with every graceful art
To charm the fancy and yet reach the heart——
Must we displace her ? And instead advance
The goddess of the woful countenance—
The sentimental Muse !—Her emblems view,
The Pilgrim's Progress, and a sprig of rue !
View her—too chaste to look like flesh and blood—
Primly portray'd on emblematic wood !

---

[1] Pointing to the figure of Comedy.

Sheridan's Dramatic Works

There, fix'd in usurpation, should she stand,
She'll snatch the dagger from her sister's hand :
And having made her votaries weep a flood,
Good heaven ! she'll end her comedies in blood—
Bid Harry Woodward break poor Dunstal's crown !
Imprison Quick, and knock Ned Shuter down ;
While sad Barsanti, weeping o'er the scene,
Shall stab herself—or poison Mrs. Green.

   Such dire encroachments to prevent in time,
Demands the critic's voice—the poet's rhyme.
Can our light scenes add strength to holy laws !
Such puny patronage but hurts the cause :
Fair virtue scorns our feeble aid to ask ;
And moral truth disdains the trickster's mask,
For here their favourite stands,[1] whose brow severe
And sad, claims youth's respect, and pity's tear ;
Who, when oppress'd by foes her worth creates,
Can point a poniard at the guilt she hates.

[1] Pointing to Tragedy.

The Rivals

ACT I

SCENE I.—*A Street.*

Enter THOMAS. *He crosses the Stage;* FAG *follows, looking after him.*

Fag. What! Thomas! sure 'tis he?—What! Thomas! Thomas!

Thos. Hey!—Odd's life! Mr. Fag!—give us your hand, my old fellow-servant.

Fag. Excuse my glove, Thomas. I'm devilish glad to see you, my lad. Why, my prince of charioteers, you look as hearty!—but who the deuce thought of seeing you in Bath?

Thos. Sure, master, Madam Julia, Harry, Mrs. Kate, and the postillion, be all come.

Fag. Indeed!

Thos. Ay, master thought another fit of the gout was coming to make him a visit; so he'd a mind to gi't the slip, and whip! we were all off at an hour's warning.

Fag. Ay, ay, hasty in everything, or it would not be Sir Anthony Absolute!

Thos. But tell us, Mr. Fag, how does young master? Odd! Sir Anthony will stare to see the captain here!

Fag. I do not serve Captain Absolute now.

Thos. Why, sure!

Fag. At present I am employed by Ensign Beverley.

Thos. I doubt, Mr. Fag, you ha'n't changed for the better.

Fag. I have not changed, Thomas.

Thos. No! Why, didn't you say you had left young master?

Fag. No. Well, honest Thomas, I must puzzle you

no further. Briefly then—Captain Absolute and Ensign Beverley are one and the same person.

Thos. The devil they are !

Fag. So it is indeed, Thomas ; and the ensign half of my master being on guard at present—the captain has nothing to do with me.

Thos. So, so ! What, this is some freak, I warrant ! Do tell us, Mr. Fag, the meaning o't — you know, I ha' trusted you.

Fag. You'll be secret, Thomas ?

Thos. As a coach horse.

Fag. Why, then, the cause of all this is—Love,— Love, Thomas, who (as you may get read to you) has been a masquerader ever since the days of Jupiter.

Thos. Ay, ay ; I guessed there was a lady in the case—but pray, why does your master pass only for ensign ? Now if he had shammed general indeed——

Fag. Ah ! Thomas, there lies the mystery o' the matter. Hark'ee, Thomas, my master is in love with a lady of a very singular taste—a lady who likes him better as a half-pay ensign than if she knew he was son and heir to Sir Anthony Absolute, a baronet of three thousand a year.

Thos. That is an odd taste indeed ! But has she got the stuff, Mr. Fag ? Is she rich, hey ?

Fag. Rich ! Why, I believe she owns half the stocks ! Zounds ! Thomas, she could pay the national debt as easily as I could my washerwoman ! She has a lapdog that eats out of gold, she feeds her parrot with small pearls, and all her thread-papers are made of bank-notes !

Thos. Bravo, faith ! Odd ! I warrant she has a set of thousands at least ; but does she draw kindly with the captain ?

The Rivals

Fag. As fond as pigeons.

Thos. May one hear her name ?

Fag. Miss Lydia Languish. But there is an old tough aunt in the way; though, by-the-bye, she has never seen my master—for we got acquainted with miss while on a visit in Gloucestershire.

Thos. Well—I wish they were once harnessed together in matrimony. But pray, Mr. Fag, what kind of a place is this Bath ? I ha' heard a deal of it—here's a mort o' merry-making, hey ?

Fag. Pretty well, Thomas, pretty well—'tis a good lounge. In the morning we go to the pump-room (though neither my master nor I drink the waters); after breakfast we saunter on the parades, or play a game at billiards; at night we dance; but damn the place, I'm tired of it; their regular hours stupefy me—not a fiddle nor a card after eleven ! However, Mr. Faulkland's gentleman and I keep it up a little in private parties. I'll introduce you there, Thomas—you'll like him much.

Thos. Sure I know Mr. Du-Peigne—you know his master is to marry Madam Julia.

Fag. I had forgot. But, Thomas, you must polish a little—indeed you must. Here now—this wig ! What the devil do you do with a wig, Thomas ? None of the London whips of any degree of *ton* wear wigs now.

Thos. More's the pity ! more's the pity ! I say. Odd's life ! when I heard how the lawyers and doctors had took to their own hair, I thought how 'twould go next. Odd rabbit it ! when the fashion had got foot on the bar, I guessed 'twould mount to the box !—but 'tis all out of character, believe me, Mr. Fag : and look'ee, I'll never gi' up mine—the lawyers and doctors may do as they will.

Fag. Well, Thomas, we'll not quarrel about that.

Thos. Why, bless you, the gentlemen of the professions ben't all of a mind—for in the village now, tho'ff Jack Gauge, the exciseman, has ta'en to his carrots, there's little Dick, the farrier, swears he'll never forsake his bob, though all the college should appear with their own heads!

Fag. Indeed! well said, Dick! But hold—mark! mark! Thomas.

Thos. Zooks! 'tis the captain. Is that the lady with him?

Fag. No, no; that is Madam Lucy, my master's mistress's maid. They lodge at that house—but I must after him to tell him the news.

Thos. Odd! he's giving her money! Well, Mr. Fag——

Fag. Good-bye, Thomas. I have an appointment in Gyde's Porch this evening at eight; meet me there, and we'll make a little party. [*Exeunt severally.*

SCENE II.—*A Dressing-room in* Mrs. MALAPROP'S *Lodgings.*

LYDIA *sitting on a sofa, with a book in her hand.* LUCY, *as just returned from a message.*

Lucy. Indeed, ma'am, I traversed half the town in search of it : I don't believe there's a circulating library in Bath I ha'n't been at.

Lyd. And could not you get *The Reward of Constancy?*

Lucy. No, indeed, ma'am.

Lyd. Nor *The Fatal Connexion?*

Lucy. No, indeed, ma'am.

Lyd. Nor *The Mistakes of the Heart?*

The Rivals

Lucy. Ma'am, as ill luck would have it, Mr. Bull said Miss Sukey Saunter had just fetched it away.

Lyd. Heigh-ho! Did you inquire for *The Delicate Distress?*

Lucy. Or, *The Memoirs of Lady Woodford?* Yes, indeed, ma'am. I asked everywhere for it; and I might have brought it from Mr. Frederick's, but Lady Slattern Lounger, who had just sent it home, had so soiled and dog's-eared it, it wa'n't fit for a Christian to read.

Lyd. Heigh-ho! Yes, I always know when Lady Slattern has been before me. She has a most observing thumb; and, I believe, cherishes her nails for the convenience of making marginal notes. Well, child, what have you brought me?

Lucy. Oh! here, ma'am. [*Taking books from under her cloak, and from her pockets.*] This is *The Gordian Knot,* and this *Peregrine Pickle.* Here are *The Tears of Sensibility,* and *Humphrey Clinker.* This is *The Memoirs of a Lady of Quality, written by herself,* and here the second volume of *The Sentimental Journey.*

Lyd. Heigh-ho! What are those books by the glass?

Lucy. The great one is only *The Whole Duty of Man,* where I press a few blonds, ma'am.

Lyd. Very well—give me the sal volatile.

Lucy. Is it in a blue cover, ma'am?

Lyd. My smelling-bottle, you simpleton!

Lucy. Oh, the drops—here, ma'am.

Lyd. Hold! Here's some one coming—quick, see who it is. [*Exit* LUCY.] Surely I heard my cousin Julia's voice.

Re-enter LUCY.

Lucy. Lud! ma'am, here is Miss Melville.

Lyd. Is it possible!—— [*Exit* LUCY.

Enter JULIA.

Lyd. My dearest Julia, how delighted am I ! [*Embrace.*] How unexpected was this happiness !

Jul. True, Lydia, and our pleasure is the greater. But what has been the matter ? You were denied to me at first !

Lyd. Ah, Julia, I have a thousand things to tell you ! But first inform me what has conjured you to Bath ? Is Sir Anthony here ?

Jul. He is—we are arrived within this hour—and I suppose he will be here to wait on Mrs. Malaprop as soon as he is dressed.

Lyd. Then before we are interrupted, let me impart to you some of my distress ! I know your gentle nature will sympathise with me, though your prudence may condemn me ! My letters have informed you of my whole connection with Beverley ; but I have lost him, Julia ! My aunt has discovered our intercourse by a note she intercepted, and has confined me ever since ! Yet, would you believe it ? she has absolutely fallen in love with a tall Irish baronet she met one night since we have been here, at Lady Macshuffle's rout.

Jul. You jest, Lydia !

Lyd. No, upon my word. She really carries on a kind of correspondence with him, under a feigned name though, till she chooses to be known to him ; but it is a Delia or a Celia, I assure you.

Jul. Then, surely, she is now more indulgent to her niece.

Lyd. Quite the contrary. Since she has discovered her own frailty, she is become more suspicious of mine. Then I must inform you of another plague !

The Rivals

That odious Acres is to be in Bath to-day; so that I protest I shall be teased out of all spirits!

Jul. Come, come, Lydia, hope for the best—Sir Anthony shall use his interest with Mrs. Malaprop.

Lyd. But you have not heard the worst. Unfortunately I had quarrelled with my poor Beverley, just before my aunt made the discovery, and I have not seen him since, to make it up.

Jul. What was his offence?

Lyd. Nothing at all! But, I don't know how it was, as often as we had been together, we had never had a quarrel, and, somehow, I was afraid he would never give me an opportunity. So, last Thursday, I wrote a letter to myself, to inform myself that Beverley was at that time paying his addresses to another woman. I signed it *your friend unknown*, showed it to Beverley, charged him with his falsehood, put myself in a violent passion, and vowed I'd never see him more.

Jul. And you let him depart so, and have not seen him since?

Lyd. 'Twas the next day my aunt found the matter out. I intended only to have teased him three days and a half, and now I've lost him for ever.

Jul. If he is as deserving and sincere as you have represented him to me, he will never give you up so. Yet, consider, Lydia, you tell me he is but an ensign, and you have thirty thousand pounds.

Lyd. But you know I lose most of my fortune if I marry without my aunt's consent, till of age; and that is what I have determined to do, ever since I knew the penalty. Nor could I love the man, who would wish to wait a day for the alternative.

Jul. Nay, this is caprice!

Lyd. What! does Julia tax me with caprice? I thought her lover Faulkland had inured her to it.

Jul. I do not love even his faults.

Lyd. But apropos—you have sent to him, I suppose?

Jul. Not yet, upon my word—nor has he the least idea of my being in Bath. Sir Anthony's resolution was so sudden, I could not inform him of it.

Lyd. Well, Julia, you are your own mistress (though under the protection of Sir Anthony), yet have you, for this long year, been a slave to the caprice, the whim, the jealousy of this ungrateful Faulkland, who will ever delay assuming the right of a husband while you suffer him to be equally imperious as a lover.

Jul. Nay, you are wrong entirely. We were contracted before my father's death. That, and some consequent embarrassments, have delayed what I know to be my Faulkland's most ardent wish. He is too generous to trifle on such a point: and for his character, you wrong him there too. No, Lydia, he is too proud, too noble to be jealous; if he is captious, 'tis without dissembling; if fretful, without rudeness. Unused to the fopperies of love, he is negligent of the little duties expected from a lover—but being un-hackneyed in the passion, his affection is ardent and sincere; and as it engrosses his whole soul, he expects every thought and emotion of his mistress to move in unison with his. Yet, though his pride calls for this full return, his humility makes him undervalue those qualities in him which would entitle him to it; and not feeling why he should be loved to the degree he wishes, he still suspects that he is not loved enough. This temper, I must own, has cost me many

The Rivals

unhappy hours; but I have learned to think myself his debtor for those imperfections which arise from the ardour of his attachment.

Lyd. Well, I cannot blame you for defending him. But tell me candidly, Julia, had he never saved your life, do you think you should have been attached to him as you are? Believe me, the rude blast that overset your boat was a prosperous gale of love to him.

Jul. Gratitude may have strengthened my attachment to Mr. Faulkland, but I loved him before he had preserved me; yet surely that alone were an obligation sufficient.

Lyd. Obligation! why, a water spaniel would have done as much! Well, I should never think of giving my heart to a man because he could swim.

Jul. Come, Lydia, you are too inconsiderate.

Lyd. Nay, I do but jest. What's here?

Re-enter LUCY *in a hurry.*

Lucy. O ma'am, here is Sir Anthony Absolute just come home with your aunt.

Lyd. They'll not come here. Lucy, do **you** watch.

[*Exit* LUCY.

Jul. Yet I must go. Sir Anthony does not know I am here, and if we meet he'll detain me to show me the town. I'll take another opportunity of paying my respects to Mrs. Malaprop, when she shall treat me, as long as she chooses, with her select words so ingeniously misapplied, without being mispronounced.

Re-enter LUCY.

Lucy. O Lud! ma'am, they are both coming up-stairs.

Lyd. Well, I'll not detain you, coz. Adieu, my dear Julia, I'm sure you are in haste to send to Faulkland. There—through my room you'll find another staircase.

Jul. Adieu!   [*Embraces* LYDIA, *and exit.*

Lyd. Here, my dear Lucy, hide these books. Quick, quick. Fling *Peregrine Pickle* under the toilet—throw *Roderick Random* into the closet—put *The Innocent Adultery* into *The Whole Duty of Man*—thrust *Lord Aimworth* under the sofa—cram *Ovid* behind the bolster—there—put *The Man of Feeling* into your pocket—so, so—now lay *Mrs. Chapone* in sight, and leave *Fordyce's Sermons* open on the table.

Lucy. Oh, burn it, ma'am! the hairdresser has torn away as far as *Proper Pride.*

Lyd. Never mind—open at *Sobriety.* Fling me *Lord Chesterfield's Letters.* Now for 'em.

[*Exit* LUCY.

Enter Mrs. MALAPROP *and* Sir ANTHONY ABSOLUTE.

Mrs. Mal. There, Sir Anthony, there sits the deliberate simpleton who wants to disgrace her family, and lavish herself on a fellow not worth a shilling.

Lyd. Madam, I thought you once——

Mrs. Mal. You thought, miss! I don't know any business you have to think at all—thought does not become a young woman. But the point we would request of you is, that you will promise to forget this fellow—to illiterate him, I say, quite from your memory.

Lyd. Ah, madam! our memories are independent of our wills. It is not so easy to forget.

Mrs. Mal. But I say it is, miss; there is nothing on earth so easy as to forget, if a person chooses to set about it. I'm sure I have as much forgot your poor dear uncle as if he had never existed—and I thought it my duty so to do ; and let me tell you, Lydia, these violent memories don't become a young woman.

Sir Anth. Why, sure she won't pretend to remember what she's ordered not !—ay, this comes of her reading !

Lyd. What crime, madam, have I committed, to be treated thus ?

Mrs. Mal. Now don't attempt to extirpate yourself from the matter ; you know I have proof controvertible of it. But tell me, will you promise to do as you're bid ? Will you take a husband of your friends' choosing ?

Lyd. Madam, I must tell you plainly, that had I no preference for any one else, the choice you have made would be my aversion.

Mrs. Mal. What business have you, miss, with preference and aversion ? They don't become a young woman ; and you ought to know, that as both always wear off, 'tis safest in matrimony to begin with a little aversion. I am sure I hated your poor dear uncle before marriage as if he'd been a blackamoor—and yet, miss, you are sensible what a wife I made ! And when it pleased Heaven to release me from him, 'tis unknown what tears I shed ! But suppose we were going to give you another choice, will you promise us to give up this Beverley ?

Lyd. Could I belie my thoughts so far as to give that promise, my actions would certainly as far belie my words.

Mrs. Mal. Take yourself to your room. You are fit company for nothing but your own ill-humours.

Lyd. Willingly, ma'am—I cannot change for the worse. *[Exit.*

Mrs. Mal. There's a little intricate hussy for you !

Sir Anth. It is not to be wondered at, ma'am—all this is the natural consequence of teaching girls to read. Had I a thousand daughters, by Heaven ! I'd as soon have them taught the black art as their alphabet !

Mrs. Mal. Nay, nay, Sir Anthony, you are an absolute misanthropy.

Sir Anth. In my way hither, Mrs. Malaprop, I observed your niece's maid coming forth from a circulating library ! She had a book in each hand—they were half-bound volumes, with marble covers ! From that moment I guessed how full of duty I should see her mistress !

Mrs. Mal. Those are vile places indeed !

Sir Anth. Madam, a circulating library in a town is as an evergreen tree of diabolical knowledge ! It blossoms through the year ! And depend on it, Mrs. Malaprop, that they who are so fond of handling the leaves, will long for the fruit at last.

Mrs. Mal. Fy, fy, Sir Anthony ! you surely speak laconically.

Sir Anth. Why, Mrs. Malaprop, in moderation now, what would you have a woman know ?

Mrs. Mal. Observe me, Sir Anthony. I would by no means wish a daughter of mine to be a progeny of learning ; I don't think so much learning becomes a young woman ; for instance, I would never let her meddle with Greek, or Hebrew, or algebra, or simony, or fluxions, or paradoxes, or such inflammatory branches of learning—neither would it be necessary for her to handle any of your mathematical, astronomical, diabolical instruments. But, Sir Anthony, I would send her, at nine years old, to a boarding-

The Rivals

school, in order to learn a little ingenuity and artifice.
Then, sir, she should have a supercilious knowledge
in accounts; and as she grew up I would have her
instructed in geometry, that she might know something of the contagious countries; but above all,
Sir Anthony, she should be mistress of orthodoxy,
that she might not misspell and mispronounce words
so shamefully as girls usually do ; and likewise that
she might reprehend the true meaning of what she is
saying. This, Sir Anthony, is what I would have a
woman know; and I don't think there is a superstitious article in it.

Sir Anth. Well, well, Mrs. Malaprop, I will dispute
the point no further with you ; though I must confess
that you are a truly moderate and polite arguer, for
almost every third word you say is on my side of the
question. But, Mrs. Malaprop, to the more important
point in debate—you say you have no objection to my
proposal ?

Mrs. Mal. None, I assure you. I am under no
positive engagement with Mr. Acres, and as Lydia is
so obstinate against him, perhaps your son may have
better success.

Sir Anth. Well, madam, I will write for the boy
directly. He knows not a syllable of this yet, though
I have for some time had the proposal in my head.
He is at present with his regiment.

Mrs. Mal. We have never seen your son, Sir
Anthony ; but I hope no objection on his side.

Sir Anth. Objection !—let him object if he dare !
No, no, Mrs. Malaprop, Jack knows that the least
demur puts me in a frenzy directly. My process was
always very simple — in their younger days, 'twas
" Jack, do this"; if he demurred, I knocked him

down, and if he grumbled at that, I always sent him out of the room.

Mrs. Mal. Ay, and the properest way, o' my conscience!—nothing is so conciliating to young people as severity. Well, Sir Anthony, I shall give Mr. Acres his discharge, and prepare Lydia to receive your son's invocations; and I hope you will represent her to the captain as an object not altogether illegible.

Sir Anth. Madam, I will handle the subject prudently. Well, I must leave you; and let me beg you, Mrs. Malaprop, to enforce this matter roundly to the girl. Take my advice—keep a tight hand. If she rejects this proposal, clap her under lock and key; and if you were just to let the servants forget to bring her dinner for three or four days, you can't conceive how she'd come about.   [*Exit.*

Mrs. Mal. Well, at any rate I shall be glad to get her from under my intuition. She has somehow discovered my partiality for Sir Lucius O'Trigger—sure, Lucy can't have betrayed me! No, the girl is such a simpleton, I should have made her confess it. Lucy! Lucy! [*Calls.*] Had she been one of your artificial ones I should never have trusted her.

Re-enter LUCY.

Lucy. Did you call, ma'am?

Mrs. Mal. Yes, girl. Did you see Sir Lucius while you was out?

Lucy. No, indeed, ma'am, not a glimpse of him.

Mrs. Mal. You are sure, Lucy, that you never mentioned——

Lucy. Oh, gemini! I'd sooner cut my tongue out.

Mrs. Mal. Well, don't let your simplicity be imposed on.

The Rivals

Lucy. No, ma'am.

Mrs. Mal. So, come to me presently, and I'll give you another letter to Sir Lucius; but mind, Lucy—if ever you betray what you are entrusted with (unless it be other people's secrets to me), you forfeit my malevolence for ever; and your being a simpleton shall be no excuse for your locality. [*Exit.*

Lucy. Ha! ha! ha! So, my dear Simplicity, let me give you a little respite. [*Altering her manner.*] Let girls in my station be as fond as they please of appearing expert, and knowing in their trusts; commend me to a mask of silliness, and a pair of sharp eyes for my own interest under it! Let me see to what account have I turned my simplicity lately. [*Looks at a paper.*] For *abetting Miss Lydia Languish in a design of running away with an ensign!—in money, sundry times, twelve pound twelve; gowns, five; hats, ruffles, caps, &c. &c., numberless! From the said ensign, within this last month, six guineas and a half*—about a quarter's pay! Item, *from Mrs. Malaprop, for betraying the young people to her*—when I found matters were likely to be discovered — *two guineas and a black paduasoy.* Item, *from Mr. Acres, for carrying divers letters*—which I never delivered—*two guineas, and a pair of buckles.* Item, *from Sir Lucius O'Trigger, three crowns, two gold pocket-pieces, and a silver snuff-box!* Well done, Simplicity! Yet I was forced to make my Hibernian believe that he was corresponding, not with the aunt, but with the niece: for though not over rich, I found he had too much pride and delicacy to sacrifice the feelings of a gentleman to the necessities of his fortune. [*Exit.*

ACT II

Scene I.—Captain Absolute's *Lodgings*.

Captain Absolute *and* Fag.

Fag. Sir, while I was there Sir Anthony came in : I told him you had sent me to inquire after his health, and to know if he was at leisure to see you.

Abs. And what did he say, on hearing I was at Bath ?

Fag. Sir, in my life I never saw an elderly gentleman more astonished !   He started back two or three paces, rapped out a dozen interjectural oaths, and asked what the devil had brought you here.

Abs. Well, sir, and what did you say ?

Fag. Oh, I lied, sir—I forget the precise lie ; but you may depend on't he got no truth from me.   Yet, with submission, for fear of blunders in future, I should be glad to fix what has brought us to Bath, in order that we may lie a little consistently.   Sir Anthony's servants were curious, sir, very curious indeed.

Abs. You have said nothing to them ?

Fag. Oh, not a word, sir—not a word !   Mr. Thomas, indeed, the coachman (whom I take to be the discreetest of whips)——

Abs. 'Sdeath !—you rascal ! you have not trusted him !

Fag. Oh no, sir,—no—no—not a syllable, upon my veracity !   He was, indeed, a little inquisitive ; but I was sly, sir—devilish sly !   My master (said I), honest Thomas (you know, sir, one says honest to one's inferiors), is come to Bath to recruit—Yes, sir, I said to recruit—and whether for men, money, or constitution, you know, sir, is nothing to him, nor any one else.

Abs. Well, recruit will do—let it be so.

Fag. O sir, recruit will do surprisingly — indeed, to give the thing an air, I told Thomas that your honour had already enlisted five disbanded chairmen, seven minority waiters, and thirteen billiard-markers.

Abs. You blockhead, never say more than is necessary.

Fag. I beg pardon, sir—I beg pardon—but, with submission, a lie is nothing unless one supports it. Sir, whenever I draw on my invention for a good current lie, I always forge indorsements as well as the bill.

Abs. Well, take care you don't hurt your credit, by offering too much security. Is Mr. Faulkland returned ?

Fag. He is above, sir, changing his dress.

Abs. Can you tell whether he has been informed of Sir Anthony and Miss Melville's arrival ?

Fag. I fancy not, sir ; he has seen no one since he came in but his gentleman, who was with him at Bristol. I think, sir, I hear Mr. Faulkland coming down——

Abs. Go, tell him I am here.

Fag. Yes, sir. [*Going.*] I beg pardon, sir, but should Sir Anthony call, you will do me the favour to remember that we are recruiting, if you please.

Abs. Well, well.

Fag. And in tenderness to my character, if your honour could bring in the chairmen and waiters, I should esteem it as an obligation ; for though I never scruple a lie to serve my master, yet it hurts one's conscience to be found out.   [*Exit.*

Abs. Now for my whimsical friend; if he does not know that his mistress is here, I'll tease him a little before I tell him.

Enter FAULKLAND.

Faulkland, you're welcome to Bath again; you are punctual in your return.

Faulk. Yes; I had nothing to detain me, when I had finished the business I went on. Well, what news since I left you? How stand matters between you and Lydia?

Abs. Faith, much as they were. I have not seen her since our quarrel; however, I expect to be recalled every hour.

Faulk. Why don't you persuade her to go off with you at once?

Abs. What, and lose two-thirds of her fortune? You forget that, my friend. No, no, I could have brought her to that long ago.

Faulk. Nay, then, you trifle too long; if you are sure of her, propose to the aunt in your own character, and write to Sir Anthony for his consent.

Abs. Softly, softly; for though I am convinced my little Lydia would elope with me as Ensign Beverley, yet am I by no means certain that she would take me with the impediment of our friends' consent, a regular humdrum wedding, and the reversion of a good fortune on my side—no, no; I must prepare her gradually for the discovery, and make myself necessary to her, before I risk it. Well, but Faulkland, you'll dine with us to-day at the hotel?

Faulk. Indeed I cannot; I am not in spirits to be of such a party.

Abs. By heavens! I shall forswear your company.

The Rivals

You are the most teasing, captious, incorrigible lover!
Do love like a man.

Faulk. I own I am unfit for company.

Abs. Am not I a lover; ay, and a romantic one
too? Yet do I carry everywhere with me such a
confounded farrago of doubts, fears, hopes, wishes,
and all the flimsy furniture of a country miss's
brain?

Faulk. Ah! Jack, your heart and soul are not, like
mine, fixed immutably on one only object. You
throw for a large stake, but losing, you could stake
and throw again; but I have set my sum of happiness
on this cast, and not to succeed, were to be stripped
of all.

Abs. But, for Heaven's sake! what grounds for
apprehension can your whimsical brain conjure up
at present?

Faulk. What grounds for apprehension, did you
say? Heavens! are there not a thousand? I fear
for her spirits, her health, her life. My absence may
fret her; her anxiety for my return, her fears for me
may oppress her gentle temper: and for her health,
does not every hour bring me cause to be alarmed?
If it rains, some shower may even then have chilled
her delicate frame! If the wind be keen, some rude
blast may have affected her! The heat of noon, the
dews of the evening, may endanger the life of her for
whom only I value mine. O Jack! when delicate and
feeling souls are separated, there is not a feature in
the sky, not a movement of the elements, not an
aspiration of the breeze, but hints some cause for
a lover's apprehension!

Abs. Ay, but we may choose whether we will take
the hint or not. So then, Faulkland, if you were

convinced that Julia were well and in spirits, you would be entirely content?

Faulk. I should be happy beyond measure. I am anxious only for that.

Abs. Then to cure your anxiety at once—Miss Melville is in perfect health, and is at this moment in Bath.

Faulk. Nay, Jack—don't trifle with me.

Abs. She is arrived here with my father within this hour.

Faulk. Can you be serious?

Abs. I thought you knew Sir Anthony better than to be surprised at a sudden whim of this kind. Seriously, then, it is as I tell you—upon my honour.

Faulk. My dear friend! Hollo, Du Peigne! my hat. My dear Jack, now nothing on earth can give me a moment's uneasiness.

Re-enter FAG.

Fag. Sir, Mr. Acres, just arrived, is below.

Abs. Stay, Faulkland, this Acres lives within a mile of Sir Anthony, and he shall tell you how your mistress has been ever since you left her. Fag, show the gentleman up.   [*Exit* FAG.

Faulk. What, is he much acquainted in the family?

Abs. Oh, very intimate: I insist on your not going; besides, his character will divert you.

Faulk. Well, I should like to ask him a few questions.

Abs. He is likewise a rival of mine—that is, of my other self's, for he does not think his friend, Captain Absolute, ever saw the lady in question; and it is ridiculous enough to hear him complain to me of one Beverley, a concealed, skulking rival, who——

Faulk. Hush! he's here.

[3ı6]

The Rivals

Enter ACRES.

Acres. Ha! my dear friend, noble captain, and honest Jack, how do'st thou? Just arrived, faith, as you see. Sir, your humble servant. Warm work on the roads, Jack! Odds whips and wheels! I've travelled like a comet, with a tail of dust all the way as long as the Mall.

Abs. Ah! Bob, you are indeed an eccentric planet, but we know your attraction hither. Give me leave to introduce Mr. Faulkland to you; Mr. Faulkland, Mr. Acres.

Acres. Sir, I am most heartily glad to see you: sir, I solicit your connections. Hey, Jack—what, this is Mr. Faulkland, who——

Abs. Ay, Bob, Miss Melville's Mr. Faulkland.

Acres. Oddso! she and your father can be but just arrived before me. I suppose you have seen them. Ah, Mr. Faulkland, you are indeed a happy man.

Faulk. I have not seen Miss Melville yet, sir; I hope she enjoyed full health and spirits in Devonshire?

Acres. Never knew her better in my life, sir—never better. Odds blushes and blooms! she has been as healthy as the German Spa.

Faulk. Indeed! I did hear that she had been a little indisposed.

Acres. False, false, sir—only said to vex you: quite the reverse, I assure you.

Faulk. There, Jack, you see she has the advantage of me; I had almost fretted myself ill.

Abs. Now, are you angry with your mistress for not having been sick?

Faulk. No, no, you misunderstand me; yet surely a little trifling indisposition is not an unnatural con-

[317]

sequence of absence from those we love. Now, confess—isn't there something unkind in this violent,
robust, unfeeling health ?

Abs. Oh, it was very unkind of her to be well in
your absence, to be sure !

Acres. Good apartments, Jack.

Faulk. Well, sir, but you was saying that Miss
Melville has been so exceedingly well—what, then,
she has been merry and gay, I suppose ? Always
in spirits, hey ?

Acres. Merry, odds crickets ! she has been the belle
and spirit of the company wherever she has been—so
lively and entertaining ! so full of wit and humour !

Faulk. There, Jack, there. Oh, by my soul ! there
is an innate levity in woman that nothing can overcome. What ! happy, and I away !

Abs. Have done. How foolish this is ! just now
you were only apprehensive for your mistress's spirits.

Faulk. Why, Jack, have I been the joy and spirit of
the company ?

Abs. No, indeed, you have not.

Faulk. Have I been lively and entertaining ?

Abs. Oh, upon my word, I acquit you.

Faulk. Have I been full of wit and humour ?

Abs. No, faith, to do you justice, you have been
confoundedly stupid indeed.

Acres. What's the matter with the gentleman ?

Abs. He is only expressing his great satisfaction at
hearing that Julia has been so well and happy, that's
all—hey, Faulkland ?

Faulk. Oh ! I am rejoiced to hear it—yes, yes, she
has a happy disposition !

Acres. That she has indeed—then she is so accomplished—so sweet a voice—so expert at her harpsichord

The Rivals

—such a mistress of flat and sharp, squallante, rum-blante, and quiverante ! There was this time month—odds minims and crotchets ! how she did chirrup at Mrs. Piano's concert !

Faulk. There again, what say you to this ? You see she has been all mirth and song—not a thought of me !

Abs. Pho ! man, is not music the food of love ?

Faulk. Well, well, it may be so. Pray, Mr. ——, what's his damned name ? Do you remember what songs Miss Melville sung ?

Acres. Not I indeed.

Abs. Stay, now, they were some pretty melancholy purling-stream airs, I warrant ; perhaps you may re-collect. Did she sing, *When absent from my soul's delight?*

Acres. No, that wa'n't it.

Abs. Or, *Go, gentle gales !*   [*Sings.*

Acres. Oh no ! nothing like it. Odds ! now I re-collect one of them—*My heart's my own, my will is free.*   [*Sings.*

Faulk. Fool ! fool that I am ! to fix all my happiness on such a trifler ! 'Sdeath ! to make herself the pipe and ballad-monger of a circle ! to soothe her light heart with catches and glees ! What can you say to this, sir ?

Abs. Why, that I should be glad to hear my mistress had been so merry, sir.

Faulk. Nay, nay, nay—I'm not sorry that she has been happy—no, no, I am glad of that—I would not have had her sad or sick ; yet surely a sympathetic heart would have shown itself even in the choice of a song—she might have been temperately healthy, and somehow, plaintively gay — but she has been dancing too, I doubt not !

Acres. What does the gentleman say about dancing?

Abs. He says the lady we speak of dances as well as she sings.

Acres. Ay, truly does she—there was at our last race ball——

Faulk. Hell and the devil! There!—there—I told you so! I told you so! Oh! she thrives in my absence! Dancing! but her whole feelings have been in opposition with mine. I have been anxious, silent, pensive, sedentary—my days have been hours of care, my nights of watchfulness. She has been all health! spirit! laugh! song! dance! Oh! damned, damned levity!

Abs. For Heaven's sake, Faulkland, don't expose yourself so! Suppose she has danced, what then? Does not the ceremony of society often oblige——

Faulk. Well, well, I'll contain myself—perhaps as you say—for form's sake. What, Mr. Acres, you were praising Miss Melville's manner of dancing a minuet —hey?

Acres. Oh, I dare insure her for that—but what I was going to speak of was her country-dancing. Odds swimmings! she has such an air with her!

Faulk.—Now disappointment on her! Defend this, Absolute; why don't you defend this? Country-dances! jigs and reels! am I to blame now? A minuet I could have forgiven—I should not have minded that—I say I should not have regarded a minuet—but country-dances! Zounds! had she made one in a cotillion—I believe I could have forgiven even that—but to be monkey-led for a night!—to run the gauntlet through a string of amorous palming puppies! to show paces like a managed filly! O Jack, there never can be but one man in the world whom a truly modest and delicate woman ought to pair with in a country-dance; and, even then, the rest of the couples should be her great-uncles and aunts!

Abs. Ay, to be sure!—grandfathers and grandmothers!

Faulk. If there be but one vicious mind in the set,'twill spread like a contagion—the action of their pulse beats to the lascivious movement of the jig—their quivering, warm-breathed sighs impregnate the very air—the atmosphere becomes electrical to love, and each amorous spark darts through every link of the chain! I must leave you. I own I am somewhat flurried—and that confounded looby has perceived it. [*Going.*

Abs. Nay, but stay, Faulkland, and thank Mr. Acres for his good news.

Faulk. Damn his news! [*Exit.*

Abs. Ha! ha! ha! poor Faulkland, five minutes since—"nothing on earth could give him a moment's uneasiness!"

Acres. The gentleman wa'n't angry at my praising his mistress, was he?

Abs. A little jealous, I believe, Bob.

Acres. You don't say so? Ha! ha! jealous of me—that's a good joke.

Abs. There's nothing strange in that, Bob; let me tell you, that sprightly grace and insinuating manner of yours will do some mischief among the girls here.

Acres. Ah! you joke—ha! ha! mischief—ha! ha! but you know I am not my own property, my dear Lydia has forestalled me. She could never abide me in the country, because I used to dress so badly—but odds frogs and tambours! I shan't take matters so here, now ancient madam has no voice in it: I'll make my old clothes know who's master. I shall straightway cashier the hunting-frock, and render my leather breeches incapable. My hair has been in training some time.

Abs. Indeed !

Acres. Ay—and tho'ff the side curls are a little restive, my hind-part takes it very kindly.

Abs. Oh, you'll polish, I doubt not.

Acres. Absolutely I propose so—then if I can find out this Ensign Beverley, odds triggers and flints ! I'll make him know the difference o't.

Abs. Spoke like a man ! But pray, Bob, I observe you have got an odd kind of a new method of swearing——

Acres. Ha ! ha ! you've taken notice of it — 'tis genteel, isn't it ? I didn't invent it myself though ; but a commander in our militia, a great scholar, I assure you, says that there is no meaning in the common oaths, and that nothing but their antiquity makes them respectable ; because, he says, the ancients would never stick to an oath or two, but would say, by Jove ! or by Bacchus ! or by Mars ! or by Venus ! or by Pallas ! according to the sentiment : so that to swear with propriety, says my little major, the oath should be an echo to the sense ; and this we call the *oath referential*, or *sentimental swearing*—ha ! ha ! 'tis genteel, isn't it ?

Abs. Very genteel, and very new, indeed !—and I dare say will supplant all other figures of imprecation.

Acres. Ay, ay, the best terms will grow obsolete. Damns have had their day.

Re-enter FAG.

Fag. Sir, there is a gentleman below desires to see you. Shall I show him into the parlour ?

The Rivals

Abs. Ay—you may.

Acres. Well, I must be gone——

Abs. Stay; who is it, Fag?

Fag. Your father, sir.

Abs. You puppy, why didn't you show him up directly?
　　　　　　　　　　　　　　　　　　[Exit FAG.

Acres. You have business with Sir Anthony. I expect a message from Mrs. Malaprop at my lodgings. I have sent also to my dear friend, Sir Lucius O'Trigger. Adieu, Jack! we must meet at night, when you shall give me a dozen bumpers to little Lydia.

Abs. That I will with all my heart. *[Exit* ACRES.] Now for a parental lecture—I hope he has heard nothing of the business that has brought me here—I wish the gout had held him fast in Devonshire, with all my soul!

Enter SIR ANTHONY ABSOLUTE.

Sir, I am delighted to see you here looking so well! Your sudden arrival at Bath made me apprehensive for your health.

Sir Anth. Very apprehensive, I dare say, Jack. What, you are recruiting here, hey?

Abs. Yes, sir, I am on duty.

Sir Anth. Well, Jack, I am glad to see you, though I did not expect it, for I was going to write to you on a little matter of business. Jack, I have been considering that I grow old and infirm, and shall probably not trouble you long.

Abs. Pardon me, sir, I never saw you look more strong and hearty; and I pray frequently that you may continue so.

Sir Anth. I hope your prayers may be heard, with

[323]

all my heart. Well then, Jack, I have been considering that I am so strong and hearty I may continue to plague you a long time. Now, Jack, I am sensible that the income of your commission, and what I have hitherto allowed you, is but a small pittance for a lad of your spirit.

Abs. Sir, you are very good.

Sir Anth. And it is my wish, while yet I live, to have my boy make some figure in the world. I have resolved, therefore, to fix you at once in a noble independence.

Abs. Sir, your kindness overpowers me — such generosity makes the gratitude of reason more lively than the sensations even of filial affection.

Sir Anth. I am glad you are so sensible of my attention—and you shall be master of a large estate in a few weeks.

Abs. Let my future life, sir, speak my gratitude ; I cannot express the sense I have of your munificence. Yet, sir, I presume you would not wish me to quit the army ?

Sir Anth. Oh, that shall be as your wife chooses.

Abs. My wife, sir !

Sir Anth. Ay, ay, settle that between you—settle that between you.

Abs. A wife, sir, did you say ?

Sir Anth. Ay, a wife—why, did not I mention her before ?

Abs. Not a word of her, sir.

Sir Anth. Odd so !—I mustn't forget her though. Yes, Jack, the independence I was talking of is by a marriage—the fortune is saddled with a wife—but I suppose that makes no difference.

Abs. Sir ! sir !—you amaze me !

The Rivals

Sir Anth. Why, what the devil's the matter with the fool ? Just now you were all gratitude and duty.

Abs. I was, sir ; you talked to me of independence and a fortune, but not a word of a wife.

Sir Anth. Why—what difference does that make ? Odds life, sir ! if you have the estate, you must take it with the live stock on it, as it stands.

Abs. If my happiness is to be the price, I must beg leave to decline the purchase. Pray, sir, who is the lady ?

Sir Anth. What's that to you, sir ? Come, give me your promise to love, and to marry her directly.

Abs. Sure, sir, this is not very reasonable, to summon my affections for a lady I know nothing of !

Sir Anth. I am sure, sir, 'tis more unreasonable in you to object to a lady you know nothing of.

Abs. Then, sir, I must tell you plainly that my inclinations are fixed on another—my heart is engaged to an angel.

Sir Anth. Then pray let it send an excuse. It is very sorry—but business prevents its waiting on her.

Abs. But my vows are pledged to her.

Sir Anth. Let her foreclose, Jack ; let her foreclose ; they are not worth redeeming. Besides, you have the angel's vows in exchange, I suppose ; so there can be no loss there.

Abs. You must excuse me, sir, if I tell you, once for all, that in this point I cannot obey you.

Sir Anth. Hark'ee, Jack ; I have heard you for some time with patience—I have been cool—quite cool ; but take care. You know I am compliance itself—when I am not thwarted ; no one more easily led—when I have my own way ; but don't put me in a frenzy.

Abs. Sir, I must repeat it—in this I cannot obey you.

Sir Anth. Now damn me! if ever I call you Jack again while I live!

Abs. Nay, sir, but hear me.

Sir Anth. Sir, I won't hear a word—not a word! not one word! So give me your promise by a nod— and I'll tell you what, Jack—I mean, you dog—if you don't, by——

Abs. What, sir, promise to link myself to some mass of ugliness! to——

Sir Anth. Zounds! sirrah! the lady shall be as ugly as I choose : she shall have a hump on each shoulder; she shall be as crooked as the crescent; her one eye shall roll like the bull's in Cox's Museum; she shall have a skin like a mummy, and the beard of a Jew— she shall be all this, sirrah!—yet I will make you ogle her all day, and sit up all night to write sonnets on her beauty.

Abs. This is reason and moderation indeed!

Sir Anth. None of your sneering, puppy! no grinning, jackanapes!

Abs. Indeed, sir, I never was in a worse humour for mirth in my life.

Sir Anth. 'Tis false, sir, I know you are laughing in your sleeve; I know you'll grin when I am gone, sirrah!

Abs. Sir, I hope I know my duty better.

Sir Anth. None of your passion, sir! none of your violence, if you please! It won't do with me, I promise you.

Abs. Indeed, sir, I never was cooler in my life.

Sir Anth. 'Tis a confounded lie! I know you are in a passion in your heart; I know you are, you hypocritical young dog! but it won't do.

The Rivals

Abs. Nay, sir, upon my word——

Sir Anth. So you will fly out! can't you be cool like me? What the devil good can passion do? Passion is of no service, you impudent, insolent, over-bearing reprobate! There, you sneer again! don't provoke me!—but you rely upon the mildness of my temper—you do, you dog! You play upon the meekness of my disposition! Yet take care—the patience of a saint may be overcome at last!—but mark! I give you six hours and a half to consider of this: if you then agree, without any condition, to do everything on earth that I choose, why—confound you! I may in time forgive you. If not, zounds! don't enter the same hemisphere with me! don't dare to breathe the same air, or use the same light with me; but get an atmosphere and a sun of your own! I'll strip you of your commission; I'll lodge a five-and-threepence in the hands of trustees, and you shall live on the interest. I'll disown you, I'll disinherit you, I'll unget you! and damn me! if ever I call you Jack again!

[*Exit.*

Abs. Mild, gentle, considerate father—I kiss your hands! What a tender method of giving his opinion in these matters Sir Anthony has! I dare not trust him with the truth. I wonder what old wealthy hag it is that he wants to bestow on me! Yet he married himself for love, and was in his youth a bold intriguer and a gay companion!

Re-enter FAG.

Fag. Assuredly, sir, your father is wrath to a degree; he comes downstairs eight or ten steps at a time—muttering, growling, and thumping the banisters all the way. I and the cook's dog stand bowing at the door—rap! he gives me a stroke on the head with his cane; bids me carry that to my master; then kicking the poor turnspit into the area, damns us all, for a puppy triumvirate! Upon my credit, sir, were I in your place, and found my father such very bad company, I should certainly drop his acquaintance.

Abs. Cease your impertinence, sir, at present. Did you come in for nothing more? Stand out of the way! [*Pushes him aside, and exit.*

Fag. So! Sir Anthony trims my master: he is afraid to reply to his father, then vents his spleen on poor Fag! When one is vexed by one person, to revenge one's self on another who happens to come in the way is the vilest injustice! Ah! it shows the worst temper—the basest——

Enter BOY.

Boy. Mr. Fag! Mr. Fag! your master calls you.

Fag. Well, you little dirty puppy, you need not bawl so! The meanest disposition! the——

Boy. Quick, quick, Mr. Fag!

Fag. Quick! quick! you impudent jackanapes! Am I to be commanded by you too, you little impertinent, insolent, kitchen-bred——

[*Exit kicking and beating him.*

SCENE II.—*The North Parade.*

Enter LUCY.

Lucy. So—I shall have another rival to add to my mistress's list—Captain Absolute. However, I shall not enter his name till my purse has received notice in form. Poor Acres is dismissed! Well, I have done him a last friendly office in letting him know that Beverley was here before him. Sir Lucius is

The Rivals

generally more punctual, when he expects to hear from his *dear Dalia,* as he calls her. I wonder he's not here! I have a little scruple of conscience from this deceit; though I should not be paid so well if my hero knew that Delia was near fifty, and her own mistress.

Enter Sir Lucius O'Trigger.

Sir Luc. Ha! my little ambassadress—upon my conscience, I have been looking for you; I have been on the South Parade this half-hour.

Lucy. [*Speaking simply.*] Oh, gemini! and I have been waiting for your worship here on the North.

Sir Luc. Faith! maybe that was the reason we did not meet; and it is very comical, too, how you could go out and I not see you, for I was only taking a nap at the Parade Coffee-house, and I chose the window on purpose that I might not miss you.

Lucy. My stars! Now I'd wager a sixpence I went by while you were asleep.

Sir Luc. Sure enough it must have been so—and I never dreamt it was so late, till I waked. Well, but my little girl, have you got nothing for me?

Lucy. Yes, but I have—I've got a letter for you in my pocket.

Sir Luc. Oh, faith! I guessed you weren't come empty-handed. Well, let me see what the dear creature says.

Lucy. There, Sir Lucius. [*Gives him a letter.*

Sir Luc. [Reads.] *Sir,—There is often a sudden incentive impulse in love that has a greater induction than years of domestic combination: such was the commotion I felt at the first superfluous view of Sir Lucius O'Trigger.*
—Very pretty, upon my word.—*Female punctuation for-*

bids me to say more; yet let me add that it will give me joy infallible to find Sir Lucius worthy the last criterion of my affections.—DELIA. Upon my conscience, Lucy, your lady is a great mistress of language. Faith, she's quite the queen of the dictionary!—for the devil a word dare refuse coming at her call—though one would think it was quite out of hearing.

Lucy. Ay, sir, a lady of her experience——

Sir Luc. Experience! what, at seventeen?

Lucy. Oh, true, sir—but then she reads so—my stars! how she will read off-hand!

Sir Luc. Faith, she must be very deep read to write this way—though she is rather an arbitrary writer too—for here are a great many poor words pressed into the service of this note that would get their *habeas corpus* from any court in Christendom.

Lucy. Ah! Sir Lucius, if you were to hear how she talks of you!

Sir Luc. Oh, tell her I'll make her the best husband in the world, and Lady O'Trigger into the bargain! But we must get the old gentlewoman's consent, and do everything fairly.

Lucy. Nay, Sir Lucius, I thought you wa'n't rich enough to be so nice!

Sir Luc. Upon my word, young woman, you have hit it; I am so poor that I can't afford to do a dirty action. If I did not want money, I'd steal your mistress and her fortune with a great deal of pleasure. However, my pretty girl [*Gives her money*], here's a little something to buy you a ribbon; and meet me in the evening, and I'll give you an answer to this. So, hussy, take a kiss beforehand to put you in mind.

[*Kisses her.*

Lucy. O Lud! Sir Lucius—I never seed such a

gemman! My lady won't like you if you're so impudent.

Sir Luc. Faith she will, Lucy! That same—pho! what's the name of it?—modesty—is a quality in a lover more praised by the women than liked; so, if your mistress asks you whether Sir Lucius ever gave you a kiss, tell her fifty, my dear.

Lucy. What, would you have me tell her a lie?

Sir Luc. Ah, then, you baggage! I'll make it a truth presently.

Lucy. For shame now! here is some one coming.

Sir Luc. Oh, faith, I'll quiet your conscience!

[*Exit, humming a tune.*

Enter FAG.

Fag. So, so, ma'am! I humbly beg pardon.

Lucy. O Lud! now, Mr. Fag—you flurry one so.

Fag. Come, come, Lucy, here's no one by—so a little less simplicity, with a grain or two more sincerity, if you please. You play false with us, madam. I saw you give the baronet a letter. My master shall know this—and if he don't call him out, I will.

Lucy. Ha! ha! ha! you gentlemen's gentlemen are so hasty. That letter was from Mrs. Malaprop, simpleton. She is taken with Sir Lucius's address.

Fag. How! what tastes some people have! Why, I suppose I have walked by her window a hundred times. But what says our young lady? Any message to my master?

Lucy. Sad news, Mr. Fag. A worse rival than Acres! Sir Anthony Absolute has proposed his son.

Fag. What, Captain Absolute?

Lucy. Even so—I overheard it all.

Fag. Ha! ha! ha! very good, faith! Good-bye, Lucy, I must away with this news.

Lucy. Well, you may laugh—but it is true, I assure you. [*Going.*] But, Mr. Fag, tell your master not to be cast down by this.

Fag. Oh, he'll be so disconsolate!

Lucy. And charge him not to think of quarrelling with young Absolute.

Fag. Never fear! never fear!

Lucy. Be sure—bid him keep up his spirits.

Fag. We will—we will. [*Exeunt severally.*

ACT III

Scene I.—*The North Parade.*

Enter Captain Absolute.

Abs. 'Tis just as Fag told me, indeed. Whimsical enough, faith! My father wants to force me to marry the very girl I am plotting to run away with! He must not know of my connection with her yet awhile. He has too summary a method of proceeding in these matters. However, I'll read my recantation instantly. My conversion is something sudden, indeed — but I can assure him it is very sincere. So, so—here he comes. He looks plaguy gruff. [*Steps aside.*

Enter Sir Anthony Absolute.

Sir Anth. No — I'll die sooner than forgive him. Die, did I say? I'll live these fifty years to plague him. At our last meeting his impudence had almost put me out of temper. An obstinate, passionate, self-willed boy! Who can he take after? This is my return for getting him before all his brothers and

The Rivals

sisters !—for putting him, at twelve years old, into a marching regiment, and allowing him fifty pounds a year, besides his pay, ever since ! But I have done with him ; he's anybody's son for me. I never will see him more, never—never—never.

Abs. [*Aside, coming forward.*] Now for a penitential face.

Sir Anth. Fellow, get out of my way !

Abs. Sir, you see a penitent before you.

Sir Anth. I see an impudent scoundrel before me.

Abs. A sincere penitent. I am come, sir, to acknowledge my error, and to submit entirely to your will.

Sir Anth. What's that ?

Abs. I have been revolving, and reflecting, and considering on your past goodness, and kindness, and condescension to me.

Sir Anth. Well, sir ?

Abs. I have been likewise weighing and balancing what you were pleased to mention concerning duty, and obedience, and authority.

Sir Anth. Well, puppy ?

Abs. Why then, sir, the result of my reflections is— a resolution to sacrifice every inclination of my own to your satisfaction.

Sir Anth. Why, now you talk sense—absolute sense —I never heard anything more sensible in my life. Confound you ! you shall be Jack again.

Abs. I am happy in the appellation.

Sir Anth. Why then, Jack, my dear Jack, I will now inform you who the lady really is. Nothing but your passion and violence, you silly fellow, prevented my telling you at first. Prepare, Jack, for wonder and rapture — prepare. What think you of Miss Lydia Languish ?

Abs. Languish ! What, the Languishes of Worcestershire ?

Sir Anth. Worcestershire ! no. Did you never meet Mrs. Malaprop and her niece, Miss Languish, who came into our country just before you were last ordered to your regiment ?

Abs. Malaprop ! Languish ! I don't remember ever to have heard the names before. Yet, stay—I think I do recollect something. Languish ! Languish ! She squints, don't she ? A little red-haired girl ?

Sir Anth. Squints ! A red-haired girl ! Zounds ! no.

Abs. Then I must have forgot ; it can't be the same person.

Sir Anth. Jack ! Jack ! what think you of blooming, love-breathing seventeen ?

Abs. As to that, sir, I am quite indifferent. If I can please you in the matter, 'tis all I desire.

Sir Anth. Nay, but Jack, such eyes ! such eyes ! so innocently wild ! so bashfully irresolute ! not a glance but speaks and kindles some thought of love ! Then, Jack, her cheeks ! her cheeks, Jack ! so deeply blushing at the insinuations of her tell-tale eyes ! Then, Jack, her lips ! O Jack, lips smiling at their own discretion ; and if not smiling, more sweetly pouting ; more lovely in sullenness !

Abs. That's she, indeed. Well done, old gentleman.   [*Aside.*

Sir Anth. Then, Jack, her neck ! O Jack ! Jack !

Abs. And which is to be mine, sir, the niece or the aunt ?

Sir Anth. Why, you unfeeling, insensible puppy, I despise you ! When I was of your age, such a description would have made me fly like a rocket ! The aunt indeed ! Odds life ! when I ran away with your mother, I would not have touched anything old or ugly to gain an empire.

Abs. Not to please your father, sir ?

Sir Anth. To please my father ! zounds ! not to please—— Oh, my father—odd so !—yes—yes ; if my father indeed had desired—that's quite another matter. Though he wa'n't the indulgent father that I am, Jack.

Abs. I dare say not, sir.

Sir Anth. But, Jack, you are not sorry to find your mistress is so beautiful ?

Abs. Sir, I repeat it—if I please you in this affair, 'tis all I desire. Not that I think a woman the worse for being handsome ; but, sir, if you please to recollect, you before hinted something about a hump or two, one eye, and a few more graces of that kind. Now, without being very nice, I own I should rather choose a wife of mine to have the usual number of limbs, and a limited quantity of back ; and though one eye may be very agreeable, yet as the prejudice has always run in favour of two, I would not wish to affect a singularity in that article.

Sir Anth. What a phlegmatic sot it is ! Why, sirrah, you're an anchorite !—a vile, insensible stock. You a soldier !—you're a walking block, fit only to dust the company's regimentals on ! Odds life ! I have a great mind to marry the girl myself.

Abs. I am entirely at your disposal, sir. If you should think of addressing Miss Languish yourself, I suppose you would have me marry the aunt ; or if you should change your mind, and take the old lady —'tis the same to me—I'll marry the niece.

Sir Anth. Upon my word, Jack, thou'rt either a very great hypocrite, or — but come, I know your

indifference on such a subject must be all a lie—I'm
sure it must—come, now—damn your demure face !—
come, confess, Jack—you have been lying—ha'n't you ?
You have been playing the hypocrite, hey !—I'll never
forgive you, if you ha'n't been lying and playing the
hypocrite.

Abs. I'm sorry, sir, that the respect and duty which
I bear to you should be so mistaken.

Sir Anth. Hang your respect and duty ! But come
along with me ; I'll write a note to Mrs. Malaprop,
and you shall visit the lady directly. Her eyes shall
be the Promethean torch to you—come along. I'll
never forgive you if you don't come back stark mad
with rapture and impatience—if you don't, egad, I will
marry the girl myself ! [*Exeunt.*

SCENE II.—JULIA'S *Dressing-room.*

FAULKLAND *discovered alone.*

Faulk. They told me Julia would return directly ; I
wonder she is not yet come ! How mean does this
captious, unsatisfied temper of mine appear to my
cooler judgment ! Yet I know not that I indulge it
in any other point ; but on this one subject, and to
this one subject, whom I think I love beyond my life,
I am ever ungenerously fretful and madly capricious !
I am conscious of it—yet I cannot correct myself !
What tender, honest joy sparkled in her eyes when
we met ! how delicate was the warmth of her expressions ! I was ashamed to appear less happy—though
I had come resolved to wear a face of coolness and
upbraiding. Sir Anthony's presence prevented my
proposed expostulations ; yet I must be satisfied that
she has not been so very happy in my absence. She

The Rivals

is coming ! Yes !—I know the nimbleness of her tread, when she thinks her impatient Faulkland counts the moments of her stay.

Enter JULIA.

Jul. I had not hoped to see you again so soon.

Faulk. Could I, Julia, be contented with my first welcome—restrained as we were by the presence of a third person ?

Jul. O Faulkland, when your kindness can make me thus happy, let me not think that I discovered something of coldness in your first salutation.

Faulk. 'Twas but your fancy, Julia. I was rejoiced to see you—to see you in such health. Sure I had no cause for coldness ?

Jul. Nay, then, I see you have taken something ill. You must not conceal from me what it is.

Faulk. Well, then—shall I own to you that my joy at hearing of your health and arrival here, by your neighbour Acres, was somewhat damped by his dwelling much on the high spirits you had enjoyed in Devonshire — on your mirth — your singing — dancing, and I know not what ! For such is my temper, Julia, that I should regard every mirthful moment in your absence as a treason to constancy. The mutual tear that steals down the cheek of parting lovers is a compact that no smile shall live there till they meet again.

Jul. Must I never cease to tax my Faulkland with this teasing minute caprice ? Can the idle reports of a silly boor weigh in your breast against my tried affection ?

Faulk. They have no weight with me, Julia. No, no—I am happy if you have been so—yet only say that you did not sing with mirth—say that you thought of Faulkland in the dance.

Jul. I never can be happy in your absence. If I wear a countenance of content, it is to show that my mind holds no doubt of my Faulkland's truth. If I seemed sad, it were to make malice triumph, and say that I had fixed my heart on one who left me to lament his roving and my own credulity. Believe me, Faulkland, I mean not to upbraid you when I say that I have often dressed sorrow in smiles, lest my friends should guess whose unkindness had caused my tears.

Faulk. You were ever all goodness to me. Oh, I am a brute when I but admit a doubt of your true constancy !

Jul. If ever without such cause from you, as I will not suppose possible, you find my affections veering but a point, may I become a proverbial scoff for levity and base ingratitude.

Faulk. Ah ! Julia, that last word is grating to me. I would I had no title to your gratitude ! Search your heart, Julia ; perhaps what you have mistaken for love is but the warm effusion of a too thankful heart.

Jul. For what quality must I love you ?

Faulk. For no quality ! To regard me for any quality of mind or understanding were only to esteem me. And for person—I have often wished myself deformed, to be convinced that I owed no obligation there for any part of your affection.

Jul. Where nature has bestowed a show of nice attention in the features of a man, he should laugh at it as misplaced. I have seen men, who in this vain article, perhaps, might rank above you ; but my heart has never asked my eyes if it were so or not.

Faulk. Now this is not well from you, Julia—I

The Rivals

despise person in a man—yet if you loved me as I wish, though I were an Æthiop, you'd think none so fair.

Jul. I see you are determined to be unkind! The contract which my poor father bound us in gives you more than a lover's privilege.

Faulk. Again, Julia, you raise ideas that feed and justify my doubts. I would not have been more free. No! I am proud of my restraint. Yet—yet—perhaps your high respect alone for this solemn compact has fettered your inclinations, which else had made a worthier choice. How shall I be sure, had you remained unbound in thought and promise, that I should still have been the object of your persevering love?

Jul. Then try me now. Let us be free as strangers as to what is past. My heart will not feel more liberty!

Faulk. There now! so hasty, Julia! so anxious to be free! If your love for me were fixed and ardent, you would not lose your hold, even though I wished it!

Jul. Oh! you torture me to the heart! I cannot bear it.

Faulk. I do not mean to distress you. If I loved you less I should never give you an uneasy moment. But hear me. All my fretful doubts arise from this. Women are not used to weigh and separate the motives of their affections. The cold dictates of prudence, gratitude, or filial duty may sometimes be mistaken for the pleadings of the heart. I would not boast—yet let me say that I have neither age, person, nor character, to found dislike on; my fortune such as few ladies could be charged with indis-

cretion in the match. O Julia! when love receives
such countenance from prudence, nice minds will be
suspicious of its birth.

Jul. I know not whither your insinuations would
tend; but as they seem pressing to insult me, I will
spare you the regret of having done so. I have given
you no cause for this! [*Exit in tears.*

Faulk. In tears! Stay, Julia; stay but for a
moment.—The door is fastened!—Julia! my soul!—
but for one moment! I hear her sobbing!—'Sdeath!
what a brute am I to use her thus! Yet stay.—Ay,
she is coming now. How little resolution there is in
woman! How a few soft words can turn them!
No, faith! she is not coming either. Why, Julia—
my love—say but that you forgive me—come but to
tell me that—now this is being too resentful. Stay!
she is coming too—I thought she would—no steadiness in anything: her going away must have been a
mere trick then—she sha'nt see that I was hurt by it.
I'll affect indifference. [*Hums a tune: then listens.*]
No—zounds! she's not coming!—nor don't intend it,
I suppose. This is not steadiness, but obstinacy!
Yet I deserve it. What, after so long an absence to
quarrel with her tenderness! 'Twas barbarous and
unmanly! I should be ashamed to see her now. I'll
wait till her just resentment is abated; and when I
distress her so again, may I lose her for ever! and be
linked instead to some antique virago, whose gnawing
passions and long-hoarded spleen shall make me
curse my folly half the day and all the night. [*Exit.*

The Rivals

Mrs. Malaprop, *with a letter in her hand, and*
Captain Absolute.

Mrs. Mal. Your being Sir Anthony's son, captain,
would itself be a sufficient accommodation; but
from the ingenuity of your appearance, I am convinced you deserve the character here given of you.

Abs. Permit me to say, madam, that as I never yet
have had the pleasure of seeing Miss Languish, my
principal inducement in this affair at present is the
honour of being allied to Mrs. Malaprop, of whose
intellectual accomplishments, elegant manners, and
unaffected learning, no tongue is silent.

Mrs. Mal. Sir, you do me infinite honour! I beg,
captain, you'll be seated. [*They sit.*] Ah! few
gentlemen nowadays know how to value the ineffec-
tual qualities in a woman! Few think how a little
knowledge becomes a gentlewoman! Men have no
sense now but for the worthless flower of beauty!

Abs. It is but too true, indeed, ma'am; yet I fear
our ladies should share the blame. They think our
admiration of beauty so great, that knowledge in them
would be superfluous. Thus, like garden trees, they
seldom show fruit, till time has robbed them of the
more specious blossom. Few, like Mrs. Malaprop
and the orange-tree, are rich in both at once!

Mrs. Mal. Sir, you overpower me with good breeding.—He is the very pine-apple of politeness!—You
are not ignorant, captain, that this giddy girl has
somehow contrived to fix her affections on a beggarly,
strolling, eavesdropping ensign, whom none of us
have seen, and nobody knows anything of.

Abs. Oh, I have heard the silly affair before. I'm not at all prejudiced against her on that account.

Mrs. Mal. You are very good and very considerate, captain. I am sure I have done everything in my power since I exploded the affair; long ago I laid my positive conjunctions on her never to think on the fellow again. I have since laid Sir Anthony's preposition before her; but, I am sorry to say, she seems resolved to decline every particle that I enjoin her.

Abs. It must be very distressing indeed, ma'am.

Mrs. Mal. Oh! it gives me the hydrostatics to such a degree. I thought she had persisted from corresponding with him; but behold, this very day, I have interceded another letter from the fellow. I believe I have it in my pocket.

Abs. Oh, the devil! my last note.   [*Aside.*

Mrs. Mal. Ay, here it is.

Abs. Ay, my note indeed! Oh, the little traitress Lucy.   [*Aside.*

Mrs. Mal. There, perhaps you may know the writing.   [*Gives him the letter.*

Abs. I think I have seen the hand before—yes, I certainly must have seen this hand before——

Mrs. Mal. Nay, but read it, captain.

Abs. [Reads.] *My soul's idol, my adored Lydia!*— Very tender indeed.

Mrs. Mal. Tender; ay, and profane too, o' my conscience.

Abs. [Reads.] *I am excessively alarmed at the intelligence you send me, the more so as my new rival*——

Mrs. Mal. That's you, sir.

Abs. [Reads.] *has universally the character of being an accomplished gentleman and a man of honour.*—Well, that's handsome enough.

Mrs. Mal. Oh, the fellow has some design in writing so.

Abs. That he had, I'll answer for him, ma'am.

Mrs. Mal. But go on, sir—you'll see presently.

Abs. [Reads.] *As for the old weather-beaten she-dragon who guards you*—Who can he mean by that?

Mrs. Mal. Me, sir!—me!—he means me! There —what do you think now? But go on a little further.

Abs. Impudent scoundrel! [Reads.] *it shall go hard, but I will elude her vigilance, as I am told that the same ridiculous vanity which makes her dress up her coarse features, and deck her dull chat with hard words which she don't understand——*

Mrs. Mal. There, sir, an attack upon my language! What do you think of that?—an aspersion upon my parts of speech!—was ever such a brute! Sure, if I reprehend anything in this world, it is the use of my oracular tongue, and a nice derangement of epitaphs!

Abs. He deserves to be hanged and quartered! Let me see. [Reads.] *same ridiculous vanity——*

Mrs. Mal. You need not read it again, sir.

Abs. I beg pardon, ma'am. [Reads.] *does also lay her open to the grossest deceptions from flattery and pretended admiration*—an impudent coxcomb!—*so that I have a scheme to see you shortly with the old harridan's consent, and even to make her a go-between in our interview.*—Was ever such assurance!

Mrs. Mal. Did you ever hear anything like it? He'll elude my vigilance, will he? Yes, yes! ha! ha! he's very likely to enter these doors! We'll try who can plot best!

Abs. So we will, ma'am—so we will! Ha! ha! ha! a conceited puppy, ha! ha! ha! Well, but Mrs. Malaprop, as the girl seems so infatuated by this fellow, suppose you were to wink at her corresponding with him for a little time—let her even plot an elopement with him; then do you connive at her escape—while I, just in the nick, will have the fellow laid by the heels, and fairly contrive to carry her off in his stead.

Mrs. Mal. I am delighted with the scheme; never was anything better perpetrated!

Abs. But, pray, could not I see the lady for a few minutes now? I should like to try her temper a little.

Mrs. Mal. Why, I don't know—I doubt she is not prepared for a visit of this kind. There is a decorum in these matters.

Abs. O Lord! she won't mind me. Only tell her Beverley——

Mrs. Mal. Sir!

Abs. Gently, good tongue.   [*Aside.*

Mrs. Mal. What did you say of Beverley?

Abs. Oh, I was going to propose that you should tell her, by way of jest, that it was Beverley who was below. She'd come down fast enough then—ha! ha! ha!

Mrs. Mal. 'Twould be a trick she well deserves; besides, you know, the fellow tells her he'll get my consent to see her—ha! ha! Let him if he can, I say again. Lydia, come down here! [*Calling.*] He'll make me a go-between in their interviews!—ha! ha! ha! Come down, I say, Lydia! I don't wonder at your laughing—ha! ha! ha! His impudence is truly ridiculous.

Abs. 'Tis very ridiculous, upon my soul, ma'am—ha! ha! ha!

Mrs. Mal. The little hussy won't hear. Well, I'll

go and tell her at once who it is—she shall know that Captain Absolute is come to wait on her. And I'll make her behave as becomes a young woman.

Abs. As you please, ma'am.

Mrs. Mal. For the present, captain, your servant. Ah! you've not done laughing yet, I see—elude my vigilance; yes, yes; ha! ha! ha!   [*Exit.*

Abs. Ha! ha! ha! one would think now that I might throw off all disguise at once, and seize my prize with security; but such is Lydia's caprice, that to undeceive were probably to lose her. I'll see whether she knows me.

[*Walks aside, and seems engaged in looking at the pictures.*

Enter LYDIA.

Lyd. What a scene am I now to go through! Surely nothing can be more dreadful than to be obliged to listen to the loathsome addresses of a stranger to one's heart. I have heard of girls persecuted as I am, who have appealed in behalf of their favoured lover to the generosity of his rival: suppose I were to try it. There stands the hated rival— an officer, too!—but oh, how unlike my Beverley! I wonder he don't begin; truly he seems a very negligent wooer!—quite at his ease, upon my word! I'll speak first. Mr. Absolute!   [*Turns round.*

Abs. Ma'am.

Lyd. O heavens! Beverley!

Abs. Hush!—hush, my life!—softly! be not surprised!

Lyd. I am so astonished, and so terrified, and so overjoyed! For Heaven's sake! how came you here?

Abs. Briefly, I have deceived your aunt. I was informed that my new rival was to visit here this evening, and contriving to have him kept away, have passed myself on her for Captain Absolute.

Lyd. Oh, charming! And she really takes you for young Absolute?

Abs. Oh, she's convinced of it.

Lyd. Ha! ha! ha! I can't forbear laughing to think how her sagacity is overreached!

Abs. But we trifle with our precious moments—such another opportunity may not occur; then let me now conjure my kind, my condescending angel, to fix the time when I may rescue her from undeserving persecution, and with a licensed warmth plead for my reward.

Lyd. Will you, then, Beverley, consent to forfeit that portion of my paltry wealth?—that burden on the wings of love?

Abs. Oh, come to me—rich only thus—in loveliness! Bring no portion to me but thy love. 'Twill be generous in you, Lydia—for well you know, it is the only dower your poor Beverley can repay.

Lyd. How persuasive are his words!—how charming will poverty be with him!   [*Aside.*

Abs. Ah! my soul, what a life will we then live! Love shall be our idol and support!—we will worship him with a monastic strictness; abjuring all worldly toys, to centre every thought and action there. Proud of calamity, we will enjoy the wreck of wealth; while the surrounding gloom of adversity shall make the flame of our pure love show doubly bright. By Heavens! I would fling all goods of fortune from me with a prodigal hand, to enjoy the scene where I might clasp my Lydia to my bosom and say, the

The Rivals

world affords no smile to me but here. [*Embracing her.*] If she holds out now, the devil is in it !

[*Aside.*

Lyd. Now could I fly with him to the antipodes ! but my persecution is not yet come to a crisis.

[*Aside.*

Re-enter MRS. MALAPROP, *listening.*

Mrs. Mal. I am impatient to know how the little hussy deports herself. [*Aside.*

Abs. So pensive, Lydia ! Is, then, your warmth abated ?

Mrs. Mal. Warmth abated !—so !—she has been in a passion, I suppose. [*Aside.*

Lyd. No—nor ever can while I have life.

Mrs. Mal. An ill-tempered little devil ! She'll be in a passion all her life, will she ? [*Aside.*

Lyd. Think not the idle threats of my ridiculous aunt can ever have any weight with me.

Mrs. Mal. Very dutiful, upon my word ! [*Aside.*

Lyd. Let her choice be Captain Absolute, but Beverley is mine.

Mrs. Mal. I am astonished at her assurance !—to his face—this is to his face ! [*Aside.*

Abs. Thus, then, let me enforce my suit. [*Kneeling.*

Mrs. Mal. [*Aside.*] Ay, poor young man ! Down on his knees entreating for pity ! I can contain no longer. [*Coming forward.*] Why, thou vixen ! I have overheard you.

Abs. Oh, confound her vigilance ! [*Aside.*

Mrs. Mal. Captain Absolute, I know not how to apologise for her shocking rudeness.

Abs. [*Aside.*] So all's safe, I find. [*Aloud.*] I have hopes, madam, that time will bring the young lady——

Sheridan's Dramatic Works

Mrs. Mal. Oh, there's nothing to be hoped for from her ! She's as headstrong as an allegory on the banks of Nile.

Lyd. Nay, madam, what do you charge me with now ?

Mrs. Mal. Why, thou unblushing rebel—didn't you tell this gentleman to his face that you loved another better ? Didn't you say you never would be his ?

Lyd. No, madam—I did not.

Mrs. Mal. Good Heavens ! what assurance ! Lydia, Lydia, you ought to know that lying don't become a young woman ! Didn't you boast that Beverley, that stroller Beverley, possessed your heart ? Tell me that, I say.

Lyd. 'Tis true, ma'am, and none but Beverley——

Mrs. Mal. Hold !—hold, Assurance !—you shall not be so rude.

Abs. Nay, pray, Mrs. Malaprop, don't stop the young lady's speech ; she's very welcome to talk thus —it does not hurt me in the least, I assure you.

Mrs. Mal. You are too good, captain—too amiably patient—but come with me, miss. Let us see you again soon, captain. Remember what we have fixed.

Abs. I shall, ma'am.

Mrs. Mal. Come, take a graceful leave of the gentleman.

Lyd. May every blessing wait on my Beverley, my loved Bev——

Mrs. Mal. Hussy ! I'll choke the word in your throat !—come along—come along.

> [*Exeunt severally ;* CAPTAIN ABSOLUTE *kissing his hand to* LYDIA—MRS. MALAPROP *stopping her from speaking.*

The Rivals

ACRES, *as just dressed, and* DAVID.

Acres. Indeed, David—do you think I become it so ?

Dav. You are quite another creature, believe me, master. By the mass ! an' we've any luck we shall see the Devon monkerony in all the print-shops in Bath !

Acres. Dress does make a difference, David.

Dav. 'Tis all in all, I think. Difference ! why, an' you were to go now to Clod Hall, I am certain the old lady wouldn't know you : Master Butler wouldn't believe his own eyes, and Mrs. Pickle would cry, Lard presarve me ! our dairymaid would come giggling to the door, and I warrant Dolly Tester, your honour's favourite, would blush like my waistcoat. Oons ! I'll hold a gallon, there an't a dog in the house but would bark, and I question whether Phillis would wag a hair of her tail !

Acres. Ay, David, there's nothing like polishing.

Dav. So I says of your honour's boots ; but the boy never heeds me !

Acres. But, David, has Mr. De-la-grace been here ? I must rub up my balancing, and chasing, and boring.

Dav. I'll call again, sir.

Acres. Do—and see if there are any letters for me at the post-office.

Dav. I will. By the mass ! I can't help looking at your head !—if I hadn't been by at the cooking, I wish I may die if I should have known the dish again myself !   [*Exit.*

Acres. [*Practising a dancing-step.*] Sink, slide —

coupee. Confound the first inventors of cotillons!
say I—they are as bad as algebra to us country
gentlemen. I can walk a minuet easy enough when
I am forced !—and I have been accounted a good
stick in a country-dance. Odds jigs and tabors ! I
never valued your cross-over to couple—figure in—
right and left—and I'd foot it with e'er a captain in the
county !—but these outlandlish heathen allemandes
and cotillons are quite beyond me ! I shall never
prosper at 'em, that's sure — mine are true - born
English legs — they don't understand their curst
French lingo !—their *pas* this, and *pas* that, and *pas*
t'other ! Damn me ! my feet don't like to be called
paws ! No, 'tis certain I have most Antigallican toes !

Enter SERVANT.

Serv. Here is Sir Lucius O'Trigger to wait on you,
sir.

Acres. Show him in.   [*Exit* SERVANT.

Enter SIR LUCIUS O'TRIGGER.

Sir Luc. Mr. Acres, I am delighted to embrace you.

Acres. My dear Sir Lucius, I kiss your hands.

Sir Luc. Pray, my friend, what has brought you so
suddenly to Bath ?

Acres. Faith ! I have followed Cupid's Jack-a-
lantern, and find myself in a quagmire at last. In
short, I have been very ill-used, Sir Lucius. I don't
choose to mention names, but look on me as on a
very ill-used gentleman.

Sir Luc. Pray what is the case ? I ask no names.

Acres. Mark me, Sir Lucius, I fall as deep as need
be in love with a young lady—her friends take my
part—I follow her to Bath—send word of my arrival ;

and receive answer that the lady is to be otherwise disposed of. This, Sir Lucius, I call being ill-used.

Sir Luc. Very ill, upon my conscience. Pray, can you divine the cause of it ?

Acres. Why, there's the matter ; she has another lover, one Beverley, who, I am told, is now in Bath. Odds slanders and lies ! he must be at the bottom of it.

Sir Luc. A rival in the case, is there ? And you think he has supplanted you unfairly ?

Acres. Unfairly ! to be sure he has. He never could have done it fairly.

Sir Luc. Then sure you know what is to be done ?

Acres. Not I, upon my soul !

Sir Luc. We wear no swords here, but you understand me.

Acres. What ! fight him !

Sir Luc. Ay, to be sure. What can I mean else ?

Acres. But he has given me no provocation.

Sir Luc. Now, I think he has given you the greatest provocation in the world. Can a man commit a more heinous offence against another than to fall in love with the same woman ? Oh, by my soul ! it is the most unpardonable breach of friendship.

Acres. Breach of friendship ! Ay, ay, but I have no acquaintance with this man. I never saw him in my life.

Sir Luc. That's no argument at all—he has the less right, then, to take such a liberty.

Acres. Gad, that's true—I grow full of anger, Sir Lucius ! I fire apace ! Odds hilts and blades ! I find a man may have a deal of valour in him and not know it ! But couldn't I contrive to have a little right of my side ?

Sheridan's Dramatic Works

Sir Luc. What the devil signifies right when your honour is concerned ? Do you think Achilles, or my little Alexander the Great, ever inquired where the right lay ? No, by my soul ! they drew their broadswords, and left the lazy sons of peace to settle the justice of it.

Acres. Your words are a grenadier's march to my heart ! I believe courage must be catching ! I certainly do feel a kind of valour rising as it were—a kind of courage, as I may say. Odds flints, pans, and triggers ! I'll challenge him directly.

Sir Luc. Ah, my little friend, if I had Blunderbuss Hall here, I could show you a range of ancestry, in the O'Trigger line, that would furnish the new room ; every one of whom had killed his man ! For though the mansion - house and dirty acres have slipped through my fingers, I thank Heaven our honour and the family-pictures are as fresh as ever.

Acres. Oh, Sir Lucius ! I have had ancestors too !— every man of 'em colonel or captain in the militia ! Odds balls and barrels ! say no more—I'm braced for it. The thunder of your words has soured the milk of human kindness in my breast. Zounds ! as the man in the play says, *I could do such deeds !*

Sir Luc. Come, come, there must be no passion at all in the case—these things should always be done civilly.

Acres. I must be in a passion, Sir Lucius—I must be in a rage. Dear Sir Lucius, let me be in a rage, if you love me. Come, here's pen and paper. [*Sits down to write.*] I would the ink were red ! Indite, I say indite ! How shall I begin ? Odds bullets and blades ! I'll write a good bold hand, however.

Sir Luc. Pray compose yourself.

The Rivals

Acres. Come—now, shall I begin with an oath? Do, Sir Lucius, let me begin with a damme.

Sir Luc. Pho! pho! do the thing decently, and like a Christian. Begin now—*Sir*——

Acres. That's too civil by half.

Sir Luc. To prevent the confusion that might arise——

Acres. Well——

Sir Luc. From our both addressing the same lady——

Acres. Ay, there's the reason—*same lady*—well——

Sir Luc. I shall expect the honour of your company——

Acres. Zounds! I'm not asking him to dinner.

Sir Luc. Pray be easy.

Acres. Well, then, *honour of your company*——

Sir Luc. To settle our pretensions——

Acres. Well.

Sir Luc. Let me see—ay, King's-Mead-Fields will do—*in King's-Mead-Fields.*

Acres. So, that's done. Well, I'll fold it up presently; my own crest—a hand and dagger—shall be the seal.

Sir Luc. You see now this little explanation will put a stop at once to all confusion or misunderstanding that might arise between you.

Acres. Ay, we fight to prevent any misunderstanding.

Sir Luc. Now, I'll leave you to fix your own time. Take my advice, and you'll decide it this evening if you can; then let the worst come of it, 'twill be off your mind to-morrow.

Acres. Very true.

Sir Luc. So I shall see nothing more of you, unless it be by letter, till the evening. I would do myself the honour to carry your message ; but, to tell you a secret, I believe I shall have just such another affair on my own hands. There is a gay captain here, who put a jest on me lately at the expense of my country, and I only want to fall in with the gentleman to call him out.

Acres. By my valour, I should like to see you fight first ! Odds life ! I should like to see you kill him if it was only to get a little lesson.

Sir Luc. I shall be very proud of instructing you. Well, for the present—but remember now, when you meet your antagonist, do everything in a mild and agreeable manner. Let your courage be as keen, but at the same time as polished, as your sword.

[*Exeunt severally.*

ACT IV

SCENE I.—ACRES' *Lodgings.*

ACRES *and* DAVID.

Dav. Then, by the mass, sir ! I would do no such thing—ne'er a Sir Lucius O'Trigger in the kingdom should make me fight, when I wa'n't so minded. Oons ! what will the old lady say, when she hears o't ?

Acres. Ah ! David, if you had heard Sir Lucius ! Odds sparks and flames ! he would have roused your valour.

Dav. Not he, indeed. I hate such bloodthirsty cormorants. Look'ee, master, if you'd wanted a bout at boxing, quarter-staff, or short-staff, I should never be the man to bid you cry off : but for your curst sharps and snaps, I never knew any good come of 'em.

Acres. But my honour, David, my honour ! I must be very careful of my honour.

The Rivals

Dav. Ay, by the mass! and I would be very careful of it; and I think in return my honour couldn't do less than to be very careful of me.

Acres. Odds blades! David, no gentleman will ever risk the loss of his honour!

Dav. I say, then, it would be but civil in honour never to risk the loss of a gentleman. Look'ee, master, this honour seems to me to be a marvellous false friend: ay, truly, a very courtier-like servant. Put the case, I was a gentleman (which, thank God, no one can say of me); well—my honour makes me quarrel with another gentleman of my acquaintance. So—we fight. (Pleasant enough that!) Boh!— I kill him—(the more's my luck!) now, pray, who gets the profit of it? Why, my honour. But put the case that he kills me!—by the mass! I go to the worms, and my honour whips over to my enemy.

Acres. No, David—in that case! Odds crowns and laurels! your honour follows you to the grave.

Dav. Now, that's just the place where I could make a shift to do without it.

Acres. Zounds! David, you are a coward! It doesn't become my valour to listen to you. What, shall I disgrace my ancestors? Think of that, David —think what it would be to disgrace my ancestors!

Dav. Under favour, the surest way of not disgracing them, is to keep as long as you can out of their company. Look'ee now, master, to go to them in such haste—with an ounce of lead in your brains— I should think might as well be let alone. Our ancestors are very good kind of folks; but they are the last people I should choose to have a visiting acquaintance with.

Acres. But, David, now, you don't think there is

such very, very, very great danger, hey? Odds life! people often fight without any mischief done!

Dav. By the mass, I think 'tis ten to one against you! Oons! here to meet some lion-headed fellow, I warrant, with his damned double-barrelled swords, and cut-and-thrust pistols! Lord bless us! it makes me tremble to think o't! Those be such desperate bloody-minded weapons! Well, I never could abide 'em—from a child I never could fancy 'em! I suppose there an't been so merciless a beast in the world as your loaded pistol!

Acres. Zounds! I won't be afraid! Odds fire and fury! you shan't make me afraid. Here is the challenge, and I have sent for my dear friend Jack Absolute to carry it for me.

Dav. Ay, i' the name of mischief, let him be the messenger. For my part, I wouldn't lend a hand to it for the best horse in your stable. By the mass! it don't look like another letter! It is, as I may say, a designing and malicious-looking letter; and I warrant smells of gunpowder like a soldier's pouch! Oons! I wouldn't swear it mayn't go off!

Acres. Out, you poltroon! you han't the valour of a grasshopper.

Dav. Well, I say no more—'twill be sad news, to be sure, at Clod Hall! but I ha' done. How Phillis will howl when she hears of it! Ay, poor bitch, she little thinks what shooting her master's going after! And I warrant old Crop, who has carried your honour, field and road, these ten years, will curse the hour he was born.   [*Whimpering*.

Acres. It won't do, David—I am determined to fight—so get along, you coward, while I'm in the mind.

The Rivals

Enter SERVANT.

Ser. Captain Absolute, sir.

Acres. Oh ! show him up. [*Exit* SERVANT.

Dav. Well, Heaven send we be all alive this time to-morrow.

Acres. What's that ? Don't provoke me, David !

Dav. Good-bye, master. [*Whimpering.*

Acres. Get along, you cowardly, dastardly, croaking raven ! [*Exit* DAVID.

Enter CAPTAIN ABSOLUTE.

Abs. What's the matter, Bob ?

Acres. A vile, sheep-hearted blockhead ! If I hadn't the valour of St. George and the dragon to boot——

Abs. But what did you want with me, Bob ?

Acres. Oh ! There—— [*Gives him the challenge.*

Abs. [*Aside*]. *To Ensign Beverley.* So—what's going on now ! [*Aloud.*] Well, what's this ?

Acres. A challenge !

Abs. Indeed ! Why, you won't fight him ; will you, Bob ?

Acres. Egad, but I will, Jack. Sir Lucius has wrought me to it. He has left me full of rage—and I'll fight this evening, that so much good passion mayn't be wasted.

Abs. But what have I to do with this ?

Acres. Why, as I think you know something of this fellow, I want you to find him out for me, and give him this mortal defiance.

Abs. Well, give it to me, and trust me he gets it.

Acres. Thank you, my dear friend, my dear Jack ; but it is giving you a great deal of trouble.

Abs. Not in the least—I beg you won't mention it. No trouble in the world, I assure you.

Acres. You are very kind. What it is to have a friend! You couldn't be my second, could you, Jack?

Abs. Why no, Bob—not in this affair—it would not be quite so proper.

Acres. Well, then, I must get my friend Sir Lucius. I shall have your good wishes, however, Jack?

Abs. Whenever he meets you, believe me.

Re-enter SERVANT.

Ser. Sir Anthony Absolute is below, inquiring for the captain.

Abs. I'll come instantly. [*Exit* SERVANT.] Well, my little hero, success attend you.   [*Going.*

Acres. Stay—stay, Jack. If Beverley should ask you what kind of a man your friend Acres is, do tell him I am a devil of a fellow—will you, Jack?

Abs. To be sure I shall. I'll say you are a determined dog—hey, Bob?

Acres. Ay, do, do—and if that frightens him, egad, perhaps he mayn't come. So tell him I generally kill a man a week—will you, Jack?

Abs. I will, I will; I'll say you are called in the country Fighting Bob.

Acres. Right—right—'tis all to prevent mischief; for I don't want to take his life if I clear my honour.

Abs. No! that's very kind of you.

Acres. Why, you don't wish me to kill him—do you, Jack?

Abs. No, upon my soul, I do not. But a devil of a fellow, hey?   [*Going.*

Acres. True, true—but stay—stay, Jack—you may add, that you never saw me in such a rage before—a most devouring rage!

The Rivals

Abs. I will, I will.

Acres. Remember, Jack—a determined dog!

Abs. Ay, ay, Fighting Bob!   [*Exeunt severally.*

Scene II.—Mrs. Malaprop's *Lodgings.*

Mrs. Malaprop *and* Lydia.

Mrs. Mal. Why, thou perverse one! tell me what you can object to him? Isn't he a handsome man? —tell me that. A genteel man? a pretty figure of a man?

Lyd. [*Aside.*] She little thinks whom she is praising! [*Aloud.*] So is Beverley, ma'am.

Mrs. Mal. No caparisons, miss, if you please. Caparisons don't become a young woman. No! Captain Absolute is indeed a fine gentleman!

Lyd. Ay, the Captain Absolute you have seen.

[*Aside.*

Mrs. Mal. Then he's so well bred—so full of alacrity and adulation!—and has so much to say for himself—in such good language too! His physiognomy so grammatical! Then his presence is so noble! I protest, when I saw him, I thought of what Hamlet says in the play :—

> " Hesperian curls—the front of Job himself!—
>   An eye, like March, to threaten at command !—
>   A station, like Harry Mercury, new—"

Something about kissing—on a hill—however, the similitude struck me directly.

Lyd. How enraged she'll be presently, when she discovers her mistake! [*Aside.*

Enter SERVANT.

Ser. Sir Anthony and Captain Absolute are below, ma'am.

Mrs. Mal. Show them up here. [*Exit* SERVANT.] Now, Lydia, I insist on your behaving as becomes a young woman. Show your good breeding, at least, though you have forgot your duty.

Lyd. Madam, I have told you my resolution! I shall not only give him no encouragement, but I won't even speak to, or look at him.

[*Flings herself into a chair, with her face from the door.*

Enter SIR ANTHONY ABSOLUTE *and* CAPTAIN ABSOLUTE.

Sir Anth. Here we are, Mrs. Malaprop; come to mitigate the frowns of unrelenting beauty—and difficulty enough I had to bring this fellow. I don't know what's the matter; but if I had not held him by force, he'd have given me the slip.

Mrs. Mal. You have infinite trouble, Sir Anthony, in the affair. I am ashamed for the cause! [*Aside to* LYDIA.] Lydia, Lydia, rise, I beseech you!—pay your respects!

Sir Anth. I hope, madam, that Miss Languish has reflected on the worth of this gentleman, and the regard due to her aunt's choice, and my alliance. [*Aside to* CAPTAIN ABSOLUTE.] Now, Jack, speak to her.

Abs. [*Aside.*] What the devil shall I do! [*Aside to* SIR ANTHONY.] You see, sir, she won't even look at me whilst you are here. I knew she wouldn't! I told you so. Let me entreat you, sir, to leave us together.

[*Seems to expostulate with his father.*

The Rivals

Lyd. [*Aside.*] I wonder I han't heard my aunt exclaim yet! Sure she can't have looked at him!—perhaps their regimentals are alike, and she is something blind.

Sir Anth. I say, sir, I won't stir a foot yet!

Mrs. Mal. I am sorry to say, Sir Anthony, that my affluence over my niece is very small. [*Aside to* LYDIA.] Turn round, Lydia: I blush for you!

Sir Anth. May I not flatter myself, that Miss Languish will assign what cause of dislike she can have to my son! [*Aside to* CAPTAIN ABSOLUTE.] Why don't you begin, Jack? Speak, you puppy—speak!

Mrs. Mal. It is impossible, Sir Anthony, she can have any. She will not say she has. [*Aside to* LYDIA.] Answer, hussy! why don't you answer?

Sir Anth. Then, madam, I trust that a childish and hasty predilection will be no bar to Jack's happiness. [*Aside to* CAPTAIN ABSOLUTE.] Zounds! sirrah! why don't you speak?

Lyd. [*Aside.*] I think my lover seems as little inclined to conversation as myself. How strangely blind my aunt must be!

Abs. Hem! hem! madam—hem! [*Attempts to speak, then returns to* SIR ANTHONY.] Faith! sir, I am so confounded!—and—so—so—confused! I told you I should be so, sir—I knew it. The—the—tremor of my passion entirely takes away my presence of mind.

Sir Anth. But it don't take away your voice, fool, does it? Go up, and speak to her directly!

[CAPTAIN ABSOLUTE *makes signs to* MRS. MALAPROP *to leave them together.*

Mrs. Mal. Sir Anthony, shall we leave them to-

Sheridan's Dramatic Works

gether? [*Aside to* LYDIA.] Ah! you stubborn little vixen!

Sir Anth. Not yet, ma'am, not yet! [*Aside to* CAPTAIN ABSOLUTE.] What the devil are you at? Unlock your jaws, sirrah, or——

Abs. [*Aside.*] Now Heaven send she may be too sullen to look round! I must disguise my voice. [*Draws near* LYDIA, *and speaks in a low hoarse tone.*] Will not Miss Languish lend an ear to the mild accents of true love? Will not——

Sir Anth. What the devil ails the fellow? Why don't you speak out?—not stand croaking like a frog in a quinsy!

Abs. The—the—excess of my awe, and my—my—my modesty, quite choke me!

Sir Anth. Ah! your modesty again! I'll tell you what, Jack; if you don't speak out directly and glibly too, I shall be in such a rage! Mrs. Malaprop, I wish the lady would favour us with something more than a side-front.

[MRS. MALAPROP *seems to chide* LYDIA.

Abs. [*Aside.*] So all will out, I see! [*Goes up to* LYDIA, *speaks softly.*] Be not surprised, my Lydia; suppress all surprise at present.

Lyd. [*Aside.*] Heavens! 'tis Beverley's voice! Sure he can't have imposed on Sir Anthony too! [*Looks round by degrees, then starts up.*] Is this possible!—my Beverley!—how can this be?—my Beverley?

Abs. Ah! 'tis all over. [*Aside.*

Sir Anth. Beverley!—the devil—Beverley! What can the girl mean? This is my son, Jack Absolute.

Mrs. Mal. For shame, hussy! for shame! your head runs so on that fellow, that you have him

The Rivals

always in your eyes! Beg Captain Absolute's pardon directly.

Lyd. I see no Captain Absolute, but my loved Beverley!

Sir Anth. Zounds! the girl's mad!—her brain's turned by reading.

Mrs. Mal. O' my conscience, I believe so! What do you mean by Beverley, hussy? You saw Captain Absolute before to-day. There he is—your husband that shall be.

Lyd. With all my soul, ma'am—when I refuse my Beverley——

Sir Anth. Oh! she's as mad as Bedlam!—or has this fellow been playing us a rogue's trick! Come here, sirrah, who the devil are you?

Abs. Faith, sir, I am not quite clear myself; but I'll endeavour to recollect.

Sir Anth. Are you my son or not? Answer for your mother, you dog, if you won't for me.

Mrs. Mal. Ay, sir, who are you? Oh, mercy! I begin to suspect!—

Abs. [*Aside.*] Ye powers of impudence, befriend me! [*Aloud.*] Sir Anthony, most assuredly I am your wife's son, and that I sincerely believe myself to be yours also, I hope my duty has always shown. Mrs. Malaprop, I am your most respectful admirer, and shall be proud to add affectionate nephew. I need not tell my Lydia, that she sees her faithful Beverley, who, knowing the singular generosity of her temper, assumed that name and station, which has proved a test of the most disinterested love, which he now hopes to enjoy in a more elevated character.

Lyd. So!—there will be no elopement after all!

[*Sullenly.*

Sheridan's Dramatic Works

Sir Anth. Upon my soul, Jack, thou art a very impudent fellow ! To do you justice, I think I never saw a piece of more consummate assurance !

Abs. Oh, you flatter me, sir—you compliment—'tis my modesty, you know, sir—my modesty that has stood in my way.

Sir Anth. Well, I am glad you are not the dull, insensible varlet you pretended to be, however ! I'm glad you have made a fool of your father, you dog—I am. So this was your *penitence*, your *duty* and *obedience !* I thought it was damned sudden ! *You never heard their names before*, not you !—*what, the Languishes of Worcestershire*, hey ?—*if you could please me in the affair it was all you desired !* Ah ! you dissembling villain ! What ! [*Pointing to* LYDIA] *she squints, don't she ? — a little red-haired girl !* — hey ? Why, you hypocritical young rascal ! I wonder you an't ashamed to hold up your head !

Abs. 'Tis with difficulty, sir. I am confused—very much confused, as you must perceive.

Mrs. Mal. O Lud ! Sir Anthony ! — a new light breaks in upon me !—hey !—how ! what ! captain, did you write the letters then ? What ! am I to thank you for the elegant compilation of *an old weather-beaten she-dragon*—hey ? Oh, mercy ! Was it you that reflected on my parts of speech ?

Abs. Dear sir ! my modesty will be overpowered at last, if you don't assist me—I shall certainly not be able to stand it !

Sir Anth. Come, come, Mrs. Malaprop, we must forget and forgive—odds life ! matters have taken so clever a turn all of a sudden, that I could find in my heart to be so good-humoured ! and so gallant ! —hey ! Mrs. Malaprop ?

[364]

The Rivals

Mrs. Mal. Well, Sir Anthony, since you desire it, we will not anticipate the past!—so mind, young people—our retrospection will be all to the future.

Sir Anth. Come, we must leave them together; Mrs. Malaprop, they long to fly into each other's arms, I warrant! Jack—isn't the cheek as I said, hey?—and the eye, you rogue!—and the lip—hey? Come, Mrs. Malaprop, we'll not disturb their tenderness—theirs is the time of life for happiness! *Youth's the season made for joy*—[*Sings*]—hey!—Odds life! I'm in such spirits—I don't know what I could not do! Permit me, ma'am. [*Gives his hand to* MRS. MALAPROP.] Tol-de-rol—'gad, I should like to have a little fooling myself. Tol-de-rol! de-rol.

[*Exit, singing and handing* MRS. MALAPROP.— LYDIA *sits sullenly in her chair.*

Abs. [*Aside.*] So much thought bodes me no good. [*Aloud.*] So grave, Lydia!

Lyd. Sir!

Abs. [*Aside.*] So!—egad! I thought as much!— that damned monosyllable has froze me! [*Aloud.*] What, Lydia, now that we are as happy in our friends' consent, as in our mutual vows——

Lyd. Friends' consent indeed!   [*Peevishly.*

Abs. Come, come, we must lay aside some of our romance—a little wealth and comfort may be endured after all. And for your fortune the lawyers shall make such settlements as——

Lyd. Lawyers! I hate lawyers!

Abs. Nay, then, we will not wait for their lingering forms, but instantly procure the licence, and——

Lyd. The licence! I hate licence!

Abs. Oh my love! be not so unkind!—thus let me entreat——   [*Kneeling.*

[365]

Sheridan's Dramatic Works

Lyd. Psha !— what signifies kneeling, when you know I must have you ?

Abs. [*Rising.*] Nay, madam, there shall be no constraint upon your inclinations, I promise you. If I have lost your heart—I resign the rest. [*Aside.*] 'Gad, I must try what a little spirit will do.

Lyd. [*Rising.*] Then, sir, let me tell you, the interest you had there was acquired by a mean, unmanly imposition, and deserves the punishment of fraud. What, you have been treating me like a child !— humouring my romance ! and laughing, I suppose, at your success !

Abs. You wrong me, Lydia, you wrong me—only hear——

Lyd. So, while I fondly imagined we were deceiving my relations, and flattered myself that I should outwit and incense them all—behold my hopes are to be crushed at once, by my aunt's consent and approbation — and I am myself the only dupe at last ! [*Walking about in a heat.*] But here, sir, here is the picture—Beverley's picture ! [*taking a miniature from her bosom*] which I have worn, night and day, in spite of threats and entreaties ! There, sir ; [*flings it to him*] and be assured I throw the original from my heart as easily.

Abs. Nay, nay, ma'am, we will not differ as to that. Here—[*taking out a picture*] here is Miss Lydia Languish. What a difference !—ay, there is the heavenly assenting smile that first gave soul and spirit to my hopes !—those are the lips which sealed a vow, as yet scarce dry in Cupid's calendar ! and there the half-resentful blush, that would have checked the ardour of my thanks ! Well, all that's past ! — all over indeed ! There, madam—in beauty, that copy is not

[366]

The Rivals

equal to you, but in my mind its merit over the original, in being still the same, is such—that—I cannot find in my heart to part with it.

[Puts it up again.

Lyd. [*Softening*] 'Tis your own doing, sir—I—I—I suppose you are perfectly satisfied.

Abs. Oh, most certainly—sure now this is much better than being in love !—ha ! ha ! ha !—there's some spirit in this ! What signifies breaking some scores of solemn promises ?—all that's of no consequence, you know. To be sure people will say that miss don't know her own mind — but never mind that ! Or, perhaps, they may be ill-natured enough to hint, that the gentleman grew tired of the lady and forsook her —but don't let that fret you.

Lyd. There is no bearing his insolence.

[Bursts into tears.

Re-enter MRS. MALAPROP *and* SIR ANTHONY ABSOLUTE.

Mrs. Mal. Come, we must interrupt your billing and cooing awhile.

Lyd. This is worse than your treachery and deceit, you base ingrate ! *[Sobbing.*

Sir Anth. What the devil's the matter now ? Zounds ! Mrs. Malaprop, this is the oddest billing and cooing I ever heard ! — but what the deuce is the meaning of it ? I am quite astonished !

Abs. Ask the lady, sir.

Mrs. Mal. Oh, mercy ! I'm quite analysed, for my part ! Why, Lydia, what is the reason of this ?

Lyd. Ask the gentleman, ma'am.

Sir Anth. Zounds ! I shall be in a frenzy ! Why, Jack, you are not come out to be any one else, are you ?

Sheridan's Dramatic Works

Mrs. Mal. Ay, sir, there's no more trick, is there?
—you are not like Cerberus, three gentlemen at once,
are you?

Abs. You'll not let me speak. I say the lady
can account for this much better than I can.

Lyd. Ma'am, you once commanded me never to
think of Beverley again. There is the man—I now
obey you! for, from this moment, I renounce him for
ever.   [*Exit.*

Mrs. Mal. Oh, mercy! and miracles! what a turn
here is—why sure, captain, you haven't behaved disrespectfully to my niece.

Sir Anth. Ha! ha! ha!—ha! ha! ha!—now I see
it. Ha! ha! ha!—now I see it. You have been too
lively, Jack.

Abs. Nay, sir, upon my word——

Sir Anth. Come, no lying, Jack—I'm sure 'twas so.

Mrs. Mal. O Lud! Sir Anthony!—Oh, fy, captain!

Abs. Upon my soul, ma'am——

Sir Anth. Come, no excuses, Jack; why, your
father, you rogue, was so before you — the blood of
the Absolutes was always impatient. Ha! ha! ha!
poor little Lydia! Why, you've frightened her, you
dog, you have.

Abs. By all that's good, sir——

Sir Anth. Zounds! say no more, I tell you—Mrs.
Malaprop shall make your peace. You must make
his peace, Mrs. Malaprop. You must tell her 'tis
Jack's way—tell her 'tis all our ways—it runs in the
blood of our family! Come away, Jack. Ha! ha!
ha! Mrs. Malaprop—a young villain!

[*Pushing him out.*

Mrs. Mal. Oh! Sir Anthony!—Oh, fy, captain!

[*Exeunt severally.*

The Rivals

SCENE III.—*The North Parade.*

Enter SIR LUCIUS O'TRIGGER.

Sir Luc. I wonder where this Captain Absolute hides himself! Upon my conscience! these officers are always in one's way in love affairs. I remember I might have married Lady Dorothy Carmine, if it had not been for a little rogue of a major, who ran away with her before she could get a sight of me! And I wonder, too, what it is the ladies can see in them to be so fond of them—unless it be a touch of the old serpent in 'em, that makes the little creatures be caught, like vipers, with a bit of red cloth. Ha! isn't this the captain coming?—faith it is! There is a probability of succeeding about that fellow, that is mighty provoking! Who the devil is he talking to?

[*Steps aside.*

Enter CAPTAIN ABSOLUTE.

Abs. [*Aside.*] To what fine purpose I have been plotting!—a noble reward for all my schemes, upon my soul!—a little gipsy! I did not think her romance could have made her so damned absurd either. 'Sdeath, I never was in a worse humour in my life! I could cut my own throat, or any other person's, with the greatest pleasure in the world!

Sir Luc. Oh, faith! I'm in the luck of it. I never could have found him in a sweeter temper for my purpose—to be sure, I'm just come in the nick! Now to enter into conversation with him, and so quarrel genteelly. [*Goes up to* CAPTAIN ABSOLUTE.] With regard to that matter, captain, I must beg leave to differ in opinion with you.

Abs. Upon my word, then, you must be a very

subtle disputant, because, sir, I happened just then to be giving no opinion at all.

Sir Luc. That's no reason. For give me leave to tell you, a man may think an untruth as well as speak one.

Abs. Very true, sir; but if a man never utters his thoughts, I should think they might stand a chance of escaping controversy.

Sir Luc. Then, sir, you differ in opinion with me, which amounts to the same thing.

Abs. Hark'ee, Sir Lucius, if I had not before known you to be a gentleman, upon my soul, I should not have discovered it at this interview; for what you can drive at, unless you mean to quarrel with me, I cannot conceive!

Sir Luc. I humbly thank you, sir, for the quickness of your apprehension. [*Bowing.*] You have named the very thing I would be at.

Abs. Very well, sir, I shall certainly not balk your inclinations. But I should be glad you would please to explain your motives.

Sir Luc. Pray, sir, be easy; the quarrel is a very pretty quarrel as it stands, we should only spoil it by trying to explain it. However, your memory is very short, or you could not have forgot an affront you passed on me within this week. So, no more, but name your time and place.

Abs. Well, sir, since you are so bent on it, the sooner the better; let it be this evening—here, by the Spring Gardens. We shall scarcely be interrupted.

Sir Luc. Faith! that same interruption in affairs of this nature shows very great ill-breeding. I don't know what's the reason, but in England, if a thing of this kind gets wind, people make such a pother, that a gentleman can never fight in peace and quietness. However, if it's the same to you, captain, I should take it as a particular kindness if you'd let us meet in King's-Mead-Fields, as a little business will call me there about six o'clock, and I may despatch both matters at once.

Abs. 'Tis the same to me exactly. A little after six, then, we will discuss this matter more seriously.

Sir Luc. If you please, sir; there will be very pretty small-sword light, though it won't do for a long shot. So that matter's settled, and my mind's at ease !

[*Exit.*

Enter FAULKLAND.

Abs. Well met ! I was going to look for you. O Faulkland ! all the demons of spite and disappointment have conspired against me ! I'm so vexed, that if I had not the prospect of a resource in being knocked o' the head by-and-by, I should scarce have spirits to tell you the cause.

Faulk. What can you mean ? Has Lydia changed her mind ? I should have thought her duty and inclination would now have pointed to the same object.

Abs. Ay, just as the eyes do of a person who squints. When her love-eye was fixed on me, t'other, her eye of duty, was finely obliqued : but when duty bid her point that the same way, off t'other turned on a swivel, and secured its retreat with a frown !

Faulk. But what's the resource you——

Abs. Oh, to wind up the whole, a good-natured Irishman here has [*Mimicking* SIR LUCIUS] begged leave to have the pleasure of cutting my throat ; and I mean to indulge him—that's all.

Faulk. Prithee, be serious !

[371]

Sheridan's Dramatic Works

Abs. 'Tis fact, upon my soul! Sir Lucius O'Trigger—you know him by sight—for some affront, which I am sure I never intended, has obliged me to meet him this evening at six o'clock. 'Tis on that account I wished to see you; you must go with me.

Faulk. Nay, there must be some mistake, sure. Sir Lucius shall explain himself, and I dare say matters may be accommodated. But this evening, did you say? I wish it had been any other time.

Abs. Why? there will be light enough; there will (as Sir Lucius says) be very pretty small-sword light, though it will not do for a long shot. Confound his long shots!

Faulk. But I am myself a good deal ruffled by a difference I have had with Julia. My vile tormenting temper has made me treat her so cruelly, that I shall not be myself till we are reconciled.

Abs. By Heavens! Faulkland, you don't deserve her!

Enter SERVANT, *gives* FAULKLAND *a letter, and exit.*

Faulk. Oh, Jack! this is from Julia. I dread to open it! I fear it may be to take a last leave!—perhaps to bid me return her letters, and restore—— Oh, how I suffer for my folly!

Abs. Here, let me see. [*Takes the letter and opens it.*] Ay, a final sentence, indeed!—'tis all over with you, faith!

Faulk. Nay, Jack, don't keep me in suspense!

Abs. Hear then. [Reads.] *As I am convinced that my dear Faulkland's own reflections have already up-braided him for his last unkindness to me, I will not add a word on the subject. I wish to speak with you as soon as possible. Yours ever and truly,* JULIA. There's stubbornness and resentment for you! [*Gives him the letter.*] Why, man, you don't seem one whit the happier at this!

Faulk. Oh yes, I am; but—but——

Abs. Confound your buts! you never hear anything that would make another man bless himself, but you immediately damn it with a but!

Faulk. Now, Jack, as you are my friend, own honestly—don't you think there is something forward, something indelicate, in this haste to forgive? Women should never sue for reconciliation: that should always come from us. They should retain their coldness till wooed to kindness; and their pardon, like their love, should "not unsought be won."

Abs. I have not patience to listen to you! Thou'rt incorrigible! so say no more on the subject. I must go to settle a few matters. Let me see you before six, remember, at my lodgings. A poor industrious devil like me, who have toiled, and drudged, and plotted to gain my ends, and am at last disappointed by other people's folly, may in pity be allowed to swear and grumble a little; but a captious sceptic in love, a slave to fretfulness and whim, who has no difficulties but of his own creating, is a subject more fit for ridicule than compassion. [*Exit.*

Faulk. I feel his reproaches; yet I would not change this too exquisite nicety for the gross content with which he tramples on the thorns of love! His engaging me in this duel has started an idea in my head, which I will instantly pursue. I'll use it as the touchstone of Julia's sincerity and disinterestedness. If her love prove pure and sterling ore, my name will rest on it with honour; and once I've stamped it there, I lay aside my doubts for ever! But if the dross of selfishness, the alloy of pride, predominate, 'twill be best to leave her as a toy for some less cautious fool to sigh for !   [*Exit.*

ACT V

Scene I.—Julia's *Dressing-Room.*

Julia *discovered alone.*

Jul. How this message has alarmed me ! what dreadful accident can he mean ? why such charge to be alone ? O Faulkland !—how many unhappy moments—how many tears have you cost me !

Enter Faulkland.

Jul. What means this ?—why this caution, Faulkland ?

Faulk. Alas! Julia, I am come to take a long farewell.

Jul. Heavens ! what do you mean ?

Faulk. You see before you a wretch, whose life is forfeited.   Nay, start not !—the infirmity of my temper has drawn all this misery on me.   I left you fretful and passionate—an untoward accident drew me into a quarrel—the event is, that I must fly this kingdom instantly.   O Julia, had I been so fortunate as to have called you mine entirely, before this mischance had fallen on me, I should not so deeply dread my banishment !

Jul. My soul is oppressed with sorrow at the nature of your misfortune.   Had these adverse circumstances arisen from a less fatal cause, I should have felt strong comfort in the thought that I could now chase from your bosom every doubt of the warm sincerity of my love.   My heart has long known no other guardian— I now entrust my person to your honour—we will

The Rivals

fly together. When safe from pursuit, my father's will may be fulfilled—and I receive a legal claim to be the partner of your sorrows and tenderest comforter. Then on the bosom of your wedded Julia, you may lull your keen regret to slumbering; while virtuous love, with a cherub's hand, shall smooth the brow of upbraiding thought, and pluck the thorn from compunction.

Faulk. O Julia! I am bankrupt in gratitude! but the time is so pressing, it calls on you for so hasty a resolution. Would you not wish some hours to weigh the advantages you forego, and what little compensation poor Faulkland can make you beside his solitary love?

Jul. I ask not a moment. No, Faulkland, I have loved you for yourself; and if I now, more than ever, prize the solemn engagement which so long has pledged us to each other, it is because it leaves no room for hard aspersions on my fame, and puts the seal of duty to an act of love. But let us not linger. Perhaps this delay——

Faulk. 'Twill be better I should not venture out again till dark. Yet am I grieved to think what numberless distresses will press heavy on your gentle disposition!

Jul. Perhaps your fortune may be forfeited by this unhappy act. I know not whether 'tis so; but sure that alone can never make us unhappy. The little I have will be sufficient to support us; and exile never should be splendid.

Faulk. Ay, but in such an abject state of life, my wounded pride perhaps may increase the natural fretfulness of my temper, till I become a rude, morose companion, beyond your patience to endure. Perhaps the recollection of a deed my conscience cannot justify may haunt me in such gloomy and unsocial fits that I shall hate the tenderness that would relieve me, break from your arms, and quarrel with your fondness.

Jul. If your thoughts should assume so unhappy a bent, you will the more want some mild and affectionate spirit to watch over and console you : one who, by bearing your infirmities with gentleness and resignation, may teach you so to bear the evils of your fortune.

Faulk. Julia, I have proved you to the quick ! and with this useless device I throw away all my doubts. How shall I plead to be forgiven this last unworthy effect of my restless, unsatisfied disposition ?

Jul. Has no such disaster happened as you related ?

Faulk. I am ashamed to own that it was pretended ; yet in pity, Julia, do not kill me with resenting a fault which never can be repeated : but sealing, this once, my pardon, let me to-morrow, in the face of Heaven, receive my future guide and monitress, and expiate my past folly by years of tender adoration.

Jul. Hold, Faulkland !—that you are free from a crime, which I before feared to name, Heaven knows how sincerely I rejoice ! These are tears of thankfulness for that ! But that your cruel doubts should have urged you to an imposition that has wrung my heart, gives me now a pang more keen than I can express !

Faulk. By Heavens ! Julia——

Jul. Yet hear me. My father loved you, Faulkland ! and you preserved the life that tender parent gave me ; in his presence I pledged my hand—joyfully pledged it—where before I had given my heart. When, soon after, I lost that parent, it seemed to me that Providence had, in Faulkland, shown me whither to transfer without a pause, my grateful duty, as well as my affection : hence, I have been content to bear from you what pride and delicacy would have forbid me from another. I will not upbraid you, by repeating how you have trifled with my sincerity——

Faulk. I confess it all ! yet hear——

Jul. After such a year of trial, I might have flattered myself that I should not have been insulted with a new probation of my sincerity, as cruel as unnecessary ! I now see it is not in your nature to be content or confident in love. With this conviction—I never will be yours. While I had hopes that my persevering attention, and unreproaching kindness, might in time reform your temper, I should have been happy to have gained a dearer influence over you ; but I will not furnish you with a licensed power to keep alive an incorrigible fault, at the expense of one who never would contend with you.

Faulk. Nay, but, Julia, by my soul and honour, if after this——

Jul. But one word more. As my faith has once been given to you, I never will barter it with another. I shall pray for your happiness with the truest sincerity ; and the dearest blessing I can ask of Heaven to send you will be to charm you from that unhappy temper, which alone has prevented the performance of our solemn engagement. All I request of you is, that you will yourself reflect upon this infirmity, and when you number up the many true delights it has deprived you of, let it not be your least regret, that it lost you the love of one who would have followed you in beggary through the world !   [*Exit.*

Faulk. She's gone—for ever ! There was an awful resolution in her manner that riveted me to my place. O fool !—dolt !—barbarian ! Cursed as I am, with more imperfections than my fellow-wretches, kind Fortune sent a heaven-gifted cherub to my aid, and, like a ruffian, I have driven her from my side ! I must now haste to my appointment. Well, my mind is tuned for such a scene. I shall wish only to become a principal in it, and reverse the tale my cursed folly put me upon forging here. O Love !—tormentor !—fiend !—whose influence, like the moon's, acting on men of dull souls, makes idiots of them, but meeting subtler spirits, betrays their course, and urges sensibility to madness !   [*Exit.*

Enter LYDIA *and* MAID.

Maid. My mistress, ma'am, I know, was here just now—perhaps she is only in the next room.   [*Exit.*

Lyd. Heigh-ho ! Though he has used me so, this fellow runs strangely in my head. I believe one lecture from my grave cousin will make me recall him. [*Re-enter* JULIA.] O Julia, I am come to you with such an appetite for consolation. Lud ! child, what's the matter with you ? You have been crying !—I'll be hanged if that Faulkland has not been tormenting you !

Jul. You mistake the cause of my uneasiness ! Something has flurried me a little. Nothing that you can guess at. [*Aside.*] I would not accuse Faulkland to a sister !

Lyd. Ah ! whatever vexations you may have, I can

The Rivals

assure you mine surpass them. You know who Beverley proves to be?

Jul. I will now own to you, Lydia, that Mr. Faulkland had before informed me of the whole affair. Had young Absolute been the person you took him for, I should not have accepted your confidence on the subject, without a serious endeavour to counteract your caprice.

Lyd. So, then, I see I have been deceived by every one. But I don't care—I'll never have him.

Jul. Nay, Lydia——

Lyd. Why, is it not provoking? when I thought we were coming to the prettiest distress imaginable, to find myself made a mere Smithfield bargain of at last! There, had I projected one of the most sentimental elopements!—so becoming a disguise!—so amiable a ladder of ropes!—conscious moon—four horses—Scotch parson—with such surprise to Mrs. Malaprop—and such paragraphs in the newspapers! Oh, I shall die with disappointment!

Jul. I don't wonder at it!

Lyd. Now—sad reverse!—what have I to expect, but, after a deal of flimsy preparation with a bishop's licence, and my aunt's blessing, to go simpering up to the altar; or perhaps be cried three times in a country church, and have an unmannerly fat clerk ask the consent of every butcher in the parish to join John Absolute and Lydia Languish, spinster! Oh that I should live to hear myself called spinster!

Jul. Melancholy indeed!

Lyd. How mortifying, to remember the dear delicious shifts I used to be put to, to gain half a minute's conversation with this fellow! How often have I stole forth, in the coldest night in January, and found him in the garden, stuck like a dripping statue! There would he kneel to me in the snow, and sneeze and cough so pathetically!—he shivering with cold and I with apprehension!—and while the freezing blast numbed our joints, how warmly would he press me to pity his flame, and glow with mutual ardour! Ah, Julia, that was something like being in love.

Jul. If I were in spirits, Lydia, I should chide you only by laughing heartily at you; but it suits more the situation of my mind, at present, earnestly to entreat you not to let a man, who loves you with sincerity, suffer that unhappiness from your caprice, which I know too well caprice can inflict.

Lyd. O Lud! what has brought my aunt here?

Enter MRS. MALAPROP, FAG, *and* DAVID.

Mrs. Mal. So! so! here's fine work!—here's fine suicide, parricide, and simulation, going on in the fields! and Sir Anthony not to be found to prevent the antistrophe!

Jul. For Heaven's sake, madam, what's the meaning of this?

Mrs. Mal. That gentleman can tell you—'twas he enveloped the affair to me.

Lyd. Do, sir—will you, inform us?   [*To* FAG.

Fag. Ma'am, I should hold myself very deficient in every requisite that forms the man of breeding, if I delayed a moment to give all the information in my power to a lady so deeply interested in the affair as you are.

Lyd. But quick! quick, sir!

Fag. True, ma'am, as you say, one should be quick in divulging matters of this nature; for should we

The Rivals

be tedious, perhaps while we are flourishing on the subject, two or three lives may be lost !

Lyd. Oh, patience ! Do, ma'am, for Heaven's sake ! tell us what is the matter ?

Mrs. Mal. Why, murder's the matter ! slaughter's the matter ! killing's the matter !—but he can tell you the perpendiculars.

Lyd. Then, prithee, sir, be brief.

Fag. Why, then, ma'am, as to murder—I cannot take upon me to say—and as to slaughter, or man-slaughter, that will be as the jury finds it.

Lyd. But who, sir—who are engaged in this ?

Fag. Faith, ma'am, one is a young gentleman whom I should be very sorry anything was to happen to—a very pretty behaved gentleman ! We have lived much together, and always on terms.

Lyd. But who is this ? Who ! who ! who ?

Fag. My master, ma'am—my master—I speak of my master.

Lyd. Heavens ! What, Captain Absolute ?

Mrs. Mal. Oh, to be sure, you are frightened now !

Jul. But who are with him, sir ?

Fag. As to the rest, ma'am, this gentleman can inform you better than I.

Jul. Do speak, friend.   [*To* DAVID.

Dav. Look'ee, my lady—by the mass ! there's mischief going on. Folks don't use to meet for amusement with fire-arms, firelocks, fire-engines, fire-screens, fire-office, and the devil knows what other crackers beside ! This, my lady, I say, has an angry favour.

Jul. But who is there beside Captain Absolute, friend ?

Dav. My poor master—under favour for mention-

ing him first. You know me, my lady—I am David
—and my master of course is, or was, Squire Acres.
Then comes Squire Faulkland.

Jul. Do, ma'am, let us instantly endeavour to
prevent mischief.

Mrs. Mal. Oh, fy ! it would be very inelegant in
us. We should only participate things.

Dav. Ah ! do, Mrs. Aunt, save a few lives—they
are desperately given, believe me. Above all, there is
that bloodthirsty Philistine, Sir Lucius O'Trigger.

Mrs. Mal. Sir Lucius O'Trigger ? Oh, mercy ! have
they drawn poor little dear Sir Lucius into the
scrape ? Why, how you stand, girl ! You have no
more feeling than one of the Derbyshire petrifac-
tions !

Lyd. What are we to do, madam ?

Mrs. Mal. Why, fly with the utmost felicity, to be
sure, to prevent mischief ! Here, friend, you can
show us the place ?

Fag. If you please, ma'am, I will conduct you.
David, do you look for Sir Anthony. [*Exit* DAVID.

Mrs. Mal. Come, girls ! this gentleman will exhort
us. Come, sir, you're our envoy—lead the way, and
we'll precede.

Fag. Not a step before the ladies for the world !

Mrs. Mal. You're sure you know the spot ?

Fag. I think I can find it, ma'am ; and one good
thing is, we shall hear the report of the pistols as we
draw near, so we can't well miss them—never fear,
ma'am, never fear. [*Exeunt, he talking.*

The Rivals

SCENE II.—*The South Parade.*

Enter CAPTAIN ABSOLUTE, *putting his sword under his greatcoat.*

Abs. A sword seen in the streets of Bath would raise as great an alarm as a mad dog. How provoking this is in Faulkland !—never punctual ! I shall be obliged to go without him at last. Oh, the devil ! here's Sir Anthony ! how shall I escape him ?
> [*Muffles up his face, and takes a circle to go off.*

Enter SIR ANTHONY ABSOLUTE.

Sir Anth. How one may be deceived at a little distance ; only that I see he don't know me, I could have sworn that was Jack !—Hey ! Gad's life ! it is. Why, Jack, what are you afraid of ? hey !—sure I'm right. Why, Jack, Jack Absolute ! [*Goes up to him.*

Abs. Really, sir, you have the advantage of me. I don't remember ever to have had the honour—my name is Saunderson, at your service.

Sir Anth. Sir, I beg your pardon—I took you— hey ?—why, zounds ! it is ! Stay. [*Looks up to his face.*] So, so—your humble servant, Mr. Saunderson ! Why, you scoundrel, what tricks are you after now ?

Abs. Oh, a joke, sir, a joke ! I came here on purpose to look for you, sir.

Sir Anth. You did ? Well, I am glad you were so lucky—but what are you muffled up so for ? What's this for ?—hey !

Abs. 'Tis cool, sir ; isn't it ?—rather chilly somehow —but I shall be late—I have a particular engagement.

Sir Anth. Stay ! Why, I thought you were looking for me ! Pray, Jack, where is't you are going ?

Abs. Going, sir ?

Sir Anth. Ay, where are you going ?

Abs. Where am I going ?

Sir Anth. You unmannerly puppy !

Abs. I was going, sir—to—to—to—to Lydia—sir, to Lydia—to make matters up if I could—and I was looking for you, sir, to—to——

Sir Anth. To go with you, I suppose. Well, come along.

Abs. Oh ! zounds ! no, sir, not for the world ! I wished to meet with you, sir—to—to—to—— You find it cool, I'm sure, sir—you'd better not stay out.

Sir Anth. Cool !—not at all. Well, Jack, and what will you say to Lydia ?

Abs. Oh, sir, beg her pardon, humour her—promise and vow. But I detain you, sir. Consider the cold air on your gout.

Sir Anth. Oh, not at all !—not at all ! I'm in no hurry. Ah ! Jack, you youngsters, when once you are wounded here. [*Putting his hand to* CAPTAIN ABSOLUTE'S *breast.*] Hey ! what the deuce have you got here ?

Abs. Nothing, sir—nothing.

Sir Anth. What's this ?—here's something damned hard.

Abs. Oh, trinkets, sir ! trinkets !—a bauble for Lydia !

Sir Anth. Nay, let me see your taste. [*Pulls his coat open, the sword falls.*] Trinkets !—a bauble for Lydia ! Zounds ! sirrah, you are not going to cut her throat, are you ?

Abs. Ha ! ha ! ha ! I thought it would divert you, sir, though I didn't mean to tell you till afterwards.

Sir Anth. You didn't ? Yes, this is a very diverting trinket, truly !

The Rivals

Abs. Sir, I'll explain to you. You know, sir, Lydia is romantic, devilish romantic, and very absurd, of course : now, sir, I intend, if she refuses to forgive me, to unsheathe this sword, and swear—I'll fall upon its point, and expire at her feet !

Sir Anth. Fall upon a fiddlestick's end ! Why, I suppose it is the very thing that would please her. Get along, you fool !

Abs. Well, sir, you shall hear of my success—you shall hear. *O Lydia!—forgive me, or this pointed steel* —says I.

Sir Anth. O booby! stab away and welcome—says she. Get along ! and damn your trinkets !

[*Exit* CAPTAIN ABSOLUTE.

Enter DAVID, *running.*

Dav. Stop him ! stop him ! Murder ! Thief ! Fire ! Stop fire ! Stop fire ! O Sir Anthony—call ! call ! bid 'm stop ! Murder ! Fire !

Sir Anth. Fire ! Murder !—Where ?

Dav. Oons ! he's out of sight ! and I'm out of breath ! for my part ! O Sir Anthony, why didn't you stop him ?—why didn't you stop him ?

Sir Anth. Zounds ! the fellow's mad ! Stop whom ? Stop Jack ?

Dav. Ay, the captain, sir !—there's murder and slaughter——

Sir Anth. Murder !

Dav. Ay, please you, Sir Anthony, there's all kinds of murder, all sorts of slaughter to be seen in the fields : there's fighting going on, sir—bloody sword-and-gun fighting !

Sir Anth. Who are going to fight, dunce ?

Dav. Everybody that I know of, Sir Anthony—

everybody is going to fight—my poor master, Sir
Lucius O'Trigger, your son, the captain——

Sir Anth. Oh, the dog! I see his tricks. Do you
know the place?

Dav. King's-Mead-Fields.

Sir Anth. You know the way?

Dav. Not an inch; but I'll call the mayor—alder-
men—constables—churchwardens—and beadles. We
can't be too many to part them.

Sir Anth. Come along—give me your shoulder!
We'll get assistance as we go—the lying villain!
Well, I shall be in such a frenzy! So—this was the
history of his trinkets! I'll bauble him! [*Exeunt.*

SCENE III.—*King's-Mead-Fields.*

Enter SIR LUCIUS O'TRIGGER *and* ACRES, *with pistols.*

Acres. By my valour! then, Sir Lucius, forty yards
is a good distance. Odds levels and aims! I say it
is a good distance.

Sir Luc. Is it for muskets or small field-pieces?
Upon my conscience, Mr. Acres, you must leave those
things to me. Stay now—I'll show you. [*Measures
paces along the stage.*] There now, that is a very
pretty distance—a pretty gentleman's distance.

Acres. Zounds! we might as well fight in a sentry-
box! I tell you, Sir Lucius, the farther he is off, the
cooler I shall take my aim.

Sir Luc. Faith! then, I suppose you would aim at
him best of all if he was out of sight!

Acres. No, Sir Lucius; but I should think forty or
eight-and-thirty yards——

Sir Luc. Pho! pho! nonsense! three or four feet
between the mouths of your pistols is as good as a mile.

The Rivals

Acres. Odds bullets, no ! By my valour ! there is no merit in killing him so near. Do, my dear Sir Lucius, let me bring him down at a long shot—a long shot, Sir Lucius, if you love me !

Sir Luc. Well, the gentleman's friend and I must settle that. But tell me now, Mr. Acres, in case of an accident, is there any little will or commission I could execute for you ?

Acres. I am much obliged to you, Sir Lucius—but I don't understand——

Sir Luc. Why, you may think there's no being shot at without a little risk—and if an unlucky bullet should carry a quietus with it—I say it will be no time then to be bothering you about family matters.

Acres. A quietus !

Sir Luc. For instance, now—if that should be the case — would you choose to be pickled and sent home ?—or would it be the same to you to lie here in the Abbey ? I'm told there is very snug lying in the Abbey.

Acres. Pickled ! Snug lying in the Abbey ! Odds tremors ! Sir Lucius, don't talk so !

Sir Luc. I suppose, Mr. Acres, you never were engaged in an affair of this kind before ?

Acres. No, Sir Lucius, never before.

Sir Luc. Ah ! that's a pity !—there's nothing like being used to a thing. Pray now, how would you receive the gentleman's shot ?

Acres. Odds files ! I've practised that ! There, Sir Lucius—there. [*Puts himself in an attitude.*] A side-front, hey ? Odd ! I'll make myself small enough ! I'll stand edgeways.

Sir Luc. Now—you're quite out—for if you stand so when I take my aim—— [*Levelling at him.*

[387]

Acres. Zounds! Sir Lucius—are you sure it is not cocked?

Sir Luc. Never fear.

Acres. But—but—you don't know—it may go off of its own head!

Sir Luc. Pho! be easy. Well now, if I hit you in the body, my bullet has a double chance—for if it misses a vital part of your right side—'twill be very hard if it don't succeed on the left!

Acres. A vital part!

Sir Luc. But there—fix yourself so. [*Placing him.*] Let him see the broadside of your full front—there. Now a ball or two may pass clean through your body, and never do any harm at all.

Acres. Clean through me!—a ball or two clean through me!

Sir Luc. Ay—may they—and it is much the genteelest attitude into the bargain.

Acres. Look'ee! Sir Lucius—I'd just as lieve be shot in an awkward posture as a genteel one; so, by my valour! I will stand edgeways.

Sir Luc. [*Looking at his watch.*] Sure, they don't mean to disappoint us—Hah! no, faith—I think I see them coming.

Acres. Hey!—what!—coming!——

Sir Luc. Ay. Who are those yonder getting over the stile?

Acres. There are two of them indeed! Well—let them come—hey, Sir Lucius!—we—we—we—we—won't run.

Sir Luc. Run!

Acres. No—I say—we won't run, by my valour!

Sir Luc. What the devil's the matter with you?

Acres. Nothing—nothing—my dear friend—my dear

The Rivals

Sir Lucius—but I—I—I don't feel quite so bold, somehow, as I did.

Sir Luc. Oh, fy!—consider your honour.

Acres. Ay—true—my honour. Do, Sir Lucius, edge in a word or two every now and then about my honour.

Sir Luc. Well, here they're coming.   [*Looking*.

Acres. Sir Lucius—if I wa'n't with you, I should almost think I was afraid. If my valour should leave me! Valour will come and go.

Sir Luc. Then pray keep it fast, while you have it.

Acres. Sir Lucius—I doubt it is going—yes— my valour is certainly going!—it is sneaking off! I feel it oozing out as it were at the palms of my hands!

Sir Luc. Your honour—your honour. Here they are.

Acres. Oh, mercy!—now—that I was safe at Clod Hall! or could be shot before I was aware!

Enter FAULKLAND *and* CAPTAIN ABSOLUTE.

Sir Luc. Gentlemen, your most obedient. Hah! what, Captain Absolute! So, I suppose, sir, you are come here, just like myself—to do a kind office, first for your friend—then to proceed to business on your own account.

Acres. What, Jack! my dear Jack! my dear friend!

Abs. Hark'ee, Bob, Beverley's at hand.

Sir Luc. Well, Mr. Acres—I don't blame your saluting th gentleman civilly. [*To* FAULKLAND.] So, Mr. Beverley, if you'll choose your weapons, the captain and I will measure the ground.

Faulk. My weapons, sir!

Acres. Odds life ! Sir Lucius, I'm not going to fight Mr. Faulkland ; these are my particular friends.

Sir Luc. What, sir, did you not come here to fight Mr. Acres ?

Faulk. Not I, upon my word, sir.

Sir Luc. Well now, that's mighty provoking ! But I hope, Mr. Faulkland, as there are three of us come on purpose for the game, you won't be so cantankerous as to spoil the party by sitting out.

Abs. Oh, pray, Faulkland, fight to oblige Sir Lucius.

Faulk. Nay, if Mr. Acres is so bent on the matter——

Acres. No, no, Mr. Faulkland ; I'll bear my disappointment like a Christian. Look'ee, Sir Lucius, there's no occasion at all for me to fight ; and if it is the same to you, I'd as lieve let it alone.

Sir Luc. Observe me, Mr. Acres—I must not be trifled with. You have certainly challenged somebody—and you came here to fight him. Now, if that gentleman is willing to represent him—I can't see, for my soul, why it isn't just the same thing.

Acres. Why no—Sir Lucius—I tell you, 'tis one Beverley I've challenged—a fellow, you see, that dare not show his face ! If he were here, I'd make him give up his pretensions directly.

Abs. Hold, Bob—let me set you right. There is no such man as Beverley in the case. The person who assumed that name is before you ; and as his pretensions are the same in both characters, he is ready to support them in whatever way you please.

Sir Luc. Well, this is lucky. Now you have an opportunity——

Acres. What, quarrel with my dear friend Jack

The Rivals

Absolute ?—not if he were fifty Beverleys ! Zounds !
Sir Lucius, you would not have me so unnatural.

Sir Luc. Upon my conscience, Mr. Acres, your
valour has oozed away with a vengeance !

Acres. Not in the least ! Odds backs and abettors !
I'll be your second with all my heart—and if you
should get a quietus, you may command me entirely.
I'll get you snug lying in the Abbey here ; or pickle
you, and send you over to Blunderbuss Hall, or anything of the kind, with the greatest pleasure.

Sir Luc. Pho ! pho ! you are little better than a
coward.

Acres. Mind, gentlemen, he calls me a coward ;
coward was the word, by my valour !

Sir Luc. Well, sir ?

Acres. Look'ee, Sir Lucius, 'tisn't that I mind the
word coward—coward may be said in joke. But
if you had called me a poltroon, odds daggers and
balls——

Sir Luc. Well, sir ?

Acres. I should have thought you a very ill-bred
man.

Sir Luc. Pho ! you are beneath my notice.

Abs. Nay, Sir Lucius, you can't have a better
second than my friend Acres. He is a most determined dog—called in the country, Fighting Bob. He
generally kills a man a week—don't you, Bob ?

Acres. Ay—at home !

Sir Luc. Well, then, captain, 'tis we must begin—so
come out, my little counsellor [*Draws his sword*],
and ask the gentleman, whether he will resign the
lady, without forcing you to proceed against him ?

Abs. Come on, then, sir [*Draws*] ; since you won't
let it be an amicable suit, here's my reply.

[391]

Sheridan's Dramatic Works

Enter SIR ANTHONY ABSOLUTE, DAVID, MRS.
MALAPROP, LYDIA, *and* JULIA.

Dav. Knock 'em all down, sweet Sir Anthony;
knock down my master in particular; and bind his
hands over to their good behaviour!

Sir Anth. Put up, Jack, put up, or I shall be in a
frenzy—how came you in a duel, sir?

Abs. Faith, sir, that gentleman can tell you better
than I; 'twas he called on me, and you know, sir, I
serve his majesty.

Sir Anth. Here's a pretty fellow; I catch him going
to cut a man's throat, and he tells me he serves his
majesty! Zounds! sirrah, then how durst you draw
the king's sword against one of his subjects?

Abs. Sir, I tell you! that gentleman called me out,
without explaining his reasons.

Sir Anth. 'Gad! sir, how came you to call my son
out, without explaining your reasons?

Sir Luc. Your son, sir, insulted me in a manner
which my honour could not brook.

Sir Anth. Zounds! Jack, how durst you insult the
gentleman in a manner which his honour could not
brook?

Mrs. Mal. Come, come, let's have no honour before
ladies. Captain Absolute, come here. How could
you intimidate us so? Here's Lydia has been terrified
to death for you.

Abs. For fear I should be killed, or escape, ma'am?

Mrs. Mal. Nay, no delusions to the past. Lydia is
convinced. Speak, child.

Sir Luc. With your leave, ma'am, I must put in a
word here. I believe I could interpret the young
lady's silence. Now mark——

Lyd. What is it you mean, sir?

The Rivals

Sir Luc. Come, come, Delia, we must be serious now—this is no time for trifling.

Lyd. 'Tis true, sir ; and your reproof bids me offer this gentleman my hand, and solicit the return of his affections.

Abs. Oh ! my little angel, say you so ? Sir Lucius— I perceive there must be some mistake here, with regard to the affront which you affirm I have given you. I can only say, that it could not have been intentional. And as you must be convinced that I should not fear to support a real injury—you shall now see that I am not ashamed to atone for an inadvertency—I ask your pardon. But for this lady, while honoured with her approbation, I will support my claim against any man whatever.

Sir Anth. Well said, Jack, and I'll stand by you, my boy.

Acres. Mind, I give up all my claim—I make no pretensions to anything in the world ; and if I can't get a wife without fighting for her, by my valour ! I'll live a bachelor.

Sir Luc. Captain, give me your hand : an affront handsomely acknowledged becomes an obligation ; and as for the lady, if she chooses to deny her own handwriting, here——   *[Takes out letters.*

Mrs. Mal. Oh, he will dissolve my mystery ! Sir Lucius, perhaps there's some mistake—perhaps I can illuminate——

Sir Luc. Pray, old gentlewoman, don't interfere where you have no business. Miss Languish, are you my Delia, or not ?

Lyd. Indeed, Sir Lucius, I am not.

    [Walks aside with CAPTAIN ABSOLUTE.

Mrs. Mal. Sir Lucius O'Trigger—ungrateful as you

Sheridan's Dramatic Works

are—I own the soft impeachment—pardon my blushes, I am Delia.

Sir Luc. You Delia—pho ! pho ! be easy.

Mrs. Mal. Why, thou barbarous Vandyke—those letters are mine. When you are more sensible of my benignity—perhaps I may be brought to encourage your addresses.

Sir Luc. Mrs. Malaprop, I am extremely sensible of your condescension ; and whether you or Lucy have put this trick on me, I am equally beholden to you. And, to show you I am not ungrateful, Captain Absolute, since you have taken that lady from me, I'll give you my Delia into the bargain.

Abs. I am much obliged to you, Sir Lucius ; but here's my friend, Fighting Bob, unprovided for.

Sir Luc. Hah ! little Valour—here, will you make your fortune ?

Acres. Odds wrinkles ! No. But give me your hand, Sir Lucius, forget and forgive ; but if ever I give you a chance of pickling me again, say Bob Acres is a dunce, that's all.

Sir Anth. Come, Mrs. Malaprop, don't be cast down—you are in your bloom yet.

Mrs. Mal. O Sir Anthony—men are all barbarians.

[*All retire but* JULIA *and* FAULKLAND.

Jul. [*Aside.*] He seems dejected and unhappy—not sullen ; there was some foundation, however, for the tale he told me. O woman ! how true should be your judgment when your resolution is so weak !

Faulk. Julia ! how can I sue for what I so little deserve ? I dare not presume, yet Hope is the child of Penitence.

Jul. Oh ! Faulkland, you have not been more faulty in your unkind treatment of me, than I am now in

The Rivals

wanting inclination to resent it. As my heart honestly bids me place my weakness to the account of love, I should be ungenerous not to admit the same plea for yours.

Faulk. Now I shall be blest indeed!

Sir Anth. [*Coming forward.*] What's going on here? So you have been quarrelling too, I warrant! Come, Julia, I never interfered before; but let me have a hand in the matter at last. All the faults I have ever seen in my friend Faulkland seemed to proceed from what he calls the delicacy and warmth of his affection for you. There, marry him directly, Julia; you'll find he'll mend surprisingly! [*The rest come forward.*

Sir Luc. Come, now, I hope there is no dissatisfied person but what is content; for as I have been disappointed myself, it will be very hard if I have not the satisfaction of seeing other people succeed better.

Acres. You are right, Sir Lucius. So, Jack, I wish you joy—Mr. Faulkland the same. Ladies, come now, to show you I'm neither vexed nor angry, odds tabors and pipes! I'll order the fiddles in half-an-hour to the New Rooms—and I insist on your all meeting me there.

Sir Anth. 'Gad! sir, I like your spirit; and at night we single lads will drink a health to the young couples, and a husband to Mrs. Malaprop.

Faulk. Our partners are stolen from us, Jack—I hope to be congratulated by each other—yours for having checked in time the errors of an ill-directed imagination, which might have betrayed an innocent heart; and mine for having, by her gentleness and candour, reformed the unhappy temper of one who by it made wretched whom he loved most, and tortured the heart he ought to have adored.

Abs. Well, Jack, we have both tasted the bitters, as well as the sweets of love ; with this difference only, that you always prepared the bitter cup for yourself, while I——

Lyd. Was always obliged to me for it, hey! Mr. Modesty ?——But, come, no more of that — our happiness is now as unalloyed as general.

Jul. Then let us study to preserve it so : and while Hope pictures to us a flattering scene of future bliss, let us deny its pencil those colours which are too bright to be lasting. When hearts deserving happiness would unite their fortunes, Virtue would crown them with an unfading garland of modest hurtless flowers : but ill-judging Passion will force the gaudier rose into the wreath, whose thorn offends them when its leaves are dropped !   [*Exeunt omnes.*

EPILOGUE

BY THE AUTHOR

SPOKEN BY MRS. BULKLEY

LADIES, for you—I heard our poet say—
He'd try to coax some moral from his play :
"One moral's plain," cried I, "without more fuss ;
Man's social happiness all rests on us :
Through all the drama—whether damn'd or not—
Love gilds the scene, and women guide the plot.
From every rank obedience is our due—
D'ye doubt ? The world's great stage shall prove it
    true.

The Rivals

The cit, well skill'd to shun domestic strife,
Will sup abroad ; but first he'll ask his wife :
John Trot, his friend, for once will do the same,
But then—he'll just step home to tell his dame.

The surly squire at noon resolves to rule,
And half the day—Zounds ! madam is a fool !
Convinced at night, the vanquish'd victor says,
Ah, Kate ! you women have such coaxing ways.

The jolly toper chides each tardy blade,
Till reeling Bacchus calls on Love for aid :
Then with each toast he sees fair bumpers swim,
And kisses Chloe on the sparkling brim !

Nay, I have heard that statesmen—great and wise—
Will sometimes counsel with a lady's eyes !
The servile suitors watch her various face,
She smiles preferment, or she frowns disgrace,
Curtsies a pension here—there nods a place.

Nor with less awe, in scenes of humbler life,
Is view'd the mistress, or is heard the wife.
The poorest peasant of the poorest soil,
The child of poverty, and heir to toil,
Early from radiant Love's impartial light
Steals one small spark to cheer this world of night :
Dear spark ! that oft through winter's chilling woes
Is all the warmth his little cottage knows !

The wandering tar, who not for years has press'd
The widow'd partner of his day of rest,
On the cold deck, far from her arms removed,
Still hums the ditty which his Susan loved ;
And while around the cadence rude is blown,
The boatswain whistles in a softer tone.

The soldier, fairly proud of wounds and toil,
Pants for the triumph of his Nancy's smile ;
But ere the battle should he list her cries.

Sheridan's Dramatic Works

The lover trembles—and the hero dies !
That heart, by war and honour steel'd to fear,
Droops on a sigh, and sickens at a tear !
    But ye more cautious, ye nice-judging few,
Who give to beauty only beauty's due,
Though friends to love—ye view with deep regret
Our conquests marr'd, our triumphs incomplete,
Till polish'd wit more lasting charms disclose,
And judgment fix the darts which beauty throws !
In female breasts did sense and merit rule,
The lover's mind would ask no other school ;
Shamed into sense, the scholars of our eyes,
Our beaux from gallantry would soon be wise ;
Would gladly light, their homage to improve,
The lamp of knowledge at the torch of love !"

END OF VOL. I.

Printed by BALLANTYNE, HANSON & Co
Edinburgh & London